Feeding Among The Lilies

Feeding Among
The Lilies

The Wellsprings Reader

•

Selected and Edited by
Baila Olidort

Wellsprings
Brooklyn, New York

A publication of the Student Affairs Office of
Lubavitch Youth Organization

ISBN 0-8266-0487-0

Orders:
291 Kingston Avenue / Brooklyn, New York 11213
(718) 778-0226 / FAX (718) 778-4148 kehot@aol.com

Printed in the United States of America

To my parents, with gratitude

Contents

Preface

WHEN THE OPPORTUNITY TO WORK WITH WELLSPRINGS fell into my lap some 13 years ago, I had no idea that the journal would come to impose itself so significantly on my life, and that a relationship of almost human proportions would develop between me and the journal.

I was drawn to *Wellsprings* by a personal curiosity about people I had encountered in my teenage years; people who were not born into lives of Torah observance, but traveled along a circuitous course that brought them there. For some, the odyssey was prompted by a need for stability and sanity in an often chaotic and insane world. They would embrace Judaism with an enthusiasm that, I confess, was refreshing to someone like myself who had grown up with it. For others—and of greater interest to me—it was an existential struggle that began in their cognitive years. Their turn to Judaism would not so much provide them with answers as propel them on a meaningful direction in their endless quest.

I found that Judaism, especially Chasidism, held a certain attraction for people who sought not definitive answers to specific questions but rather a perspective on the ambiguities of life; people who would not be content with ready solutions but instead sought to achieve a certain sensibility that would enable them, even empower them, to confront the dilemmas that work their way into our human lives. To these people, the questions are themselves a part of life. So that even after they would settle into a life of Torah and Judaism as they invariably did, often with marriage and family, the comfort of complacency would escape them. Stirring just below the surface would always be a longing for that elusive something that alone could redeem them from their perpetual search. Yet for all the pathos of this kind of existence, their lives are so much more keenly lived, so much more richly experienced.

Wellsprings gave me an excuse and a forum to talk to these people, to penetrate their minds and hearts, and follow them along the meandering paths they have traversed. And indeed, even those who approached Judaism with dispassionate intellect, even those who studied Torah with the detachment of an objective philosopher following principles of cold reason, would finally be drawn into it with passion, with heart. Because Judaism, especially Chasidism, if truly understood, must be lived multi-dimensionally, with both the heart and the mind, one always feeding off the other.

In *Song of Songs*, Solomon sings of G-d as the shepherd whose flock grazes among the lilies. In a play on the word *shoshanim*, the Hebrew word for lilies, the *Zohar* says the word should rather be read as *sheshonim*, as in *sheshonim bahalakhot*, which means "that are studying the laws." That is to say, G-d's sheep, the Jewish people, are beloved to G-d for they feed upon the *halakhot*, or are occupied with the study of *halakhot*.

The lily (by modern translations, the rose) with its proverbial 13 petals, is a metaphor for the 13 principles of Torah study—the principles by which the Jewish people study and interpret the Torah and her laws. But thirteen is as well, the number representing the Divine attributes of mercy—the emotive qualities. So the lily represents the contrary inclinations of both the mind and the heart as being on a par with one another.

As editor of *Wellsprings* I felt that the journal's success would depend on its ability to articulate the integration of these two. If the subject concerned an abstract issue, the writer would need to justify its relevance. Why does, or should this conceptual issue matter to the writer, or, to the reader? In this way, I had hoped to avoid essays that were no more than academic exercises. Conversely, if the article were of human interest, I'd want the writer to search his or her mind and share with us the mental process by which s/he analyzed the feelings and intuitive impulses that seemed to take hold. In that way, I had hoped that no personal essay in *Wellsprings* would ever be so subjective as to be irrelevant to a reader who hadn't shared those experiences.

This was not an easy requirement to fulfill for a journal that was supposed to be published regularly. In my stubbornness to strive for this standard rather than meet deadlines, I've dismayed many readers by the long gaps between the issues, and am sorry for this. But my regrets are only that I have not yet discovered more individuals like those who have helped *Wellsprings* grow, and upon whom the journal depends so that it will eventually be published at more frequent intervals.

The essays included in this anthology span the course of twelve years and were selected (with difficulty) from some 30 journals on a variety of topics, from the personal to the philosophical. Each of these, I think, is a gem. Or a lily.

As it turns out, the voices heard here are mostly women's voices. This is not intentional, but should probably not come as a surprise given the introspective character of many of these essays. It is true that the writers who had the ability and the willingness to probe their hearts and minds, and then make themselves vulnerable by sharing it with a public audience, were few and far between, and usually women.

•

I am grateful to each of the many individuals who have contributed to *Wellsprings* over the years. I deeply cherish the personal friendships that resulted from the journal. Most especially, Susan Handelman and Naftali Loewenthal have not only contributed regularly and so wonderfully to the journal in spite of the burdens on their schedules, but have taken a personal interest in seeing it succeed, in encouraging me when I was near burnout, and offering insight and foresight where my own were short.

In addition to her incisive essays, Tzivia Emmer has been an invaluable sounding board over the years. Varda Branfman, Tamar Frankiel, Eli Silberstein and Shmuel Klatzkin (who has been doing our book reviews that do not appear in this volume) have become familiar names to Wellsprings readers.

I owe a great debt of gratitude to the *Wellsprings* publisher, Rabbi Kasriel Kastel. He has always been supportive beyond my expectations, giving me the freedom and the encouragement to follow my instinct and to experiment with the journal and related projects. I am grateful for his confidence in my ability and his unmatched patience.

Special thanks to our generous host office, Merkos L'Inyonei Chinuch, and to Rabbi Yosef B. Friedman and Shmuel Marcus who facilitated publication of this book.

Some names do not appear on the *Wellsprings* masthead. My sister, Tila Hecht, whose discernment and sensitivity to nuance are indispensable to me in my editorial decisions, has given me a rare perspective on many an issue.

My children, Shana, Eli and Lea, who have long since counted *Wellsprings* as another sibling, have been generous and preciously tolerant of my often obsessive preoccupation with the journal, especially during those frantic few weeks before publication.

To Dovid, my husband and primary resource, thank you.

Baila Olidort

Adar 23, 5759 / March 1999

Jewish Culture

Jewish Culture and Jewish Covenant

Susan A. Handelman

A FEW YEARS AGO, A REMARKABLE EXHIBITION OF JEWISH culture toured this country. It was entitled "The Precious Legacy" and was brought here from the Judaica Museum in Prague. During World War II, the Nazis had collected a vast treasure of Judaica in Prague, composed of items stolen and expropriated from Europe's devastated Jewish communities. They collected this material to establish a museum about this soon-to-be "extinct race." What appeared in "The Precious Legacy" exhibition was just a small selection of the thousands of objects which are now still stored in warehouses in Prague. The exhibit was filled with magnificent Torah scrolls, pointers, crowns, hallah covers, Pesach plates, and so forth.

I visited the exhibit a few days after it opened in Washington, D.C. and behind me in line were two very intelligent looking, well-off Jews, probably from the affluent Washington suburbs. We were moving along a showcase of printed Hebrew books which were five or six hundred years old, but they weren't well labelled. One of the books was very small and looked at first glance like an illuminated manuscript. On closer inspection, I saw that it was opened to the first words of the *birkhat hamazon*—the ritual "blessing after meals"; and so I recognized it as a prayerbook, a *siddur.* Even today in most prayerbooks, the Hebrew letters where this blessing begins are printed in extra large letters; and so it was in this siddur.

As I looked at this prayerbook from about the year 1500, opened to the first words which I have said so often, which every schoolchild in almost every Jewish school learns to say by heart, and which many Jews who do not adhere to much else of Jewish law still often recite after they eat a Shabbat meal—I had an overwhelming feeling of unity and continuity with those Jews who 400 years ago, said those same words and read the same Hebrew letters I was staring at.

The couple came up behind me, and I heard the husband say to the wife, "What do you think that is?" She looked at it and answered, "I don't know, I think it's a children's book." At that moment, that extraordinary feeling of unity with all the Jewish people dissolved into a sharp pain—because these two intelligent and sophisticated Jews couldn't even recognize the most elementary words, couldn't even identify a prayerbook.

This experience illustrated for me the painful truth that in the end there simply isn't any enduring Jewish culture without Jewish literacy—without knowledge of the Hebrew language, and of the classical sources of Judaism. And by the sources I don't mean Bellow, Malamud, Roth, and Mailer but Bible, Talmud, and Midrash. And I want to argue here that there is also no enduring Jewish culture without Jewish covenant.

The Condition of Contemporary American Jewish Culture

What, in fact, is the cultural condition of American Jews? Harold Bloom, one of the most brilliant and best-read literary critics writing today, has been very pessimistic about what is called the condition of "American-Jewish Culture." He compares the phrase to "Holy Roman Empire" which, as he says, was neither holy, nor Roman, nor an empire. Similarly, Bloom writes, "Much that is joined together under the rubric of American-Jewish Culture is not American, not Jewish, and not culture . . . [the concept of culture] could never be Jewish, if by Jewish we mean anything religious at all, since culture is so stubbornly secular a concept."[1]

What, however, is "culture"? The word is endlessly invoked these days, especially by modern Jews in search of a Jewish identity. We look to "culture" for "values" and "traditions"; and we invoke "culture" to make all kinds of differing things coexist happily, from Israeli folk dancing to Freud, from the *Baraitah* to Saul Bellow, the Book of Deuteronomy to Dizengoff Street, the Marx Brothers to Maimonides—as if in "culture" there could be found some magic medicine to unite all Jews, to energize us, heal our wounds, and solve our spiritual dilemmas. (R. Samson Rafael Hirsch in the last century wryly said, "Only when Judaism became sick did it need 'Rabbi Doctors.'")

In Paul Mendes-Flohr's analysis, if we take culture to denote the "particular intellectual and material qualities of different people and societies," the term is distinctive of our self-consciousness as moderns, part of the pluralistic world-view of modernity. Yet the term is also paradoxical. For on the one hand, once we start speaking about varying peoples having different "cultures," we are implying a multiplicity, a plurality, an equality among them. On the other hand, when the intellectual category of "culture" was being created in the 19th century, "culture" was identified with "high culture." There was an attempt to reserve culture as a badge of prestige, associated with the intellectual and aesthetic attainments of Europe which were thought to be the most "advanced." In other words, there was from the beginning a basic conflict between a pluralist and elitist definition of the term.

And, continues Mendes-Flohr, this conflict would "confound the Jews in their efforts to find a place for themselves and their ancestral culture in the modern world." For the political emancipation of the Jews in Europe and their admission into European society was partially dependent on the Jews' being able to prove that they, too, had acquired "culture." One had to prove that she or he was learned in European culture and languages, or that Judaism, too, was an "elevated culture" and completely harmonious with modern Western thought.[2] (And that project is still being carried out by many Jews today.)

Needless to say, this acculturation through the acquisition of European languages and thought often came at the expense of the knowledge of Hebrew language and Jewish thought. And the after-effects are found in Bloom's pessimistic diagnosis of the condition of American-Jewish culture. Asks Bloom, "What has American Jewry engendered, that American higher culture has absorbed? The probable answer is that American humor has been changed by Jewish humor into certain modes of self mockery . . . I do not find much contribution to high literature."

There is of course the comic achievement of Saul Bellow, but when Bellow wants to represent authentic spirituality, he has Mr. Sammler read Meister Eckhart, or the narrator of *Humboldt's Gift* read Rudolph Steiner, which is rather a falling away even within Gentile spirituality.

Alfred Kazin, in an essay about Jewish-American literature, argues that the original, creative contribution of the Jews to America did not come from high culture, from universities, or journalists. It came instead from low culture, from pop culture, vaudeville, the Marx Brothers, Fanny Brice and Eddie Cantor and Al Jolson—all of which became today's entertainment industry. And of course, if we invoke Irving Berlin (whose original name was Israel Baylin), as a representative of American-Jewish culture, that means American Jewish culture also includes "I'm Dreaming of a White Christmas," "In Your Easter Bonnet," and "G-d Bless America."

Cynthia Ozick, an eminent contemporary American-Jewish novelist agrees with Bloom on this issue and writes, "There are no major Jewish writers. . . . There have been no Jewish literary giants in the diaspora. Marx and Freud are vast presences but they are analyzers and judgers of culture. . . . They belong to the social sciences. Imaginative writers, by contrast, are compelled to swim in the medium of culture. Literature is an instrument of culture, not a summary of it."

In her view, the role of the Jew is to be a judge of culture, not its medium.[3] And, Ozick argues, "Nothing written or thought in the diaspora has ever been able to last unless it has been centrally Jewish." That means, probably, farewell to figures such as Norman Mailer, Saul Bellow, Philip Roth, and many others.

But we're still left with a nagging problem. What is "centrally Jewish"? As one might expect from a literary critic, Bloom thinks the distinguishing feature of the Jews is that traditionally they were a "text-centered" people. And "If we still are a people it can only be because we have some texts in common." Yet as he acknowledges, most contemporary Jews have lost this obsession and special relation with Scripture and Talmud.

Ozick claims that a "centrally Jewish text" means something liturgical . . . not prayer only, but embodying what she calls a "reciprocal moral imagination as opposed to an isolated lyric imagination." She describes it as "a communal or choral voice, the echo of the Voice of the Lord of history." As an academic biblical scholar once remarked, the authentic Jewish literary genre is not the novel, the lyric, or the drama, but the anthology. And in a sense, that is what the Bible, the Talmud, the Midrash are—anthologies, collections, communal and choral voices. Voices which not only have a dialogue between many traditions, but also the voices of the Jewish people's conversation with G-d. A very special kind of dialogue, a kind of "reciprocity"—which is also a term we use to talk about covenant.

But "covenant" is also a binding relation and a certain call to responsibility. As the contemporary French-Jewish poet Edmond Jabes once wrote, "To be a Jew is to take responsibility for all books through obsession with the single book." And perhaps it was this Jewish notion of the "Book of Books," this idea of the world created by, and for, Torah that lies behind some of our deepest Western cultural notions about the spiritual edification of "literature."

Connecting Earth and Heaven

To believe in the power of books and education to "cultivate" or edify a person takes us back to the etymological roots of the word "culture." It comes, in fact, from the Latin and derives from a root which means "to cultivate, to dwell, to take care of, to tend, to preserve." That originally referred to the relation of humanity with the earth, nature. In other words, one cultivates to make something fit for human habitation. This notion became connected with the Roman reverence for tradition, for preserving the Greek tradition, and so culture became associated with the continuity of tradition.

In his great theological treatise, *The Star of Redemption*, the German-Jewish philosopher Franz Rosenzweig noted the etymological connection between the words "culture" and "cultus," the service of the earth (culture) and the service of heaven (cult). Care, veneration, worship are also the service of heaven. And Rosenzweig's paradigmatic Jewish endeavor was to connect the service of the earth with the service of heaven.

Indeed, according to Chasidic philosophy, the connection of earth and heaven is precisely the meaning of the giving of the Torah at Sinai. As the Midrash (*Shemot Rabbah* 12:3) relates, an entirely new state of being was inaugurated with the giving of the Torah: "Even though the Holy One, blessed be He, decreed that 'The heavens are the heavens of the Lord, but the earth He has given to the sons of man'. . . when He wished to give the Torah He annulled the initial decree and said, 'The lower [worlds] shall ascend to the higher, and the higher descend to the lower. And I shall take the initiative,' as it is said (Ex. 19:20) 'And the L-rd descended upon Mt. Sinai' and [afterwards] it is written (Ex. 24:1), 'And to Moses He said, Come up unto the L-rd.'"

One of the fundamental themes of Chasidic thought is that the ultimate purpose of Torah and the service of a Jew is for the earth to become a "dwelling-place" for G-d; that through human effort, the lower, material, earthly realms become infused with spirituality—not negated, but refined, elevated, and sanctified. For the Divine intention is to have a "dwelling place in the lower worlds." Holiness is not found in retreat from the world, or ascetic practice, but in engagement and transformation of the world with all one's material as well as spiritual being.

There is a similar insight into the relation of culture and covenant in the rabbinic commentary on the story of Noah. Noah's experiences building the Ark and surviving the flood are among the most familiar stories in the Torah. But a quite troubling event happens after the flood. When the waters recede and Noah emerges from the Ark, God blesses him and his children and says, "I will establish my covenant with you" (Gen 9:11). Then, however, Noah planted a vineyard, and became drunk and naked within his tent. His younger son Ham saw his nakedness and told his older brothers outside. The two other sons of Noah, Shem and Yefet, "took a cloak, laid it upon both their shoulders, and walked backwards and covered their father's nakedness" (Gen. 9:20-24).

Noah awoke and blessed Shem and Yefet: "May G-d extend Yefet, and let him dwell in the tents of Shem" (Gen. 9:27). In the next chapter, the Torah gives the "Table of Nations," tracing all the nations of the world back to Noah and his three sons. Shem is the ancestor of the Shemmites, whose lineage ultimately leads to Abraham and the Jews; among Yefet's descendants is Yavan, the ancestor of the Greeks. In the Talmud, the rabbis relate the name "Yefet" to the Hebrew word *yafeh*, "beauty," for Greece indeed was one of the primary sources of beauty and culture in the West.

Rabbi Samson Rafael Hirsch commented that the verse about Yefet dwelling in the tents of Shem means that beauty and culture are not ends in themselves but need to be illumined and guided by "Shem," i.e., by Jewish spirituality, by Torah.

In sum, Judaism has to be something more than a "culture." Even to act as Ozick's "judge" of culture, one needs some external perspective. Jewish culture must be more than folklore, ethnic pride or solidarity, patterns of birth and geography, or political structures.

To truly have Yefet dwell in the tents of Shem means to try to bring G-d into the world; or, as Chasidic thought explains, to infuse the material with the spiritual. Art and literature can participate in that attempt—as the modern philosopher Steven Schwarzschild has written: "True aesthetics, Kantian and Jewish, subsumes art indirectly but decisively to ethics. . . . It depicts the Messiah as man's anticipatory construction of the world as it ought to be, as G-d wants it to be."

A Living Jewish Culture

Jews today desperately need to learn how to bring Yefet into the tents of Shem, how to reconnect the service of earth with the service of heaven. And this means every Jew. Not just the rabbi, scholar, teacher, artist, or museum curator. True Jewish culture, finally, cannot be the culture of artists and intellectuals only. *Tzibbur* is a Hebrew word that denotes "community." *Tzibbur*, a rabbi once interpreted, is an acronym for the following three words: *tzaddikim*, meaning the "righteous ones"; *benonim*, the "average ones"; *rashayim*, the "wicked ones." *Tzibbur* thus means you have to include everybody—righteous, average, and wicked—otherwise you don't have a community. Nor do you have a living culture.

Rabbi Adin Steinsaltz is a great contemporary Israeli scholar of Talmudic and Chasidic thought—and a man well acquainted with Western culture. Rabbi Steinsaltz once described the way the Jews learn the Talmud as follows: "When you begin to learn each day, you first pick up the Talmud and you kiss it. And then you open the book, study, and pound on it as you argue about its meaning with your study partner (*havruta*). And then after you finish learning, you close the book, and you kiss it again."

Why do you kiss it? He didn't say, but perhaps you kiss it because for all your "culture," and all your intellectual ingenuity, and all your creative insight, and all your disagreements with your learning partner, you recognize there is something there that transcends you and your intellect, and which binds you to the entire Jewish past and to all other Jews.

And this is also one of the deeper meanings of the giving of the Torah. The Torah recounts that the Jews "came into the wilderness of Sinai. They encamped in the wilderness; and there Israel encamped before the Mount" (Ex 19:2). The classical commentator Rashi notes that the verb used in the phrase "And there Israel encamped (*va'yichan*)" is in the singular, not the plural. This signifies they were "like one man with one mind, whereas all the other encampments were with complaints and strife."

So while Jews argue, debate, differ with each other, we also need to remember to learn and to kiss the sacred books—and in so doing, to kiss each other and be one with G-d.

NOTES

1. Harold Bloom, "A Speculation Upon American Jewish Culture," *Judaism*, (Summer, 1982).

2. Paul Mendes-Flohr, "Culture," *Contemporary Jewish Religious Thought*, ed. A. Gohen and P. Mendes-Flohr (New York: Scribners, 1987).

3. Cynthia Ozick, "Toward a New Yiddish," *Art And Ardor* (New York: Dutton, 1983). As Alfred Kazin also writes, even the famous "New York Jewish intellectuals" who helped fashion American "high culture" after World War II, themselves idolized figures who claimed to

The Philosopher, The Writer, And The Chasidic Story

Tzivia Emmer

WHO DOESN'T LOVE A STORY? A JEWISH, CHASIDIC STORY especially—one that enters the heart like an arrow of truth and wisdom. There are stories of *tzaddikim* and of simple Jews of another era, stories that show the workings of Divine Providence in everyday life, stories that illuminate an abstract concept or a verse in the Torah, and stories that show the value of certain character traits like kindness and charity. Some stories contain little more than a play on words or a flash of wit. In the classic Chasidic tales we find traces of the vanished world of Eastern European Jewry, glimpsed across the chasm of time and destruction that separates us from that world.

"Through telling stories of *tzaddikim*," says Rabbi Nachman of Bratslav, "one draws down the light of the Moshiach into this World, and repels from it all manner of darkness and tribulations."

Chasidim are fond of saying that relating stories about the Baal Shem Tov on Saturday night is beneficial for one's livelihood—but that the aforesaid statement contains three errors: first, not only the Baal Shem Tov but any *tzaddik*; second, not only on Saturday night but at any time; and third, that it is good not only for matters of livelihood but for any worthwhile aspect of life.

Our Sages asked why the Torah, usually so sparing of words, devotes a long and repetitious segment to the activities of Abraham's servant Eliezer in acquiring a wife for Abraham's son, Isaac. The Talmud answers that the conversation of the patriarch's servants is loftier than the Torah as studied by their sons. Reb Shlomo of Radomsk wrote: "This is so because the conversation—the story-telling—of the servants of the patriarchs becomes the Torah of the sons." Tales of *tzaddikim* and authentic Jewish stories deepen our appreciation of Torah and sustain faith.

Chasidic stories are less a literary form than a part of life. They serve to enliven the classroom lecture, the Shabbat table, the discussion of serious topics, a children's party. New stories complement the old; a rich oral tradition continues to grow even as more of the oral tradition is recorded and now translated into English.

But stories must be authentic. Rabbi Shlomo Yosef Zevin, a formidable Torah scholar of recent times, notes in the introduction to his *Sippurei Chasidim al haMoadim* (English version: A Treasury of Chasidic Tales on the Festivals, translated by Uri Kaploun and published by Mesorah Publications, Ltd.) that he has "neither adapted [the stories] to suit his taste nor tampered with the facts as related, whether in content or in style."

Not so with many of the stories in books that we may encounter in a bookstore or the public library, where a word, a phrase or a nuance can easily distort the entirety. I remember reading stories by Martin Buber and coming away from them wondering what they meant. Like food sculpture in a museum they looked quite good—but you couldn't bring them home and eat them. Why didn't they nourish my soul? Even worse, there were Jewish folktales and novels filled with superstition and madness. Was this indeed Jewish culture? There was a taste of something Jewish, but nothing to inspire belief or impel further inquiry. Stories outside authentic Judaic tradition often contain traps for the unwary and subtle forms of spiritual sabotage, even when they are called "Chasidic."

The Chametz on the Shelf

"Looking back over the seder he had just completed, Reb Levi Yitzchak of Berditchev noted with satisfaction that he had succeeded in suffusing each of its successive stages with the light of kabbalistic meditation—that he had indeed done justice to each of the mystical *kavanos* at their respective moments.

"But at that moment a voice from heaven intimated to him: 'Be not proud of the manner in which you conducted your seder. In this town there lives a Jew called Chaim the Porter: his seder is loftier than yours.'"

So begins a popular story about one of the best-loved personalities of Jewish history—Rabbi Levi Yitzchak of Berditchev, defender of the people of Israel, arguer with G-d, the *Rav* who always in his abundant love for his people found something good to say about everyone, even the biggest sinner. The Berditchever, as he is called, is the central figure in many Chasidic stories.

The story continues:

"Reb Levi Yitzchak turned to address the Chasidim who had completed their seder at home and had come to observe how the *tzaddik* conducted the final stages of his seder.

"Do any of you know Reb Chaim the Porter?" he asked.

One of them knew him, but did not know where he lived.

"If it were possible to call him here I would be most pleased," said the *tzaddik*.

The Chasidim immediately fanned out over all the streets of Berditchev until they found his dilapidated cottage.

His wife opened the door gingerly and asked: "Why do you need my husband? He's in there snoring, dead drunk."

The Chasidim ignored her, walked straight in, succeeded in waking him up, and just about hauled the burly fellow on their shoulders to the home of the *tzaddik*.

Reb Levi Yitzchak offered him a chair, and said: "My dear Reb Chaim! Did you recite *Avadim Hayinu* on *Shabbos HaGadol*?"

"Yes," blinked the porter.

"Did you search your cottage for *chametz* last night?" asked the *tzaddik.*

"Yes," said the simple fellow.

Reb Levi Yitzchak had one more question: "And did you conduct the seder tonight?"

Flushed and flustered, the poor man unburdened himself. "Rebbe, I'll tell you the truth. I heard that a man's not allowed to drink vodka for eight days on end. So this morning I drank enough to last me for eight days. So of course I was sleepy, and I went to bed. When it was night-time my wife wakes me up and she starts nagging me. You know how. She starts saying like this: 'Chaim,' she says, 'why don't you make a seder like all the other Jews?'

"So I said to her, I said: 'What do you want from me? I'm an ignoramus, and my father before me was an ignoramus. I haven't got a clue what it's all about. The only thing I know is this—that our fathers were in exile amongst the gypsies. But we've got a G-d, you see, who took us out of there and made us free. And now we're all in exile again. But G-d will bring us out again, for sure!' Then I saw that on the table there were matzah and wine and eggs, so I ate the matzah and the eggs, and I drank up the wine. And then I was so exhausted that I had to go back to sleep."

The *tzaddik* told the Chasidim that they could now take the porter home. After they had left he said: "Heaven was exceedingly pleased with this man's words, because he said them with all his heart, without any ulterior motives. His sincerity was unblemished—for he knows nothing more than what he said."

We have in this story several themes common in Chasidic lore: the *tzaddik* in his mystical meditations, the ever-watchful and responsive Chasidim, the value of humility, the simple man whose sincerity pierces the heavens.

A nearly-identical story is found in *Tales of the Hasidim: Early Masters* by Martin Buber. There are several differences in the wording and details of the story. Concerning Rabbi Levi Yitzchak himself, in Rabbi Zevin's version, he "notes the level of his seder with satisfaction," while in Buber's version, Levi Yitzchak sits in his room, "joyful and proud." A small difference, barely discernible, but Buber's effect is to distance us. When Chaim the Porter is brought to the *tzaddik*, Buber's Levi Yitzchak asks, "Rabbi Chaim, dear heart, what mystic intention was in your mind when you gathered what is leavened?" Astonished at the porter's simple answer, the *tzaddik* continues, "And what consecration did you think upon in the burning of it?"

Note the very different questions asked by Rabbi Levi Yitzchak in *Sippurei Chasidim*. We are not led to the conclusion that Rabbi Levi Yitzchak—*tzaddik* and all that, but so lost in his own holy world that he does not have the critical faculties that we have. Further reinforcing the point, Buber's story lacks the framing element through which Rabbi Levi Yitzchak comments upon the meaning of the event. Surely the *tzaddik* understands its significance far better than we do, and the story becomes a lesson that he teaches.

Even more significant is another detail of Buber's story: Chaim the Porter reveals that he has forgotten to burn his chametz altogether. It is all still lying on the shelf.

Possession of *chametz* during Passover is a serious transgression of Jewish Law. The fact that the porter drank up eight-days' worth of the forbidden vodka is testimony not only to his propensity to imbibe but also to the sheer weight of the Passover laws, felt even by the simple man. There is no *chametz* on the shelf in *Sippurei Chasidim*, nor would there be. It is a symbol of the erroneous notion that Chasidism, in stressing enthusiasm and sincerity in the service of G-d, thereby somehow negated the importance of careful observance of the commandments.

The power of the *mitzvah* itself, the holy deed, runs as a theme throughout the entire body of Chasidic lore. In contrast to this is the idea that Jewish Law as it relates to physical performance represented a desiccated and dead religion of outward forms, while the Chasidic movement represented only joy, release from dry learning and dry performance. If Chasidism represented joy, it was joy in the *mitzvah* itself; if it was a release from dry learning it was a release allowing for a new depth of learning.

The Baal Shem Tov showed the value of the simple, unlearned Jew at a time when the disruptions of persecution and poverty had left the majority of the population bereft of a Torah education. But the Baal Shem Tov had an inner circle of disciples who numbered among them some of the greatest Torah scholars of the age. These disciples, too, had to learn the value of the simple, sincere, G-d-fearing person. The myth that the Baal Shem Tov himself was of such ilk is one that persists to our time. It is a myth which allows the twentieth century observer to admire the 'fervor' and holy innocence of the *tzaddikim* and Chasidim of a bygone age and at the same time remain curiously untouched and as distant as ever from Judaism.

The *tzaddikim* of the stories are meticulous and knowledgeable in the observance of the Code of Jewish Law—were they otherwise they would be charlatans and fakes—as indeed Shabbetai Zvi, the false messiah, proved to be. In one story the Baal Shem Tov senses an invalid *mezuzah* on the doorpost as soon as he walks into a room. The *mezuzah* must be written according to physically precise specifications as well as with the proper concentration in order to fulfill its spiritual function.

The role of the *mitzvah* itself is never overshadowed, in authentic Chasidic stories, by mystical contemplation or miracles. Many stories attest to a caution, as in the case of Rabbi Levi Yitzchak in the seder story, about getting carried away with the notion of Kabbalistic meditations. Not that such meditations were not—are not—a reality. It is precisely because of their power that the stories present a kind of antidote.

In the story, "Not on Purpose," when the blowing of the *shofar* prevents the sinking of a ship in a storm, Reb Simchah Bunem of Pshischah warns his disciples not to think that the *tzaddik* in this story blew the shofar in order to supernaturally calm the storm. Rather, his desire was to perform the *mitzvah* of blowing the *shofar* once more before his death. "And so holy a man was he, that the *mitzvah* saved them all."

Martin Buber was the quintessential secular Jewish philosopher, his Jewishness filtered through a haze of universalism. Long ago I came upon another book of stories by Buber, entitled *The Way of Man.* As the title implies, the stories embodied spiritual concepts that would appeal to the person who was not familiar with and perhaps not even interested in Judaism. As I remember these stories, they were ostensibly about *tzaddikim* and Chasidim, but these in reality could as well have been Sufis or Buddhists—hence their appeal for anyone hoping to find in Chasidism a purely conceptual system that is easily reconciled with other religions. (Many are the conduits that lead to Torah.) The concept here is that the "great religions of the world" contain a common core of truth, and that Moses and Buddha, for example, would have more to say to one another than the rabbis would lead us to believe. But if there is any tradition having the power to negate this concept totally it is that of Chasidism itself, a movement whose spiritual giants have had the mystical appeal to strike a responsive chord in the spiritual seeker as well as the Torah knowledge that keeps the whole thing on track.

Buber was far enough from the shtetl not to have to rebel against its ethos, not far enough from it to look back with the kind of nostalgia that produces Fiddler on the Roof, but never close enough to love and appreciate its very particular, uniquely

Jewish contribution. Writing before both the holocaust and today's Torah renaissance, he may well have thought that in recording his Chasidic stories he was preserving the last glowing embers of a moribund flame. But the reader should be aware that they are written from a point of view far from the impulse that inspired the stories to begin with.

The *chametz* is always on the shelf.

Poisoned Spears

Very different from Buber's universalism is the body of Yiddish literature exemplified by I.L. Peretz and Sholom Aleichem. They depict the vanished world of the shtetl, its rhythms, its characters, its typical scenes, with a vividness that creates its own nostalgia. Fiddler on the Roof, based upon stories by Sholom Aleichem, becomes in our time, the epitome of Jewish culture in the popular mind. But although Tevye may sing about "tradition," what we have here is tradition through the looking glass. The writing of Yiddish stories was in itself an act of moral and social rebellion against the traditional life of East European Jews of the shtetl. Many of the stories are parodies, bitterly ironic thrusts against traditional Jewish life.

The Yiddish writers scorned the religiosity that Martin Buber dusted off and put on the shelf of philosophy. Although they never scorned their Jewishness, their criticism is directed against Jews whose Judaism, in their view, prevented them from grabbing hold of history and claiming their rightful place in it.

I. L. Peretz, having left the shtetl for the intellectual salons of Warsaw, both parodied and romanticized the world of the shtetl Jews. The Jews of the shtetl lived in a world whose precarious physical existence was, if we may believe the descriptions of it, merely a tattered cover. Spurned by the world, the Jews in turn shut the world out and turned inward to a more luminous reality. This reality lay just beneath the surface, always beckoning, accessible, almost tangible, and glimpsed through the words, the prayers, the teachings, the stories of the Rebbe or his Chasidim. The Jews influenced by the haskalah ("enlightenment") rebelled against that world, believing that beyond the tattered cloak lay something far better: modernity, the intellectual glories of Western culture, economic betterment.

If the Yiddish writers saw elements in Jewish life deserving of criticism, they at least knew what Jewish life was. Writing in the late nineteenth and early twentieth centuries, neither they nor their audience were very far from the world they rejected. In their art, they drew of necessity from the very world they scorned with a love-hate relationship that we, a century later, can only comprehend from several removes. The modern reader is in danger of taking the caricature for the reality. We turn to Jewish literature in translation, or collections of Jewish folklore, unmindful of the fact that the very existence of this type of literature is an anomaly in the traditional life of the shtetl, an outgrowth of nineteenth century intellectual battles which we no longer need to fight.

Peretz drew upon Chasidic material and consciously reworked it. In the story, "Even Higher," he introduces a certain "Litvak" (Lithuanians being of the orthodox element traditionally opposed to the Chasidim) to an often-told story about Rabbi Moshe Leib of Sasov. Called here the Rabbi of Nemirov, the Rebbe would go out before dawn and, disguised in peasant's clothing, chop wood for those too poor and helpless to obtain any for themselves. Peretz's Chasidim are convinced that since the rabbi disappears each morning he must go—where else?—up to heaven. The Litvak follows the Rebbe, discovers the truth, and becomes a disciple. But when the Chasidim talk about how high the rabbi ascends in the spiritual worlds, the Litvak, presumably the alter ego of Peretz himself, whispers to himself, "Even higher. . . ."

The story seems innocent enough. There is respect for the holy deed of kindness performed by the *tzaddik*. Yet why is it that only the Litvak and the reader can see and understand the *tzaddik's* true merit? Aren't the Chasidim capable of appreciating the simple humanity in the rabbi's act? Obviously, in Peretz's view, they are not.

In other stories by Peretz, heaven becomes an unfeeling bureaucracy in which angels and devils carry out their appointed tasks with petty bureaucratic dispatch, leaking pens and all. Even the most saintly individuals are subjected to a cold and mindless heavenly justice system. We are privileged to witness the very file cabinets of hell. Kafka's *Trial* is but a step away.

In "A Pinch of Snuff," the saintly rabbi of Chelm (the mythical town created to poke fun at Torah scholars) faces challenges hurled at him by Satan and his ambitious underlings. The rabbi meets each challenge with utter rectitude, but is tricked in the end into profaning the Sabbath, while "the youthful devil, who had set out without a feather in his cap or a tooth on his neck strand, waited for the ovation to set up." The rabbi's righteousness is undone through an unwitting error committed in the pursuit of a permitted pleasure—a pinch of snuff.

A strange preoccupation with hell, magic, devils and dybbuks characterizes Yiddish writing up to our time. Isaac Bashevis Singer, the Nobel laureate whose writing spans genres as well as worlds, shares in some of his works this attraction to the bizarre. Where but in Yiddish literature do we find so much Jewish weirdness? Certainly not in Judaism itself or in authentic Jewish mysticism.

In "The Magician" Peretz once again takes a familiar theme and adds his own peculiar details. A number of Jewish stories involve a very poor person or couple who lack money for matzoh, wine and food for the approaching Passover festival. A stranger arrives in town and asks to join them for the seder. They tell him he is welcome to share whatever they have, but that indeed they have little for themselves. The stranger says he will bring provisions enough for all. At some point they notice that the stranger has vanished. The couple realize that it had been Elijah the Prophet, whose task it is to travel incognito and assist certain deserving Jews in need, and to teach Torah to others.

Elijah appears in many guises, often as a poor wayfarer—sometimes with repulsive characteristics designed to test the lovingkindness of the Jew who is the object of his mission. (Such was the case with a certain Reb Eliezer, the reward for whose patience and good will toward an obnoxious guest was the birth of a son who grew up to be a *tzaddik*, the Baal Shem Tov.)

Here is Elijah in "The Magician": "In front of the whole community he swallowed live coals as if they were noodles. He drew all kinds of ribbons from his mouth: red, green, any color you wanted—each as long as the Exile. From a bootleg, he pulled sixteen pairs of turkeys, the size of bears and lively prancing around the stage. . . . White loaves of Sabbath-bread flock like birds into the air and begin to do a wedding dance beneath the ceiling. A second whistle and, in the wink of an eye, they vanish. As if they never were. No white breads, no ribbons, no turkeys! Nothing!"[1]

Yes, Elijah provides a seder for a poor couple. Allusions to the Exile, to Sabbath bread, to a wedding dance provide just that scintilla of *yiddishkeit* that makes the story sound Jewish. But the magician is a product of Peretz's imagination rather than of a Jewish sensibility. As with Peretz's angels, devils and heavenly courts, the magician is a cartoon.

Peretz wrote a verse description of the Yiddish language which could as well describe his own stories about Jewish life:

Words that stab like
poisoned spears,
And laughter that is

full of fears,
And there is a touch of gall,
Of bitterness about it all.[2]

An authentic Jewish story remains true to the moral-ethical universe which characterizes both the Chasidic and the non-Chasidic Jewish approach to life. An authentic Jewish story has roots deep in the rich soil of Torah. Its universe is at once more human and more spiritual than that of I. L. Peretz, more accessible and tangibly Jewish than that of Martin Buber. We may not always understand it, but we can trust it. It is, after all, the storytelling of the servants which becomes the Torah of the sons.

NOTES

1. From *Selected Stories* by I. L. Peretz, edited by Irving Howe and Eliezer Greenberg, (Schoken Books, NY 1974).
2. Ibid.

The Case of Kafka

Naftali Loewenthal

IT WAS A FIRST YEAR CLASS AT THE DEPARTMENT OF Hebrew and Jewish Studies at University College, London. A rather eminent professor was giving the first lecture in the course on Modern Jewish History. He looked at the dozen or so students, some fresh from high school, some mature students with degrees in other fields. There was an uncertainty: did they know enough to begin studying Jewish history? Did they know anything? He began to mention books, people, events. Some of the students seemed to be with him, nodding vigorously. Others were less certain. Then the name of Franz Kafka came up. The professor looked around the class, almost aggressively; "I assume you have all heard of Kafka." No-one dissented; perhaps no-one dared to dissent. For the professor concerned, it was a simple matter; who could not have heard of Kafka?

This incident took place in the Sixties. Today one would not be so ready to assume that every Jewish college student has heard of Kafka. Even less would one expect the influence of Kafka's writings to dominate their thinking and their perception of the world. But there remains a considerable sector of society who can say with Rabbi Jonathan Sacks, the Chief Rabbi of Britain, in a recent perceptive article: "there was a time, as an undergraduate, when I read every word of Kafka with the shock of recognition, as if I were reading my own autobiography."[1] Franz Kafka, who died in 1924 at the age of 41, succeeded—unwittingly—in creating a generation of would-be followers. Many people who today have a crucial influence in society, especially in the Jewish world, explored his writings and to some extent absorbed his world view, at the time when they were forming their own definitions of reality.

But what was Kafka saying? What are the implications of his life and work for the world? Is his message heard?

It could indeed be a Kafka fragment. (A large proportion of Kafka's published writings are in the form of fragments of stories, a brief description of a scene or of a situation.) The great writer, famous worldwide, is totally misunderstood by his public. He declares one thing, the public hears something quite different. He is cited as an authority supporting the very activities he most decries. The more his books are published and republished, the more that adulatory critical literature is written about him, the more that films are made of his work (excuse the mild anachronism), the less his message is heard.

This is the situation of Franz Kafka. His life and his work have a message for our time which is but rarely comprehended. This might not matter very much, were it not for the fact that the issues about which Kafka is most misunderstood directly concern the relationship of the Jew to Judaism and to society, to the ideals of marriage and of bearing children, and perhaps above all, to the ultimate question of the relationship of the individual and G-d.

The Wrong Message

Let us try to present the conventional way in which Kafka's input was internalized by many of his readers. Based on his books, and common knowledge of his life, what picture of reality did they construct?

The first word is loneliness: haunting loneliness. Kafka's leading characters are usually either actually alone or deeply lonely even though surrounded by family. Gregor Samsa of Metamorphosis, one of his most famous stories, is the paradigm of this loneliness: although living in the family apartment, together with his parents, sister and others, Gregor Samsa has changed into a beetle. For those around him he is a figure of horror. There is no communication, and no apparent way of resolving the problem. In the end, he dies. Other Kafka characters, such as Joseph K. in *The Trial* or K. in *The Castle*, are lonely in their struggle. In some cases the only company is itself intolerable to the point of madness, as in the case of "Blumfeld, an elderly bachelor." This pathetic figure becomes persecuted by two bouncing ping-pong balls which enter his apartment and follow him around wherever he goes.

The loneliness in the texts is supplemented by Kafka's perception of his own loneliness in real life, even though in many ways he inhabited the fairly cohesive society of thoroughly Jewish, middle class Prague, and in fact had a number of close friends. Kafka never married, a point which clearly bothered his family (and to which we will return).

The key to his feeling of loneliness was his special condition of consciousness, beset by tension and angst. His friend Max Brod wrote of his "drive towards perfection, purity, truth," and stated that Kafka was incapable of saying anything banal. The effect of this was on the one hand the tremendous respect he was accorded in his own lifetime by some of the people who knew him, and on the other his own feelings of total inadequacy, falseness and remoteness. In his *Diaries* he describes himself, having attended a gathering of a number of his friends and like-minded people, as "feeling like a clothes-rack pushed into the middle of the room."

Kafka's harshly critical self-view and profound hopelessness were expressed in his writing: the man who is on trial, but can find no way to plead in his defense, nor even to find out the nature of the crime of which he is accused: the man who vainly struggles to enter the Castle, in order to take up a position as a land-surveyor, but is prevented from doing so by an apparently endless bureaucracy. Some readers interpreted these works as parables about political totalitarianism (like Orwell's *Animal Farm*), but for the most part they were seen as comment on the situation of the individual and the general bleakness of the human condition. They have the power of dreams, intense terrifying dreams, and for Kafka the artist, the literary virtuoso, the dream replaced reality. Indeed, descriptions of Kafka's responses to daily activities indicate that to a considerable extent he saw reality as a dream.

The result in terms of Kafka's personal life was that he never got married, as mentioned above. The most casual reader can perceive that there was much anguish for him in this situation. Despite this fact, his non-marriage helped Kafka become the archetype of the Steppenwolf, the person who stands outside conventional society and its values. Thus in a recent article by a professor of English at Sussex University, the case of Kafka is cited as support for the liberal critique of the reality of marriage.[2]

On a more profound and sensitive level, for many of his readers, Kafka expressed the triumph of being uprooted, the man of truth who makes no compromises with a false world, a world in which there is no answer to the accusation and where the Castle gates are closed. This very quest for truth resulted also in his letter to Max Brod in which Kafka, dying of consumption, asked that all his unpublished manuscripts should be destroyed. These included his famous novels *The Trial*, *The Castle* and *America*, as well as a large number of stories and fragments. Brod did not follow this instruction, and thereby ensured that Kafka became known. But the fact of the request is seen as a further expression of Kafka's ultimately negative statement about the world, about life, and about Man's relationship with G-d.

It seems almost unnecessary to add that the Kafka ideal, seen from this normative but in my view false perspective, while intensely Jewish, has no dealings with Judaism as such. Kafka was famous as a Jew, and for most of his readers his being Jewish was an integral part of his loneliness and perhaps, too, of his hopelessness, especially as understood in the years leading up to and following the Holocaust. But although Kafka's Jewishness is in the foreground, Judaism itself in such forms as Shabbat and *kashrut*, or even just in terms of Jewish marriage, is altogether out of the picture.

Kafka's Context

My claim is that we have been looking at the wrong picture. Have you ever rejected a photograph of yourself, thinking "it's not me"? True, you were there, and this is how the camera caught you: but it's still not you. Too much has been left out, important details are blurred and covered over. I think Kafka himself would reject the description above. It does not define the dominant issues in Kafka's life, as he saw them. Nor does it express the significance of Kafka's experience for the Jew looking back from the vantage point of the 1990's.

First, let us consider the general context in which Kafka lived. A century before his birth the Rabbi of Prague was the famous Rabbi Yechezkel Landau, known as the "Noda biYehuda." Prague had an important Yeshiva, and Jewish life was strong. In addition there were also many small Jewish settlements in the Bohemian countryside. But in 1782, there began a forceful onslaught on the religious and cultural life of the Jewish community, with the so-called "Decree of Toleration" passed by the Emperor Franz-Joseph II. This forbade the use of Hebrew or Yiddish in public records and business transactions, and encouraged the Jews to set up German-language elementary schools with state approved teachers and curricula. Simultaneously, non-Jewish schools and universities were opened to the Jews. In 1786 a law was passed forbidding young Jews to marry unless they had attended a German-language school. The following year, the adoption of German personal and family names was made mandatory.

These and other measures weakened Judaism in Bohemia, but did not destroy it completely. The Haskalah (Jewish Enlightenment) movement in nineteenth century Prague was mild, traditionalist, and respectful of *halakhah,* when compared with the more radical parent movement in Berlin. During the entire 19th century and into the 20th, Bohemia formed a midway point between the traditionalism of Eastern Europe and the relentless assimilation of the West. This is a key issue when considering Kafka's position, because his consciousness as a Jew and as a writer was dominated by a sense of confrontation between Western assimilation and Jewish tradition. His personal struggle, as a man, concerned this conflict. His writing expresses both his yearning and his sense of paralysis, his inability to take the crucial step towards the Judaism for which he craved.

In Kafka's family, as in those of his friends, there were fond memories of traditional Jewish life. His great grandfather, who had lived in a small country community, was a pietist, perhaps a Chasid. Kafka writes of him that he had a long white beard, and a large library of Jewish books. Every day he would bathe ritually in the river; in the winter he would break a hole in the ice (*Biography* p. 4). Such a practice in the mid-19th century was characteristic of the Chasidim. However, the generation of Kafka's parents had made the move from the country to the town. In sophisticated Prague their Jewish practice decreased.

Frantisek Langer, a contemporary of Kafka, vividly describes this process in terms of his own family. When a child, he would watch his father putting on *tefillin*; he would read the Hebrew prayers, but could not understand them. As the years passed, Frantisek's father gradually stopped putting on *tefillin. Kashrut* too would have been forgotten in their home, except that they had a very pious Christian maid, who insisted on maintaining the religious standards of the family (*Nine Gates*, p. ix). We will return shortly to the Langers, because Frantisek's younger brother Jiri, who became a *baal teshuvah* (in the modern sense of the word) and for a time lived with the Belzer Chasidim, played an important role in Kafka's Jewish development.

The fact that authentic Judaism was not far away, neither in time nor geographically, was of great importance for Franz Kafka. This fact might escape notice if one focuses only on Kafka's stories and the fragments of literary works; in these there is almost no mention of Judaism as such. However, his *Diaries* and other writings present a different view. Take for example his *Letter to his Father.*

Letter to his Father

A key issue in Kafka's life was his relationship with his father. In 1919, five years before his death, he wrote his father a letter of about 45 typed pages beginning with the words, "You asked me recently why I maintain that I am afraid of you." In fact this letter was never delivered. It is intriguing to discover that from Kafka's point of view, Judaism was an important dimension of his relationship with his father, and even had the unrealized potential to bond father and son together.

". . . It would have been thinkable that we might both have found each other in Judaism or that we even might have begun from there in harmony, *but* what sort of Judaism was it that I got from you?" (*Letter to His Father*, Shocken bilingual paperback, 1953, henceforth LF, p.75).

Kafka goes on to describe the guilt he felt as a child when he did not carry out the few points of Jewish observance, such as going to the synagogue occasionally, or fasting on Yom Kippur, which his father demanded. But when he got older his view changed.

"Later, as a young man, I could not understand how, with the insignificant scrap of Judaism you yourself possessed, you could reproach me for not making an effort (for the sake of piety at least, as you put it) to cling to a similar, insignificant scrap. It was indeed, so far as I could see, a mere nothing, a joke—not even a joke. Four days a year you went to the synagogue, where you were, to say the least, closer to the indifferent than to those who took it seriously. Patiently you went through the prayers as a formality [but] sometimes amazed me by being able to show me in the prayer book the passage which was being said at the moment" (LF, p.77).

Together with boredom, the fear of being called up to the Torah ("that was something I dreaded for years"), and a Bar mitzvah described as a mere feat of memorizing, "nothing but some ridiculous passing of an examination," this is how Kafka depicts his early experience of the synagogue. Obviously his criticism of his father is the lack of depth, of authenticity and of meaning. He is also critical of the pathetically residual level of Jewish observance in their home.

"That's how it was in the synagogue; at home it was, if possible, even poorer, being confined to the first Seder, which more and more developed into a farce, with fits of hysterical laughter, admittedly under the influence of the growing children. (Why did you have to give way to that influence? Because you had brought it about.) This was the religious material that was handed on to me, to which may be added at most the outstretched hand pointing to 'the sons of the millionaire Fuchs' who attended the synagogue with their father on the High Holy days" (LF p. 79).

In our own time, when thousands of Jews from assimilated backgrounds have made the step of rediscovering their spiritual origin, there are probably many who harbor very similar accusations about the kind of Jewish example they were given. But in this letter to his father Kafka shows great understanding of the process of assimilation in which his parents were caught. He describes the effect on his father's life of, firstly, the transition from the countryside to the town, and then of military service. He explains skillfully how the "few flimsy gestures" of Jewish practice performed by his father actually had great meaning for him, his father, because like souvenirs they carried with them all the power of the religious life in the countryside which his father had known as a youth. But how could anyone expect these "souvenirs" to transmit anything of meaning to the next generation? This is Kafka's complaint, or excuse.

"Had your Judaism been stronger, your example would have been more compelling too; this goes without saying and is, again, by no means a reproach, but only a refutation of your reproaches" (LF p. 83).

These passages show that their author did have an awareness of what genuine Judaism should be, an awareness and knowledge which he acquired as an adult, and against which he could measure his upbringing. Indeed, Kafka alludes to his later movement towards Judaism in this very letter. Again, this development is described in terms of his relationship with his father. He writes that his father had "in advance, an aversion to every one of my activities." The fact that this also applied to his beginning to take an interest in Jewish matters was particularly upsetting.

". . . One could have expected that in this case you would make a little exception. It was after all Judaism of your Judaism that was here stirring, and with it also the possibility to enter into a new relationship between us. But . . . through my intervention Judaism became abhorrent to you, Jewish writings unreadable; they 'nauseated' you" (LF p. 85).

Perhaps correctly, Kafka analyzes this response as due to a wish to hide the weakness of the Judaism with which Kafka senior had brought up his children. If he welcomed the new interest shown by his son, he would be admitting that there had been something lacking in that which he himself had provided.

If we were discussing someone living in the 1970's or '80's, we would probably not have to look far in order to find the beginning of the attempted turn towards authentic Judaism evidenced by these passages. An experience such as putting on Tefillin at the Western Wall, or in a Mitzvah Mobile in Manhattan, reading an article, seeing a leaflet. But these gateways did not exist in the world of Franz Kafka. The trends in the first quarter of the twentieth century were emphatically away from Judaism and Jewish life. We therefore have to ask how Kafka's adult interest in Judaism began. Was it from books? From people? From his own personal investigation of life? Perhaps all three?

Yiddish Theatre

Kafka's innate yet suppressed interest in traditional Judaism first began to be expressed in 1910. In May that year he went with his friend Max Brod to the Cafe Savoy where they watched the performance of a Polish-Jewish theatre group from Lemberg. The Yiddish theatre of that epoch might well be viewed as an example of traditional Jewish society giving way before the pressures of the Haskalah; yet for Kafka (and many others) it functioned as a window on another world. Kafka met the Polish-Jewish actor Isak Lowy, and was fascinated by him. According to Brod, Kafka took him back home with him (to the intense annoyance of his father) and "made this passionate person tell him all about his life, his surroundings and his development, and gained deep insight into the customs and spiritual crises of the Polish-Russian-Jews" (*Biography*, p. 111). Later Kafka tried to write a biography of Lowy, and a survey of the Yiddish theatre, based on their many conversations.

Kafka's *Diaries*, from 1911 onwards, devote much space to this Yiddish theatre group, and to the plays they performed. He describes in detail a play (by Lateiner) about a *meshumad*, a Jew who has let himself be baptized. In one scene two traditional Jews wearing caftans come to his home, collecting money. They are shocked when they see no *mezuzot* on the doors. Kafka writes that during the play, hearing some of the songs and the phrase "*Yiddishe kinderlach*" brought him close to tears (6 October, 1911).

Now Kafka began to read about Jewish history, and eagerly studied a history of Yiddish literature published in Paris in 1911. His enthusiasm for Yiddish led him to organize an evening of recitations by Isak Lowy in the banquet hall of the Prague Jewish council chamber. Kafka organized the entire event, and was quite proud of its success. He introduced Lowy with the words: "Ladies and gentlemen, I want to tell you how very much more Yiddish you understand than you think you do" (*Biography*, p. 113).

The significance of this turn towards Yiddish and Polish-Russian Jewish life should not be underestimated. The Haskalah began in Germany with the attempt (unfortunately successful) to replace Yiddish with "pure," grammatical German. By the beginning of the 20th century Yiddish was not spoken in Prague. Further, as outlined above, the continuing process of modernization was also one of Westernization; The Jew of Kafka's Prague looked West, not East, for his edification and his ideals. The Yiddish plays of the Cafe Savoy represented a reversal of this trend. But would this new direction lead to authentic Judaism?

Kafka and his friend Max Brod, an incipient Zionist, were gaining a sense of Jewish identity from their contact with the Yiddish theatre. It was another friend, Jiri Langer, who brought Kafka to the next stage of his Jewish education: contact with Chasidism, and with it, the concept of *teshuvah*.

An Early *Baal Teshuvah*

Detailed information about the spiritual journey of Jiri Langer is provided by his brother Frantisek, a well known Czech playwright and politician, in his foreword to the book of Chasidic stories which Jiri later wrote, *Nine Gates*. Jiri is almost the first known, modern European *baal teshuvah*, a person who, brought up in a more or less assimilated, Western home, in which Judaism had been reduced to a variety of Protestantism, made the step of "return" to his spiritual origin, and even attempted to enter the world of Chasidism. (Others of this time are described in Klapholtz's *Return*.)

Jiri Langer was born in Prague in 1894 into the thoroughly Westernized family described above; they kept *kashrut* only at the insistence of their pious non-Jewish maid. But young Jiri soon showed an unusual interest in religion and spirituality. At fifteen years old his discussions on this subject with his older brother Frantisek, who was to be a writer, led him not to Judaism but to the works of a somewhat mystical Czech poet recommended by his brother. Jiri read all the works of this poet, but was clearly not satisfied. A new step came when, together with another Jewish friend, he learnt Hebrew and began to study Jewish writings. There did exist in Prague at that time a small circle of traditionally orthodox Jews, who were generally ignored by the far more numerous fully Westernized Jews of the city. Presumably they helped Jiri in his first steps towards Jewish life. They taught him, lent him books, and told him about the *mitzvot* of the Torah.

At the age of seventeen, Jiri Langer began applying this new knowledge in a serious way within the context of his home, much to the consternation of his family. His older brother, then a medical student, is shocked to report that Jiri gave up all the normal pleasures of a young man: friends, sport, and even the Czech Philharmonic concerts. Jiri withdrew to his room, where he sat with his hat on his head studying the large folios of the Talmud. In order to devote himself more thoroughly to his Jewish studies he took the unprecedented step of leaving school. Every day Jiri's father would give him a little sermon entreating him to think of the practical side of life, of his future, and urging him to return to school.

At one point an incident took place which slightly reassured the Langer family. While Jiri and his father were walking in the street they were suddenly approached by one of the traditional Jews of Prague. This person was very wealthy and highly respected, and was the head of the *Chevra Kaddisha* (Burial Society), a title which still meant something. He congratulated Jiri's father on having such a wonderful son, and assured him that Jiri would one day be an eminent scholar (*Nine Gates*, p. xiv). Perhaps this was the first instance in our century of the mediation which so often has to take place when a young person turns towards a more consistent form of Judaism and thereby has to face parental criticism.

While this incident had a stabilizing effect, Jiri's quest for authentic Judaism was not yet complete. At the age of 19, he set off on a journey, telling no one but his sister. To her he confided that he was going travelling in Galicia; why, he did not say.

For the Jews of Prague in 1913, Galicia and its impoverished Chasidic communities represented the Middle Ages. Jiri, looking for *yiddishkeit* rather than just Judaism, discovered the town of Belz in Eastern Galicia. At this time Belz had a population of 3,000, half of whom were Jews. At the center, spiritually, was the Belzer Rebbe, Rabbi Yissachar Dov Rokeach, grandson of R. Sholom of Belz, founder of the Belzer dynasty. Jiri found lodging with the Belzer Chasidim, and it was from this townlet that he at last sent his anxious family a postcard, asking them not to worry. In Belz, Jiri Langer entered the daily life of the Chasidim, studying Talmud (albeit generally alone), going to the *mikveh* every morning before prayer, trying to observe the Shabbat punctiliously. He was hampered by not knowing Yiddish, in fact, he had never heard it spoken before, but gradually he made progress. The whole community buzzed with talk of the youth who came all the way from Prague. He met the Rebbe, Rabbi Yissachar Dov, who welcomed him, and spoke to him kindly about Prague, where the Maharal is buried—the ancestor of R. Yissachar Dov (*Nine Gates*, p.6).

At the same time an immense conflict was going on in the heart of Jiri Langer. Together with the reality of Judaism that he was experiencing, and the warmth of life in a small Chasidic town of 80 years ago, he was undergoing a major culture shock. Jiri was fascinated by the fact that the Rebbe would not look at women, although they were allowed to present the Rebbe with a *kvitel.* Filled with curiosity, the Prague youth once had the opportunity to peep through a keyhole and watch R. Yissachar Dov speaking to his own wife. Jiri was disturbed to see that the Rebbe turned his face away from her too, as if she were a strange woman (*Nine Gates,* p. 11). The conflict finally came to a head. Jiri writes, in his introduction to his book *Nine Gates*:

"I can endure it no longer. This life of isolation from the rest of the world is intolerable. I feel disgusted with this puritanism, this ignorance, this backwardness and dirt. I escape. I travel back to my parents in Prague. But not for long. I must perforce return to my Chasidim" (p. 12).

Jiri's brief return to Prague is documented by Frantisek, who describes in detail the absolute horror with which he was greeted by his family. Frantisek writes:

"I understood what had filled [my father] with dread as soon as I saw my brother . . . He stood before me in a frayed black overcoat, clipped like a caftan . . . His whole face and chin were covered with a red beard, and side curls in front of his ears hung in ringlets down to his shoulders. My brother had not come back from Belz to home and civilization; he had brought Belz with him" (*Nine Gates,* p. xv).

Now Jiri's behavior can be seen, for the most part, as part of a pattern familiar enough in our own time. He refused to eat in the Prague kosher restaurants; they were no longer kosher enough. He ritually washed his hands before meals, and prepared his own food at home, consisting largely of bread and onions. He did not shake hands with women and in fact whenever he spoke with one he turned his back on her. His family could, more or less, put up with all this. But they were filled with alarm and embarrassment at the effect he had on others outside the house. For three generations, the Jews of Prague had done their best to look like everyone around them. The sudden appearance of a young man dressed like a Polish Jew in the streets of a respectable Prague suburb was highly disturbing. At the request of the family, the "modern" Rabbi of the district tried to speak reason with Jiri. But Jiri refused to talk to him, regarding him as an atheist . . . (*Nine Gates*, p. xvii).

In fact, Jiri did find a way to accommodate his family somewhat, probably at the advice of wise members of the small traditional community in Prague. But soon, having had a vision of R. Yissachar Dov, he was off to Belz again. This time he was accompanied by another young Jew from Prague named Gavriel. (This might be Otto Muneles, who later went through a spiritual crisis during the war and wrote an historical work about Prague Jewry.) Jiri settled in the little town, more or less accepted as "serious" by the Chasidim. When war broke out in 1914, after what he regarded as a miraculous discharge from military service, he rejoined the Rebbe and moved together with his entourage to Hungary. Later he traveled to Prague, as did a number of other Chasidim, during the upheaval of war. When R. Yissachar Dov, due to illness, visited Marienbad, Jiri Langer was among the Chasidim who accompanied him.

After the war Jiri finally left the Belz community and returned to European life. He wrote several articles and a book attempting to examine Jewish mysticism from a Freudian perspective, and became a teacher at the Jewish College in Prague. He traveled to Paris and to Palestine, and eventually, helped by Frantisek, he published in Czech his book of Chasidic stories, Nine Gates, which appeared in 1937. He also wrote religious poems in Hebrew. During the Second World War he managed to escape to the Land of Israel, and he passed away in Tel Aviv in 1943. Although he did not continue to be a follower of Belz—the death of R. Yissachar Dov in 1926 was a crucial turning point for him—according to Frantisek he was always a fully observant orthodox Jew. In a truly remarkable way, he had made the pioneering journey from modern Western assimilation to something very close to authentic Jewish life.

Kafka and Judaism

All of this intense experience was passed on to Langer's older friend, Franz Kafka. They met during the war years, and spent much time together. Max Brod was also part of the circle. A glimpse of their relationship is seen from an entry in Kafka's *Diary*. Brod wanted Langer to read one of his books, which recently had been published. But Langer refused to waste any time that could be used for Torah study, and therefore could not read the book. However, there was one possibility; to read it on the evening before December 25th, when Chasidim have the custom not to learn Torah. But this hope too was disappointed, for in 1916, the year in question, that evening was on a Friday night, when Langer refused to read anything secular! Yet there still remained a chance: the equivalent festival in the Russian calendar, which would fall thirteen days later . . . (*Diary*, 25 December 1916).

From Langer, Kafka gained an enthusiasm for Hebrew. Without telling Max Brod, he began studying this language. Brod later records his surprise at this activity of Kafka, which was kept secret from him for a considerable time (*Biography*, p. 163). Further, as the person responsible for dealing with Kafka's manuscripts after the latter's death in 1924, Brod makes an extraordinary statement: "Of the papers he left behind, the papers filled with Hebrew exercises are not much fewer than those covered with literary works in German" (*Biography*, p.197).

Were these only "exercises"? Perhaps we will never know. But Brod's occasional descriptions of Kafka's Hebrew studies are intriguing, In his own diary Brod notes, in July 1918, that Kafka prefers the country to the town; "Here he studies Hebrew and gardening. The positive things in his life. Wants to keep these quite pure—they are the 'country things'. Would like to withdraw from everything else" (*Biography*, p. 168).

Jiri Langer told Kafka stories about the Chasidim; some occur in the *Diaries* (see entry for 6 Oct. 1915). He also tried to get him to visit them. For a time Max Brod was also enthusiastic about this. In September of 1915 a Chasidic Rebbe, a relative of the Belzer Rebbe, visited Prague and stayed in the Zhiskov suburb. Kafka records that he and Langer, together with Max Brod, went to see him. This was at the time of the Third Meal on the Sabbath. They held back from coming too close. But the Rebbe said: "You're Jews too, aren't you?" Kafka's comment is striking: "A nature as strongly paternal as possible makes a Rabbi." At the same time, Kafka was aware of the immense distance dividing this Polish Jew from his own Western upbringing. Thus he notes that the Rebbe he saw in Zhiskov "reached into the food with his fingers." But this did not prevent him from also observing that "when his hand rested on the table for a moment you saw only the whiteness of his skin, a whiteness such as you remembered having seen before only in your childhood imaginings—when one's parents, too, were pure" (*Diary*, 14 Sept. 1915).

On the way home from this encounter, discussing it with Brod, Kafka rejected the experience: "If you look at it properly, it was just as if we had been among a tribe of African savages. Sheerest superstition." Brod notes that this was not meant to be insulting, but it certainly was a sober rejection. (*Biography*, p. 153).

Despite this, during the following summer Kafka took the opportunity to deepen his acquaintance with the world of Chasidism. This time, together with Jiri Langer, he met the Belzer Rebbe himself, who was then staying in Marienbad. Kafka sent Brod a long letter describing the experience; it is objective and amused. For example, while waiting outside the Hotel National for the Rebbe to appear, it began raining. Langer expected the rain to stop when the Rebbe came out; he told Kafka about an incident he had witnessed, in which the rain suddenly stopped for the Rebbe. But this time, notes Kafka, it did not stop. Instead it rained more heavily.

Despite this objectivity, Kafka let himself be involved in the activities of the Chasidim. Thus the letter continues with a description of Kafka, Langer and another Chasid running earnestly to various springs of Marienbad in order to get water for the Rebbe. By that time in the evening the Rudolf Spring was closed, so they ran to the Ambriose Spring. But this too was closed. They returned to the hotel, and there follows a description of the Rebbe surrounded by his followers; how despite the press of the crowd, they part and regroup, in order to make room for him to walk. Kafka depicts him as a mixture of eastern royalty, father and teacher. "The sight of his back, the sight of his hand, which was on his hip, the sight of the movement of that broad back—all this gives a feeling of trust" (*Briefe*, p. 144).

Another letter by Kafka, written at the same time to the philosopher Felix Weltsch, is brief but highly expressive:

"Yes, Langer is here, for now this is in general a kind of centre-point of the Jewish world, since the Belzer Rebbe is here. I have already been twice in his entourage for the evening walk. He alone is worth the journey from Karlsbad to Marienbad" (*Briefe*, p. 146).

At this time Kafka was going through a crucial inner struggle about whether or not to get married (to "F."). His diaries indicate, too, that while in Marienbad he was reading the Bible, which became part of his struggle: "Isaac denies his wife before Abimelech, as Abraham earlier had denied his wife" (*Diary*, 14 July 1916). There are grounds for suggesting that for Kafka, the central problem of his life, marriage, was intimately connected with the question of his relationship with Judaism. The passages we have quoted suggest that he saw Chasidism as a deep expression of purity. Yet somehow, as in one of his own stories, Kafka could not walk through the gateway. Perhaps at that point the Chasidic world itself was not yet sufficiently accessible for a thoroughly Westernized Jew. Langer had been able to make the journey, at least to a great extent. But Kafka was unable to follow. Ultimately, it was for this reason that he never married.

Marriage

Kafka's intense yearning for marriage is expressed in the *Letter to his Father.* Although at the time that this letter was written Kafka was trying to devote his life to his artistry as a writer, the fact that he could record the following words betrays what in fact was his greatest problem:

"Marrying, founding a family, accepting all the children that come, supporting them in this insecure world and perhaps even guiding them a little, is, I am convinced, the utmost a human being can succeed in doing at all. That so many seem to succeed in this is no evidence to the contrary . . ." (*Letter to his Father*, p. 99).

It is interesting how closely this coincides with the traditional Jewish view of life; with the help of G-d, marriage and children are the top priority, after which all ambition and quest for success have to take second place.

The overt reasons why Kafka did not marry the young lady he refers to as "F.", whether because of dedication to his writing or his lack of money or, later, his illness—these, I suggest, are secondary. The main reason was something much more profound, relating to the special predicament of the Jew in the Western world.

In December 1917 Kafka made the final break with F., an event which was to some extent cushioned by frequent discussions with Max Brod. His statement to Brod about the impossibility of his marriage is highly revealing:

"What I have to do, I can only do alone. Become clear about the ultimate things. The Western Jew is not clear about them, and therefore has no right to marry. There are no marriages for them. Unless he is the kind that is not interested in such things—businessmen for example" (*Biography*, p. 166).

If one is concerned at all about ultimate things, the unresolved question of one's Jewishness in the Western world stands in the way of marriage, the ultimate fulfilment. Put conversely, through the resolution of one's Jewishness one is able to marry.

Kafka could not resolve his Jewishness. Today, after the dramatic opening of the portals of Judaism by the Torah leaders of our time, there is a path which someone like Kafka might strive to follow. This path has many challenges, and may sometimes seem circuitous and paradoxical. This is no surprise; after all, the first Jew had to face the challenge of the *Akeda*. Nonetheless, the road is there, clearly demarcated, whether in terms of the Code of Law, subtle Torah study, practical charity or the inner discoveries of contemplative prayer. The fact that a Jew today can now discover this direction of *teshuvah*, is the result of great dedication and self-sacrifice on the part of those Sages who determined to make it accessible over the past seventy years. There is a mystical dimension to this process, which is why it is centered on the Chasidic movement; it is no simple matter to open the gateways of repentance and change the direction of history.

In 1917, despite the example of Jiri Langer, Kafka could not move forward along this path which today has been followed by thousands. Instead, his grand and tragic attempt was to try to resolve the paradox of life through his writing, which he termed "a form of prayer." This functioned as his own, personal mystical religion. It enabled him to live on and granted him a lonely ecstasy, however unsatisfactory this might have been (as is indicated by the ending of his story *In the Penal Colony*, in which fearful, self-inflicted torture fails to provide the hoped for spiritual release). Clearly, too, his art did not give him access to marriage and children, Jewish marriage, which to him signified the only true freedom.

The morning after he made the statement quoted above, that a Western Jew cannot marry, Kafka said a final goodbye to F. Then he came to Brod's office and wept; it was the only time Brod ever saw him cry. He was weeping not only about marriage to F., but about any possibility of marriage (*Biography*, p. 166-7).

There was, however, one more attempt. This is particularly poignant, because with this Kafka came so close not only to marriage but to a form of Judaism. This was towards the end of his life, when he met Dora Diamant. Predictably, she was the daughter of an orthodox and highly respected Polish-Jewish family; her father was a Chasid. Dora had traveled on the route of the Haskalah, "escaping" from the shtetl to Breslau and Berlin. Eventually, aged 19 or 20, she met Kafka—who was trying to travel in the opposite direction. At one of their first meetings, Dora, who had a high level of Jewish education, read a chapter from Isaiah to Kafka in the original Hebrew. From then on she became his companion, caring for him until his death two years later.

Kafka wrote a letter to her father, asking for her hand in marriage. In this letter he explained that although he was not a practicing Jew in her father's sense, he was nevertheless "a repentant one, seeking 'to return'" and therefore he hoped that he might be accepted into the family of such a pious man. According to Brod, Dora's father set off with this letter to the Gerer Rebbe to ask what to do. The Rebbe read the letter and answered: "No." Shortly afterwards Kafka died (*Biography*, p. 208).

Form of Prayer

The theme of marriage, often referred to in the *Diaries*, is also found occasionally in Kafka's literary works. According to

Brod, the prose piece entitled Eleven Sons is to be understood as expressing the yearning for marriage and children. The piece presents the author as a father who gives a list of his eleven offspring, sensitively and wisely discussing their respective qualities. It is noteworthy, too, that his earlier story *Metamorphosis*, describing Gregor Samsa's transformation into a beetle, ends, after the eventual death of the beetle, with a note of hope. Now that the beetle is gone, the Samsa parents can concentrate on finding a husband for their daughter, Gregor's sister. . . . Of course, the issue is not "just" marriage. Kafka once told Brod, "with suppressed sobs," that his idea was "to be a father, and talk quietly with one's son. But then one may not have a little toy hammer in place of a heart" (*Biography* p. 140). The image of the toy hammer expresses the force of Kafka's angst and incommunicable yearning which held him back from marriage and ordinary life. Again, through his writing, which he called "a form of prayer," he attempted to assuage his immense, unspeakable problem.

But Kafka's problem is not his alone. If we postulate an extraordinary spiritual sensitivity in his heart, then his problem is precisely the problem of existence as a whole, the problem of man in relation to the Infinite. The Jewish terminology for this problem, this dislocation, is "Exile." There is the exile of the Jewish people from their land, the consequent general exile of existence from G-d, and the complementary inner exile of the individual.

In Chasidic teachings the state of Exile is sometimes described in terms to which, one feels, Kafka would have responded. Take the following passage, from *Shaarei Orah* by Rabbi Dov Ber, the Mitteler Rebbe (1773-1827):

> "When G-d is exalted, remote in His Essence, height beyond height—then the world is not His place at all . . . and all the devolution of worlds has no significance. Then even when the

> Seventy Princes [of the seventy nations] are in utter disunity, and the *Shechinah* and the Jews are in Exile . . . and even when pagans dance in His Sanctuary, when they burnt the Temple . . . all this does not have any significance at all and is not any kind of flaw in His glory. Like a spider and spider-web in the palace of a king; even if it makes a big web on the floor of the royal palace certainly none of the king's servants will take any notice at all . . . The spider could easily be caught in the hand and thrown out, yet nonetheless it crawls around the royal palace and lives among the beams or on the floor, and even sometimes walks on the couch of the king. He does not feel any lack of glory in this, nor any pain, because of its total insignificance . . . This is as the Sages said; 'the might of G-d is that pagans dance in His Sanctuary and He is silent' (*Yoma* 69b) . . . This itself is a proof of the immensity of His might" (*Shaarei Orah*, p.96).

Although Kafka heard many Chasidic stories from Jiri Langer, he did not have access to teachings of the kind just quoted. Unlike most other Chasidic groups, Chabad sought to communicate the esoteric teachings which constitute the hidden essence of *Chasidut*. The Breslov school also made a comparable endeavor. In both cases, this means not the depiction of a spirituality that transcends and flees from the world, but the revelation of certain key aspects of the cosmic struggle at the heart of the process that leads from Exile to Redemption. As the person explores the Chasidic teaching, he or she discovers with a shock of recognition that the drama of the Divine is their own personal drama as well. Chabad, in particular, also provides clear guidance as to how to respond to that struggle.

Instead of the terrifying paralysis described by Kafka, "feeling like a clothes rack pushed into the middle of the room," the person discovers how to act within their own inner world, following a path of Torah study, *mitzvot*, contemplation and prayer, and also in their homes and in society as a whole. In particular the intimate reality of marriage, children and community, for which Kafka longed, is presented as the path for both personal and universal freedom.

There have been a number of attempts to draw parallels between Kafka's writings and Jewish texts, such as the writings of Rabbi Nachman of Breslov, or a genre of Chasidic stories in which Heavenly Judgement is a central theme. In such studies scholars often point out the lack of resolution of the problem in Kafka's works when compared with these Jewish texts. Thus Professor Karl Grozinger shows that in Kafka's *The Trial*, the lawyers whom "K." tries to get to intercede on his behalf have no effect at all, while in the "Heavenly Court" genre of Chasidic stories the intercessors are generally successful. Grozinger rightly points to Kafka's situation as an assimilated, Westernized Jew as the reason for this crucial difference.[2]

The message of Kafka's writing and his life is that for the Jew the resolution of ultimate problems is through authentic Judaism. For Kafka, writing was a form of prayer, and perhaps a form of mysticism (see *Biography*, p.94). But as such, tragically, it was unsuccessful. I believe this is why Kafka left instructions that his unpublished works (including *The Trial* and *The Castle*) should be destroyed. As a spiritual guide, his writings do not work. They show the lonely anguish of exile without opening the door to redemption. For that one needs not Kafka's stories but the practical teachings of the Code of Law and the spiritual guidance of the *Tanya.*

This, indeed, is Kafka's true message to us. Lonely personal mysticism has deeply compelling qualities but ultimately does not work. The path into the "Castle" is that trodden by Abraham, Moses and Rabbi Akiva. Following that path, it is true, we each have our own struggle, which might be of terrifying proportions. But we have been given powerful keys to help us; Torah teachings and commands. Sometimes even then, it might seem, we are faced with a door we cannot open. Because we are guilty, because we have transgressed (horribly), or for some other reason. According to Rabbi Dov Ber, the Maggid of Mezeritch, we still have the ultimate resource; an axe, which can break through every door. As he explained it, this means the power of Chasidism. This aspect of the world which Kafka almost entered is expressed in concepts such as "Joy breaks through the barrier" and emphasis on the theme of *kabbalat ol malchut shamayim*, "Acceptance of the Yoke of Heaven." In practice this means not worrying, just going straight ahead and carrying out the practical (and often supremely simple) Commandment. Rabbi Dov Ber's axe also suggests the incredible transformative power of Chasidic teachings, which reach into the limiting, paralyzing "Western" dimension of consciousness and reveal the sparks of holiness waiting to be redeemed.

As Rabbi Shneur Zalman puts it, each person has to discover their own path in the Torah. But the gates are open and there is an invitation to walk through, relinquishing the hostile-like ego which keeps us stranded, immobile and helpless. The Torah and its commands open up a path which leads through the open "door of the Law" and into the "Castle." With the help of G-d the Western Jew can then transcend all limitations and get married, itself a step of confident trust in the Infinite. Hopefully, blessed by G-d, this union will bring into the world a host of children, like the eleven of Kafka's story, the *Yiddishe kinderlach* for whom he yearned.

Jewish Grandchildren

Susan A. Handelman

"A JEW TODAY," SOMEONE WROTE, "IS ANYONE WHO HAS Jewish grandchildren." The words sting—perhaps more than any others in our painful debates about Jewish identity.

Of course, the definition is only metaphorical. Innumerable Jews are unable to have children; others have chosen not to have them. Many have intermarried; others are unmarried by choice or fate. And many now openly prefer relationships with members of their own sex. Rare, indeed, is the Jew today who can be certain of having Jewish grandchildren.

It's no news that "alternate lifestyles," assimilation, challenges to traditional Jewish authority, and demographic changes have all ravaged the Jewish family. One now hears the argument that the traditional Jewish emphasis on the family is obsolete because it excludes large numbers of Jews from Jewish life. Some feminists claim that the traditional nuclear family is a repressive, patriarchal institution whose ideology has helped to exclude women from full participation in Jewish institutional life. Homosexuals argue for the validation of their lifestyle. Singles often feel hurt and condescended to, by a community which sees them as unfulfilled and not full adults as long as they are unmarried.

The other side argues that the family is the foundation of Jewish life and guarantor of Jewish survival; that the first *mitzvah* is "be fruitful and multiply" and that attacks on the Jewish family emanate not from a depth of true Jewish commitment and understanding but from an all too American ethic of self-gratification, narcissism and antinomianism. Being Jewish is not to be defined by whatever makes one feel good and self-justified. The lifestyles of Jews should not determine the Jewish style of life.

My aim here is not to engage directly in the Jewish view of homosexuality, or the challenges of feminism, or the problems of singles in the Jewish community. But these questions have raised for me a deeper, underlying question: Beyond all the usual platitudes, why is the family so important in Judaism?

To define a Jew as someone who has Jewish grandchildren—for all its irony—strikes me as conceptually profound. It defines a Jew in terms of family—but not immediate family. It validates not only biological self-reproduction but a spiritual continuance beyond the immediate, and across time. The Jew is not defined by how Jewish she or he may "feel," or how many *mitzvot* they may perform, or how much money they give, but their ability to embody (literally, in children) and transmit Judaism so vitally that these children choose to remain Jewish and are able, in turn, to pass on that spark to their own children. "Three is a *chazaka*," as Jewish tradition says. In other words, only when something is done three times, does it have the element of surety, permanence—can one trust its stability. Grandchildren are the third generation; they confirm the Judaism of the first generation. Transmission requires a biological next generation, but that is not enough; biology is shaped by spirituality, self is pulled towards other, the blindness of the present towards a vision of the future.

This is not to argue that simple survival is what being Jewish is all about. Yet, beyond all the obvious reasons for our contemporary emphasis on "survival" (the decimation of the Jewish population of the Holocaust, the continuous threats to Israel, declining birthrates and intermarriage), Judaism seems strangely obsessed with this theme and with the idea of family from the beginning. Why?

Our G-d's Concern With History

The Book of Genesis, for instance, is a book all about families, barren wives, sibling rivalries, destructions by flood and fire, constant threats to the process of transmission and continuity. These themes are narrated in part to demystify nature as an autonomous controlling force and stress the then revolutionary idea that the One G-d is in control of both nature and history.

And history is meaningful in Jewish thought precisely because G-d is passionately involved in it, and not static, emotionless, and ahistoric as the god of the Greeks. Just as G-d, the ultimate model, is intensely involved with the quarrels of families from Cain and Abel to the conflicts between the families of nations, so, too, are the biblical heroes and heroines deeply involved—in fact, defined by—the problems of their own families. Families are the great scene of spiritual struggle; both then and now, they are the paradigms of intimate connection and intense ambivalence. Unlike Greek heroes, Biblical heroes do not attain identity and glory in solitary combat away from their families; their problems are deeply domestic.

It's no accident that the critical test of Abraham was precisely the command to sacrifice his son . . . and not to be tempted in the wilderness or have to sacrifice himself. For the son was not his alone, and the crisis was not only personal; it was collective. The call to Abraham was for him to become a great nation; it was not a private covenant with a single person. Judaism, unlike other religions, does not advocate or promise "salvation" to individuals. The covenant is made not with Abraham alone but with all his descendants, the family which was to grow into the nation that Moses led to Sinai. And the revelation at Sinai again was collective, to an entire people, not to individuals.

Is this obsession with family the remnants of primitive tribalism? Is the focus on survival the result of a desert mentality and the tribulations of exile? And what does all this have to do with our modern need for individualism and self definition?

The family is central to Judaism, I think, because it is central to Jewish ideas of G-d, creation, covenant, and history. The biological family reminds us that we, like the world, are created;

we are not inevitable, necessary, autonomous. We are an effect of someone else's will—and in the best case—someone's desire to give to another. We have a history. The creation of the world—it, too, is a something from nothing, an act of faith and hope.

To refuse to give birth to the next generation is to refuse to continue G-d's creation, and thus also to refuse to live in history, and thus also to deny the covenant. For covenant is collective and historical. Torah is a guide and inheritance to a people who were to journey not just in space to the Promised Land—but in time, through the travails of history. History—the physical turmoil of this world, of its passions, temptations. "The Torah," as the book of Deuteronomy says in a famous passage, "is not in Heaven."

"Every descent," the Jewish mystics say, "is for the purpose of an ascent." The soul's descent into the scrappy physical world, the people's wanderings through the course of history, enable a great spiritual blossoming—and thus the Talmud compared the Jewish people to the olive: only when squeezed does it give forth oil.

This world, daily human relationships, are the scene of divine action, by both G-d and Israel. The world is not an allegory; spirituality is not elsewhere. The Jew is engaged in sanctifying this physical world and mundane historical time. That is why memory is so important to the Jews—it is the sanctifying and linking of past, present and future. In Jewish time, the past remembers the future. Memory, said the Baal Shem Tov, is the secret of redemption.

Generation: Jewish Responsibility

And to put it simply—there is no physical future, no history without physical reproduction. The family is the unity that creates life and is the most powerful agent of transmitting personal and collective memory. That is why there is such emphasis on "generation" in the Bible, why teaching and learning are so highly valued—because they are acts of transmission to, and reception and renewal by the next generation... of the heritage, of the gift. The threat to the covenant is that there will be no one, or the wrong one, to carry it on into history. Perhaps that is one of the meanings of the famous midrash that when G-d was about to give the Torah, he asked for guarantors who would keep it—it was not enough for the Jews themselves to pledge to keep it, only when they said, "Our children will be our guarantors," did G-d agree to reveal it.

Just as the children were pledged before they had any choice in the matter—the self is not an isolated, autonomous, totally free creation, despite the dogmas of pop American psychology. The family is a covenant. For in the family, we are continuously reminded of, obligated to, intruded upon and pained by, delighted and pleased with—others. We are in constant dialogue—even if it is angry. True, one can divorce a husband or wife. But however severe the alienation may be, a child's biological bond to a parent is indissoluble. As Robert Frost once put it: "Home is the place where, when you have to go there, they have to take you in." In this way, familial relations are a microcosm, training ground, reminder, and enactment of the Jewish people's intimate and tempestuous relation to G-d; why after all, are we called the "children" of Israel, the "children" of G-d?" The prophets, of course, exploit the full implications of these metaphors: In the book of Jeremiah, G-d may angrily "divorce" the Jewish people as his unfaithful "wife" who has played harlot but then cries yearningly for their redemption, "Return, O backsliding children."

The Integrity of Traditional Sex Values

Thus I will speculate that one of the reasons Jewish tradition opposes homosexuality is that there can be no next generation from that kind of union—no biological child; therefore, no history, no future, no covenant. Now of course—Jewish tradition holds that one who teaches another's child is as if s/he gave birth to that child. And this is a great value—but Judaism, unlike Christianity, does not allegorize away the physical commandment of the Torah and seek salvation in another world. The ideal Jewish saint is not an ascetic, or one who, as in other religions, attains purity by removal from the community, or from the demands of a family or the physical world, for these struggles are the deepest spiritual struggles. The secrets of the kabbalah were to be taught only to married men. And the kabbalah itself describes the various aspects of G-d's mystical inner being (the configurations of the *sefirot*) in terms of family metaphors, "father, mother, son, daughter."

Thus the traditional Jewish advocacy of marriage, childbearing, and heterosexuality, I think, should not be mistaken for a repressive patriarchy, an intolerance of lifestyles, a primitive tribalism, or outmoded ideology. Jewish tradition clearly teaches that a Jew is a Jew no matter what, that every Jew is holy, and part of the Jewish community. I am in no way arguing for the exclusion of those with alternate views from the Jewish community or synagogue. And I do not want to minimize in any way the personal pain this position may cause to homosexuals. But that pain is not a persuasive argument for change.

Our Jewish Duty Was And Is Clear

The family can indeed be a repressive institution—as can any relationship that is distorted, but I have tried to argue here that the Jewish concept of family is distinctive and absolutely integral to Judaism; it is not reducible to a bourgeois societal arrangement or "Lifestyle." It is deeply theological. One is free to make other choices. But what will be the grounds and values on which those choices are made? For the freedom to make choices should not be confused with the freedom to remake Jewish tradition into one's own image, with only one's present in mind. The ultimate ground of value in Judaism is not the autonomous self, but the personhood bestowed by being in and continuing G-d's creation and covenant.

Someone once said that having children made him relate to G-d a lot better. "How so?" I asked. "Because now I understand what it is like to create something you have no control over," he answered. This is ironic and also very wise. Having children is indeed an aspect of being made in the image of G-d. For G-d's creation as an act of G-d's free will, gives us free will and so makes our very actions in history meaningful, and makes the Torah ours, to be renewed in every generation. A child is both oneself and completely other. Similarly, in the process of transmission, Torah is the same and other—wholly accepted, and also changed and enlarged through newness of the next generation. As the Talmud says, "Even the innovations which a brilliant student will one day teach in front of his master were already given at Sinai." In this sense, the Latin-American writer Borges said, "Jews alone produced grandchildren, whereas in the secular Western tradition of writing and texts, *The Nights of Alexandria*, Babylon, Carthage, Memphis have never succeeded in engendering a single grandfather." Although no one can guarantee it, it is our obligation to try to make sure that we do have Jewish grandchildren.

Solomon Maimon: 18th Century Enfant Terrible

Joseph Udelson

DURING AN EPOCH OF DRASTIC HISTORICAL UPHEAVAL AND change, it is often difficult for even the most intelligent individual to discern the permanent from the merely transient. Such an epoch was the second half of the 18th century, and such an individual was the Polish-Lithuanian born Jewish philosopher, Solomon Maimon (1752-1800).

Always provocative and often exasperating, Solomon Maimon shambled his way across the continent from the bleak squalor of Polish Lithuania's ravaged Jewish villages to the most fashionable salons of Berlin. Talmudic prodigy, lifelong antagonist of the Jewish establishment, guest at the court of the Maggid of Mezeritch, and iconoclastic innovator in secular philosophy, Maimon's *Autobiography*, originally published in 1792/3, provides posterity with an extraordinary description of Western and Eastern European society, Jewish and non-Jewish, experiencing fundamental sociopolitical and ideological transformations. Maimon depicts for his readers an exceptional self-portrait of a brilliant, if sociopathological, genius gone astray in the thicket of new ideas and movements.

Most significantly, he provides extraordinary evidence concerning the origins, teachings, and practices of the new Chasidic movement, that most vibrant and lasting of the legacies of the 18th century.

This remarkable account begins in the small Polish-Lithuanian village of Nesvij (Nieswiez) on the river Niemen about the year 1752. Young Solomon, the son of a minor merchant and his wife, first resided with his parents in the homestead of his maternal grandfather, who was then farming in the territory of the Polish-Lithuanian magnate Charles Stanislaus, Prince Radzivill. One of his earliest memories was of the terrifying allegation of ritual murder lodged against his grandfather by the local Russian priest. His horror at the incident still reverberates almost forty years later. Although eventually exonerated, his grandfather never allowed his family to forget either his ordeal or his deliverance; Solomon's father "composed in Hebrew a sort of epic, in which the whole event was narrated, and the goodness of G-d sung" each year on the anniversary of the acquittal.

The tribulations of the family, however, only increased. A few years later they were evicted from their farm. Almost penniless, young Solomon's father established his family in Mohilna, another of Prince Radzivill's hamlets on the Niemen, about four miles from Nesvij, the site of the Prince's primary country residence. Of the Prince himself, Maimon recounts that "without any particular inclination for it, he abandoned himself to the most shameful sensuality; and without being cruel by nature, he nevertheless exercised towards his dependents the greatest cruelties." The Jews were particular targets of this cruelty, as the following typical incident suggests: "Once he drove his whole court to a Jewish synagogue, and without anyone to this day knowing the reason, committed the greatest havoc, smashed windows and stoves, broke all the vessels, threw on the ground the copies of the Holy Scriptures kept in the ark and so forth."

But far worse were the depredations of the Russians, whose interference in Lithuania increased in proportion to the decline of Polish royal central authority. And Prince Radzivill soon "got himself encumbered with the friendship of the Russians who plundered his estates and plunged his tenants [including Maimon's family] into the greatest destitution and misery."

Despite such vicissitudes, the boy's education was not neglected. At the age of six, Solomon's father began the lad's elementary instruction in Torah, and the following year he was sent to a cheder in Mir, of which he records only sour memories: "The school is . . . a small smoky hut, and the children are scattered, some on benches, some on the bare earth. The master, in a dirty blouse sitting on the table, holds between his knees a bowl, in which he grinds tobacco into snuff . . . while at the same time he wields his authority." Of the level of instruction Maimon was even more critical, a view he held also of the cheder he attended shortly afterwards in Iwenez, where he began to learn Talmud.

When he was but seven years old, the precocious Solomon found in his father's library a copy of Rabbi David Gans's 1592 book on astronomy and first experienced the surge of excitement at uncovering new knowledge: "In this work a new world was opened to me, and I devoted myself to its study. . . . As I was obliged during the day to occupy myself solely with the study of the Talmud. . . . I devoted the evenings to my astronomical inquiries."

Thus from his earliest youth Maimon mistakenly insisted upon an absolute chasm between Torah and secular studies, relegating the former to that which is easily grasped and therefore uninteresting, while the latter was an always elusive chimera beckoning him to escape into the uncharted vistas of the unfamiliar. Mathematics and philosophy were the chief attractions. But he failed throughout his life to comprehend that Gans himself, his mentor the Maharal of Prague, and scores of the most distinguished rabbinic scholars of his own native Poland-Lithuania unapologetically engaged in so-called "secular studies" as a legitimate adjunct to their Torah studies.

The youthful scholar's career took an abrupt detour when, at the age of eleven, his mother died. His father, burdened by mounting debts, soon afterwards agreed to the proposal proffered by a widowed proprietress of an inn in Nesvij, for his young son to marry her daughter in exchange for relief from financial hardship. The unhappy children were allowed no alternative and were wed. Solomon, characterizing mother and daughter alike as "Amazons," sought every opportunity to escape from them.

Therefore after his marriage the boy eagerly accepted the position of tutor, returning to his wife only on festivals. And eventually, after fathering a son while only in his teens, Maimon completely abandoned his wife and child in Poland while he sought enlightenment in Western Europe. He gleefully succeeded in eluding the frantic woman's agents as they sought to locate him and gain his consent to return home or, at the very least, to grant her a divorce. As Maimon later explained, "I was not inclined to divorce my wife without [discovering what I could identify as a philosophically admissible] cause." Only when, many years later, he was finally confronted in person by his distraught wife after she had traced him in Germany did he eventually agree, after a sustained period of remorseless refusal, to grant her a *get*.

While still employed in his first position as tutor in the home of a local, rather uncouth Jewish farmer, Solomon discovered two new areas of Jewish teachings, both of which he studied alone, secretly. The first was Maimonides' *Moreh Nevuchim* (The Guide of the Perplexed) which would fascinate and influence him throughout the remainder of his life; indeed from the Latinized version of the author's name, i.e. Maimonides, he chose his own surname "Maimon" as a lasting tribute.

In addition to his discovery of philosophy in the writings of Maimonides, Maimon also learned about the kabbalah, which he assiduously, if very unsystematically, studied on his own. The young tutor, presuming that he had thoroughly mastered the kabbalah's esoteric secrets, concluded that "the whole science, if it is to deserve that name, can contain nothing but the secrets of nature concealed in fables and allegories ... [and as] I wished to get insight into the sciences, not veiled in fables," he endeavored to teach himself German in order to master works in the secular sciences. And, succeeding in obtaining two dated German treatises on optics and physics, Maimon claims that "after studying these books thoroughly, my eyes were opened. I believed that I had found a key to all the secrets of nature."

In his approach and conclusions concerning these studies, the adolescent Solomon betrays three serious intellectual and character flaws that would plague him for the remainder of his life. In the first place, he never recognized that, unlike those works composed in the non-Jewish Western literary tradition that intrigued him, Torah sources—Biblical, Talmudic, philosophic, Kabbalistic, and Chasidic—cannot be mastered by the untutored autodidact, however innately clever. The Jewish literary tradition, inherently multifaceted and multilayered, requires prolonged and guided deliberation and analysis. Hence, convinced that he had ascertained the true import of Maimonides' philosophic teachings, Maimon concluded that the observance of *mitzvot* was no longer necessary, a conclusion that he never chose to reexamine.

Conceding his own hubris, Maimon says, "I looked down with pride on all others who did not yet know these things, laughed at their prejudices and superstitions, and proposed to clear up their ideas on these subjects and to enlighten their understanding." Thus, with his determination to "enlighten" anyone and everyone who seemed not to perceive what appeared so obvious to him, Maimon succeeded throughout his life to alienate would-be friends.

But, as will become obvious, the primary object of these traits was Maimon himself; an extraordinarily complex individual, he constantly challenged his own most prized and cherished philosophic certainties and abandoned them readily when the doubt could not be resolved honestly.

Another inauspicious aspect that came to bear early in Maimon's life was his dependency on the escapism of alcohol.

Married too young, unhappy in his coarse employer's home, and constantly menaced by rampaging Russian soldiers, he observes, "it may be easily imagined how pitiful was my condition here. Whisky had to form my sole comfort; it made me forget all my misery." For the remainder of his life, Maimon would frequent taverns whenever he had the opportunity, composing most of his books in such establishments and squandering his always very meager financial resources there, in addition to permanently undermining his health.

As his unhappiness intensified, the nearly destitute twenty-five year-old Solomon Maimon resolved to travel to Germany in order to pursue his quest for scientific knowledge. Setting off on his wanderings, he first arrived in the East Prussian city of Koenigsberg, where his appearance and demeanor evoked general hilarity and derision.

Encouraged to direct his quest for knowledge elsewhere, Maimon decided to travel to the Prussian capital, a hub of 18th century philosophic and scientific debate.

Arriving in Berlin completely indigent, the homeless migrant was housed and fed for the evening in a facility operated by the local Jewish community. But the following day, when it was discovered that Maimon possessed no employable skills nor intended to seek gainful employment, he was summarily expelled from the city. Mortified, the young man found "the object of all my hopes and wishes was all beyond my reach, just when it had been so near. . . . I threw myself on the ground and began to weep bitterly," and soon fell into a serious fever. Granted only a single day in which to recover his health, he was once again sent packing.

Bedraggled, destitute and friendless, he tramped his way back to Poland, where, in the city of Posen, he encountered the local Chief Rabbi. This remarkable, saintly person is, in fact, the only individual Maimon praises unreservedly throughout his entire *Autobiography*:

"He [was] a great scholar and a pious man, who by extraordinary misfortunes had fallen into a very miserable condition. The Chief Rabbi, who was an excellent man, an acute Talmudist, and of a very gentle character, was touched by my distress. . . . The good-hearted rabbi bade me . . . to lay aside all anxiety . . . gave me what money he had by him, invited me to dine with him every Sabbath, as long as I remained here, and bade his boy procure a respectable lodging for me. . . . . The Chief Rabbi also ordered some new linen for me . . . [and] dressed in my new linen and new suit I went to the Chief Rabbi. I was going to express my gratitude to him, but could scarcely get out a few broken words . . . . He waved aside my thanks, and said that I was not to think too highly of him for this, as what he had done for me was a mere trifle not worth mentioning."

And it was also through the good offices of the rabbi that Maimon secured a position as tutor, employment he held for two years. Later he would recall that "this period was undoubtedly the happiest and most honourable in my life."

Much as he admired Posen's Chief Rabbi, Maimon learned nothing from him. Ever the reckless gadfly, he found himself called upon ceaselessly to "enlighten" members of the Jewish community regarding various aspects of their beliefs and behavior that he regarded as "superstitions." Finally, through his persistent and ostentatious display of contempt for the most cherished values of the community that had so generously welcomed him into its homes, Maimon, much to his astonishment, succeeded in alienating most members of the local community. Dismayed by what he could only interpret as their "fanaticism," he decided to abandon Poland forever and to return once again to his quest for enlightenment in Berlin.

Respectably attired and possessing the remnants of the wages he earned in Posen, this second visit to the Prussian capital proved far more promising than the first. Favorably impressing Moses Mendelsohn, then the most renowned member of Jewish society in Berlin and the leading advocate of Jewish political emancipation, Maimon was introduced to the most fashionable salons of the capital. He also began serious studies of the major competing 17th and 18th century philosophers of the Western European Enlightenment.

Maimon's keen intellect quickly recognized logical flaws in these contending philosophic schools. As eager as ever to explain theoretical shortcomings he had discovered, no matter the personal cost, he swiftly alienated his friends in Berlin as he had those in Posen. As he confesses a little too disingenuously, "As a man altogether without experience, I carried my frankness at times a little too far, and brought upon myself many vexations in consequence." However, Maimon does seem truly puzzled by the persistence of his benefactors' continued adherence to their own views; rather ungenerously he could only ascribe this to a deliberate obtuseness on the part of the friends, or to less than honorable motives.

After exhausting his welcome in Berlin, Maimon traveled to the Netherlands, where again he offended his Jewish hosts. Eventually returning to Germany depressed and impoverished, Maimon briefly considered converting to Christianity for profit. Once again, however, he managed to receive financial assistance from the German Jewish community. This enabled him to attend a gymnasium, allowing him to improve his proficiency in German. Eventually, he returned to Berlin and undertook an intensive study of the writing of Immanuel Kant, with whom he conducted a correspondence concerning troubling flaws Maimon had identified in the Koenigsberg philosopher's opinions. These studies inaugurated Maimon's most productive period, the final decade of the 18th century.

Maimon's *Autobiography*, written during this decade, as well as his more specialized studies, provides invaluable insights particularly into the two quite different sociopolitical ideological issues confronting the Jewish people in Europe during the 18th century. The first involves his investigations into the unresolved fundamental dilemmas inherent in Enlightenment philosophy, and, therefore, in its discussions of equality for Western European Jewry. Eventually conceding these flaws in Enlightenment rationalism, Maimon was led to question Moses Mendelsohn's views, not only in philosophy, but equally on the ethical consequences that were supposed to result from this rationalism.

The second issue treated in his *Autobiography*, which we will discuss here, includes his observations of the social conditions surrounding the rise of the Chasidic movement among Eastern European Jewry, and his account of the movement's teachings and practices as he observed them at the time of his own visit to the court of the second leader of the movement, the Maggid of Mezeritch.

Distinctive in the experience of Eastern European Jewry during the 18th century was the progressive deterioration of the central authority of the Polish-Lithuanian state. It has recently been argued by scholars that the salient social factor contributing to the rise of Chasidism is not to be located in some internal Marxist-style class conflict within Polish Jewry (viz., between rabbinic scholars and common people), but, rather, the external erosion of the power of the Polish-Lithuanian state and the ensuing consequences for the established Jewish social structure.

Thus, in addition to the now ever lurking danger of physical violence by local peasants and pillaging Russian troops, it is evident from Maimon's account that daily life for Polish-Lithuanian Jewry was becoming more precarious, and that the community's social institutions were increasingly unable to fulfill their traditional tasks. Chasidism provided a dynamic and innovative response to the despair of people despoiled of their livelihoods, repeatedly subjected to the random violence of marauding bands of ruffians, and bereft of those familiar social institutions that previously had so effectively served the communal needs and knit its members into a vibrant integrated society.

That the Chasidic leadership consciously dispatched emissaries to communicate its teachings to all strata of Polish-Lithuanian society is evident from Maimon's account of his own encounter with the new movement. As he explains, although he had heard rumors about Chasidism "it was not till I met with a young man who had already been initiated into the [Chasidic] society and had enjoyed the good fortune of conversing with its superiors. This man happened to be traveling through the place of my abode, and I seized the opportunity of asking for some information . . . [and I learned that] as far as the mode of admission was concerned, he assured me that was the simplest thing in the world. Any man who felt a desire for perfection, but did not know how to satisfy it, or wished to remove hindrances to its satisfaction, had nothing to do but apply to the superiors of the society, and automatically he became a member."

And the adolescent Solomon did just that. He set off for Mezeritch, the center of the Chasidic movement under the Maggid, R. Dovber. His account of his visit and of what he learned there provides a rare historical testimony by an outsider concerning the teachings and practices of the new movement.

Concerning the fundamental teaching of Chasidism, Maimon reports:

"The true service of G-d, according to them, consists in exercises of devotion with exertion of all our powers, and annihilation of self before G-d [i.e., *bitul*]; for they maintain that man, in accordance with his destiny, can reach the highest perfection only when he regards himself, not as a being that exists and works for himself, but as an organ of the G-dhead. Their worship consisted in a voluntary elevation above the body, that is, in abstracting their thoughts from all things except G-d, even from the individual self, and in union with G-d. In their public worship . . . they became so absorbed in the idea of Divine perfection, that they lost the idea of everything else, even their own body, which became in this state wholly devoid of feeling. The principle of self-annihilation, taught by them is, when well understood, nothing else than the foundation of self-activity."

A second fundamental characteristic of the new movement noted by Maimon was its emphasis on joyful Divine service. This innovative approach provided a potent anodyne for the common people's fundamental longing to attain the spirituality for which they longed while suffering under the hardships of their deteriorating socioeconomic conditions and crumbling communal institutions, conditions which had led them increasingly to spurn the more ascetic and quietistic pietism of the *mussar* [i.e. ethical] and Kabbalistic homilies still being recommended by religious approaches carried over from a more tranquil and prosperous era.

Maimon, himself a child of these times and its burdens, was therefore forcefully impressed by the Chasidic movement's ubiquitous emphasis on the joyful service of G-d:

"They maintained that true piety does not consist in chastisement of the body, which disturbs the spiritual quiet and cheerfulness necessary for the knowledge and love of G-d. On the contrary, they maintain that man must satisfy all his bodily needs, and seek to enjoy the pleasures of the senses, so far as may be necessary for the development of his feelings, since G-d creates all for His glory. . . . [Rejecting asceticism], those who sought to enlighten the people required, as an indispensable condition of true virtue, a cheerful state of mind disposed to every form of active exertion; and they not only allowed, but even recommended a moderate enjoyment of all kinds of pleasure as necessary for the attainment of this cheerful disposition. By doing away with gloomy piety, their doctrines met with acceptance among the lively youth."

Finally, Maimon provides fascinating historical testimony concerning the distinctive oral style that, from its origins to the present, characterizes the Chasidic leaders' method of teaching and guiding their adherents:

"Their sermons and moral teachings were not, as these things commonly are, thought over and arranged in an orderly manner beforehand. This method is proper only to the man who regards himself as a being existing and working for himself apart from G-d. [On the other hand, Chasidic leaders] hold that their teachings are Divine and therefore only when they are the result of self-annihilation [i.e., *bitul*] before G-d, that is, when they are suggested to them ex tempore, by the exigency of circumstances without their contributing anything themselves. These [Chasidic leaders] understood the art of communicating truths of reason by means of sublime figures, and of translating these figurative representations into truths of reason."

Ultimately, the youthful Solomon decided not to join those "foolish, unintelligible, confused" Chasidim. However, unlike the many other instances where he explains his rejection of some religious or philosophic outlook at length, Maimon is strangely silent concerning his reasons for repudiating the Chasidism that he had initially found so very attractive. No doubt his rejection of all but self-instruction and his unfamiliarity with the multifaceted and multilayered nature of all Torah teachings both contributed to his decision.

In the final analysis, however, the decisive factor both in his rejection of the Maggid's teachings and his silence concerning the choice is rooted in his most serious character flaw, his egotism and hubris, the diametric antithesis of the Maggid's emphasis on selflessness, on *bitul.*

Precisely because *bitul* constitutes such a potent threat to the spurious pretensions of hubris, the self-willed young Solomon, loath to acknowledge and apply the Maggid's teachings on *bitul,* had no alternative but to "flee Mezeritch" if he was to sustain his feelings of superiority. Similarly, he could never allow himself to admit the true cause for this decision, for to have done so would have been to undermine all the subsequent pretensions of intellectual and philosophic superiority he was so eager to document for posterity in the Autobiography.

His rejection of the new movement, in fact, testifies to Maimon's ignorance of the most essential instruction of his most revered teacher, Maimonides. For in his *Guide of the Perplexed,* section III, chapter 51, Maimonides presents a parable of his own invention. It tells of the ruler of a city and of his subjects, the latter divided into seven categories graded according to their nearness to the ruler's habitation. The lowest category is of those he compares to irrational animals possessing but the external form of human beings. The second category consisting of those who are within the city, but have turned their backs upon the rulers's habitation, are people who have opinions either because of some great error that befell them in the course of their speculation or because of their following the traditional authority of one who had fallen into error. Accordingly because of these opinions, the more these people walk, the greater is their distance from the ruler's habitation.

As explicitly interpreted by Maimonides, it is only in the third category, which consists of those who observe *mitzvot* in all simplicity, that one begins to approach the ruler's habitation. Accordingly, in rejecting Torah and *mitzvot,* Maimon imprisoned himself in the second lowest of the seven categories. But as his mentor, Maimonides, had emphasized, only by proceeding to the third category may one then progress still closer toward the ruler's habitation; this, indeed, constituted the exalted goal which Maimonides sought to impart in writing the *Guide* itself.

And, precisely, guidance in advancing upward through these categories constituted the fundamental lesson expounded in Mezeritch, which would soon be systematically explained in the teachings of the youngest of the Maggid's disciples, Rabbi Shneur Zalman of Liadi. His *Shulchan Aruch* is, *inter alia*, a halakhic manual for the practice of *mitzvot* and hence for Maimonides's third category, and his *Tanya*, a Chasidic manual illuminating the pathway for progress toward the still higher categories.

Such were the radiant possibilities the young Solomon abandoned as he turned his back on Mezeritch to tread instead the lonely road to Koenigsberg.

Ultimately, Maimon was never able to overcome the estrangement and suicidal depression he had experienced while at the Hague and in Hamburg. Adamantly declining all offers of practical employment and recklessly continuing to offend would-be friends in the Berlin Jewish community, the increasingly unkempt Solomon Maimon began spending most of his time and almost all of his meager funds on miserable lodgings and in shabby taverns, where, usually in an alcoholic haze and in declining health, he struggled to compose lucid studies exploring the most profound dilemmas confronting the various schools of Enlightenment thought.

Eventually, a German nobleman, impressed by Maimon's philosophic efforts, brought him to his estate in Freistadt in Lower Silesia. And it was there, with only a local Protestant pastor for his companion, that this exemplar and chronicler of a Europe turned upside down finally died, on November 22, 1800.

Reflections On The Baal Teshuvah Movement:

Tzivia Emmer

IT WAS AT A SHABBAT TABLE RECENTLY THAT SOMEONE mentioned the subject of messianic predictions. One such prophecy asserted that an auspicious time for the coming of the Messiah had been the year 1970. We thought back. He hadn't come. What did happen in that year?

"That was about the time of the beginning of the *baal teshuvah* movement," I said, remembering my arrival in Crown Heights in 1974.

My guest bristled. "What do you mean, 'movement,'" he said. "I wasn't part of any movement. I did this on my own."

He was mollified when I changed the word to "phenomenon." But his response brought to mind those old, inconclusive college discussions (Do great men shape history or vice versa? What kind of music would Mozart have written had he lived in the nineteenth century?) as well as the spectre of those other "movements" more typically associated with that time period: the peace/leftist political movement and the counterculture.

These two streams, overlapping in time and in membership, to a large extent shaped the life of anyone growing up during the sixties and seventies. The turmoil of that time was like an unforeseen volcanic eruption whose ash drifted over the earth and affected the climate for years to come.

Many in the Jewish world look upon the counterculture years as a time of unbridled hedonism, lack of discipline and reckless destructiveness which led directly to the breakdown of family life and morality in America. But to those involved, the ideals which sought expression in "anti-establishment" behavior were real. They were a search for spirituality and aliveness, in opposition to what was perceived as materialism and petrification in American life. It was a desire for justice among individuals and among nations. Typical of the many threads of thought was the notion that through transformation of oneself and one's immediate environment one could transform all of society and thereby initiate a new age of moral perfection.

Based on such observations, one psychologist has pointed out that in the counterculture "we were participants in a recreation of the great saga of personal and national redemption, for which Judaism is the fundamental archetype. . . . The counterculture as a redemptive movement in Western history, however brief, took on the elements of all such redemptive movements, for which Judaism serves as the basic model."

It should come as no surprise, therefore, that many of us who marched on Washington in 1968 or converged in Woodstock in 1969 would, by 1979, be sitting in yeshivot and learning Torah. The generation of Bob Dylan may have rejected the Hebrew school teachers of their youth, but they could see themselves as the spiritual heirs of the Baal Shem Tov, of Levi Yitzchak of Berditchev.

I attended a liberal arts experiment in the late sixties (not to be confused with a college education in the usual sense) in which the student body consisted of less than two hundred juniors and seniors who had left other institutions for one reason or another. We were divided into two groups: those studying humanities and those studying social science. It became increasingly obvious that one group was primarily interested in leftist politics and the other in spiritual or artistic self-development. We called one another respectively the revolutionaries and the belly-button contemplators.

Several of the humanities people ended up as followers of Gurdjieff, an eclectic Russian mystic of earlier in this century whose disciples carried on his work in America. We lived in a community which stressed hard work and self-discovery. We disdained the title "hippie" and, under the direction of an elderly gentleman of Dutch origin, stayed away from drugs and other frivolities. We thought it odd and unaccountable that the local, rural population continued to refer to us as hippies nonetheless.

Looking back, it is easy to see that although we considered ourselves distinct from so many contemporary goings-on, we were part and parcel of our times and of the "counterculture." Need I point out that many of us were Jewish? A characteristic of such movements has always been a disproportionate number of Jews among both the leadership and the rank and file. The radical political movements and the spiritual groups were both fueled by Jews who had lost all conscious ties with their heritage, but whose passion for justice and for a form of personal and societal redemption can easily be traced to the culture that barely two generations back had performed *mitzvot* and believed in the coming of the Messiah.

It took a generation groomed to the idea of revolution to show the way back to tradition. Those who were accustomed to pointing the finger of logic at the inconsistencies of government and society were ready to point a finger as well at the bagel and lox Judaism and the lavish Bar and Bat mitzvahs with which their parents seemed content.

A longing for absolutes infused the counterculture—if the government had faults, it was all bad; if a convention could not be justified then it could be totally abandoned. "Middle class morality" was attacked because it seemed to have no underpinning of compelling absolutism. If this were merely a convention, and if conventions are relative, then this convention too was as dispensable as last year's fashions. The reasons given for "getting married" (specifically, to someone Jewish), settling down, and so forth were never good enough—because they weren't good enough. No one told us we were supposed to get married because G-d said we were supposed to.

Or maybe someone did, but neither speaker nor listener really believed it. Here our secular education had done its job. Atheism or uninformed agnosticism were the only acceptable theological positions open. But many of us who came of age in the time when everyone was being told to "question authority," ended up doing just that and eventually questioning the voice that said, "There is no absolute authority."

Then came the spirituality of the East, bringing not moral absolutes but a kind of absolute, alternative reality that seemed the best way to understand and justify existence. This, we thought, was what was lacking in Western, American life. The older generation was shocked and disturbed. They could not have seen then that the counterculture itself was an eruption of the same forces that would later lead many of its advocates to seek an authentic experience of Judaism. The road to the ashram or to drugs could under the right circumstances become instead the road back to *yiddishkeit*; this is the paradox of our generation.

But there is a radical discontinuity between the counterculture and Judaism. "It was quite by accident," wrote the psychologist, "that many Jews seemed to stumble upon the true meaning of Judaism and began to recognize their religion as embodying many, if not most, of the 60's counterculture ideals." Judaism, however, is obviously more than the realization of a counterculture dream. And nothing happens by accident. We have to entertain the possibility that the counterculture itself was the result of something much broader.

It is hard to imagine the *baal teshuvah* movement, if we will call it that, taking place, say, in the fifties. When the Lubavitcher Rebbe told his Chasidim in the late 1950's to start preparing ways and means to deal with the young people who were searching for the truth and would soon arrive at their doorstep, a good many heads under black hats and *sheitels* must have turned to each other in bewilderment. What youth, searching for what? This was the time, remember, of fraternities, beach parties, and Sputnik, Postwar prosperity, television and suburbia were new. Dwight Eisenhower was in the White House, and Father Knew Best.

The Rebbe's prescience here is indicative of events taking place on a plane and on a scale larger than any one person's experience. From this point of view, the *baal teshuvah* of the seventies and eighties was indeed part of a movement, not the less for having struggled quite individually and uniquely in his or her own life.

One of the most eloquent accounts of the spiritual odyssey of a *baal teshuvah* of that time was written by Dr. Miriam Grossman in her article, "Antidote for the Existential Blues" (Wellsprings, Dec/Jan 1989). She describes her need which began in childhood to understand a higher, or other, reality which was only hinted at in the tangible world. The meager Judaism to which she was exposed did not, of course, give her that understanding.

Dr. Grossman doesn't give the impression at all that her search was conducted in the company of like-minded friends or companions. If anything, it is the image of the solitary voyager setting out on an expedition with only lamps, guidebooks and perhaps a temporary guide, but without crew or fellow explorers. Yet her experience reflects a pattern in the life of so many others, differing in details but not in theme.

How did you become *frum*? How often has every *baal teshuvah* been asked the question? Our answers, as Dr. Grossman points out regarding herself, are almost always superficial, designed to provide a dollop of biographical information but telling nothing of the inner process that may span many stages of a person's life.

Finally, though, as fascinating as the "full story" may be, and as instructive to those who will find in them a point of departure for similar journeys, there is something strangely missing from all such stories. How do you get from there to here, really? It's hard to know. We went to such and such a place, met someone, perhaps a friend or a friend of a friend, or a rabbi, or even got off at the wrong train station. It was that tenuous. Sometimes even a guru told someone to go home to Judaism. Outrageous coincidences combined with an openness bred in the seventies toward things spiritual brought many of us to places we never thought we'd find ourselves: yeshivahs, Jewish communities, Chasidic *farbrengens*, the Western Wall.

But the journey can be explained in great detail only up until the point of arrival. Even Miriam Grossman, when it comes to really explaining what happened, describes a series of visits to Crown Heights during which she grows more comfortable with the ideas and the people of Lubavitch. But to go from appreciating *Shabbat*, or even acknowledging G-d, to incorporating into one's life the daily preoccupation with a system of *mitzvot* that are not always convenient, not always comfortable, and not necessarily comprehensible, involves a quantum leap that is not easy to explain. Like the image of the two faces of the goblet used in perception psychology, one can see things in one way or in another, but not both ways simultaneously. Either you perceive two heads facing one another or you perceive a wine glass. Either Judaism consists of antiquated superstitions or it embodies the wisdom of G-d for all time. When does one perception give way to the other? How do you get from there to here?

"I didn't need a guru," Dr. Grossman finally exclaims, "I needed my grandmother!" What could our grandmothers have told us? Would we have believed them? Perhaps they were there all along, guiding and pushing in the right direction. We are the sum not only of our own experience but of the genetic and cultural currents of many generations. To paraphrase Rabbi Aryeh Kaplan, behind every person who becomes a *baal teshuvah*, there is a chain of events that stretches back through the eons. Each person has sixteen great-great-grandparents and 32 great-great-great grandparents. Going back ten generations, one has 1,024 ancestors. Perhaps, without them, one couldn't get from there to here at all. It was the Jewish neshamah, with a little help, asserting itself—poking out through years of intellectual debris and spiritual alienation, through layers of I Love Lucy and the Beatles, through all the baggage piled on top.

This brings to mind an analogy that many of us have heard many times: that each Jew is like an engraved letter in the Torah tablets, and not like a letter written on parchment which can be erased. Maybe the real story, and the reason it is one that cannot easily be told, is simply that someone blew away some dust and revealed what was already there. It is really the only *baal teshuvah* story that makes total sense and the only way to explain in the grand journey called the *baal teshuvah* movement how anyone ever got from there to here. Is it a movement? Did the Messiah come, almost, and did we almost feel it? All I know is that we needed our grandmother and, somehow, we found her.

Halakhah

Halakhah in a Postmodern Age: A Meditation

Susan A. Handelman

This letter was first published in Wellsprings, *and subsequently in its full version as "Crossing and Recrossing the Void: A Letter to Gene," the concluding meditation in Peter Ochs and Eugene Borowitz's,* Reviewing The Covenant. Eugene Borowitz and the Postmodern Renewal of Jewish Theology *to be published by Albany, Suny Press.*

Dear Gene,

I AM WRITING THIS IN THE FORM OF A LETTER TO YOU for many reasons. I struggled through many drafts of this essay until I finally realized that it should be a direct address. For one thing, only that form would enact and embody the direct I—thou encounter between persons at the cornerstone of your theology of covenant, community, and revelation.

Another reason that I am writing in letter form is that the task assigned to me [here] was to "meditate" on this entire collective dialogue as it relates to postmodern Jewish renewal, on the living consequences for us as Jews, for where we may be going, for what our possibilities are.

So let me begin with the Hebrew word for "meditation," *hagut*, which comes from the root *hagah*. In the Bible, the verb *haga, la-hagot*, encompasses several meanings: "to pronounce, speak, utter, articulate, to study, meditate, moan, murmur, coo." And, interesting enough, *hogeh deot* means "thinker, philosopher." From the root *hagah* also comes the word *higayon* meaning "logic," "rationality" and "common sense." So in a sense, *hagut* already implies a "postmodern" notion of thought: To think, to meditate, is not to conduct a silent, solitary set of rational deliberations in the Cartesian sense, but is an act of social utterance in relation to an other. To meditate also means to study a text, and as Jewish law prescribes, study must be oral, the words must be vocalized, given body, sung out. One does not fulfill his duty of Torah study unless s/he actually utters the words with the lips. (*Berachot* 24b; *Eruvin* 54a*; Shulchan Aruch, Orach Chayim* 62:3)

And "reading," as the Hebrew word *kriyah* instructs us, should be a "calling out." It has been noted that each of the first Rashi commentaries on the first line of each of the first five books of the Bible expresses the love of G-d for Israel: and so it is in Rashi's first comment on the word *va-yikra*, "and He called" which is the first word of the Book of Leviticus. Says Rashi, "Before all instances of 'speak' [i.e. when G-d speaks], and before all instances of 'say,' and before all instances of 'command,' the term 'call' [*kriyah*] preceded; it is an expression of endearment." *Kriyah*: reading as calling out, as endearment: I want to bear this in mind, for I think we often forget in all our postmodern academic "theories of reading," "intertextuality," "semiotic systems," and "discursive practices," that our readings should be callings out to G-d and to each other. So much of postmodern discourse in the humanities is a hermeneutics of suspicion, an attempt to "overcome oppression" by unmasking hidden ideologies, unconscious desires, and unjust power relations. One of the tasks of a Jewish postmodernism, I think, is to give a soul back to postmodernism. It is here, Gene, that you and I are allies, that we have a common project.

The Soul of Postmodernism

At its best, I would say, postmodernism can be a way for Jews who have passed through the fragmentation and secularization wrought by modernity to renew themselves Jewishly. This is the focus of your book, and my central concern here. How can the search for postmodern or postsecular "spirituality" cross the void that modernity opened up? In what way does it reconnect to and reconfigure a "pre-modern" faith? After modernity, can we come to a "second naivete"—but one which does not deny or suppress all that we have learned and experienced in modernity?

Yet, on the other hand, isn't renewal and return, *teshuvah*, the eternal task of the Jewish people? *Teshuvah*, as the ancient rabbis said, preceded even the creation of the world. And we are, as Simone Rawidowicz so aptly characterized us, the "ever-dying people." Constantly confronting disasters, catastrophes, the undermining of our foundations—and then reconstructing them and renewing ourselves. Even the Book of Genesis, from a certain point of view, is a book of collapse, destruction, concealment of G-d and fragile survival. Let alone the Book of Job.

So, I believe, we also need to overcome a certain hubris about our generation and its challenges. Indeed, whereas the ideologies of modernism had apocalyptic overtones, there is an ironic self-awareness in postmodernism, a deflation of the self and its pretensions to final understandings, revolutionary upheaval . . . or what you so aptly call the "human *tzimtzum*." Peter Ochs has also characterized postmodernism as "redemptive" of modernity—and that is a distinctively Jewish perspective without which secular postmodernism can degenerate into another form of radical skepticism and irony.

I must pause here, though, and express my discomfort with large categorical statements about what postmodernism "is." There are many kinds of postmodernism, from the philosophical intricacies of Deconstruction, to complex global political developments, to certain artistic and cultural practices . . . down to "MTV." I certainly do not want to engage here in another abstract debate about what is and isn't postmodernism. It is a mixed genre . . . as is your own book. . . .

Nevertheless, the thinkers whom you rely on, and those whom I am inspired by—such as Levinas and Rosenzweig—all follow that path of return to Judaism, of "post-assimilation." It is also the path you autobiographically describe, and it is my path too. However we define the self, postmodernism requires us to try to delineate the location of that self and how it came to be "constructed," to trace the intersection of forces, cultures, languages which give rise to it. In your epilogue, you write of your grandparents and parents being a mix of rationalist Litvaks and Hungarian Hasidim. As a native American, your formative Jewish experiences came from an upbringing in Columbus, Ohio in the 1930's . . . in a very small Jewish community with inadequate institutions. In your studies for the rabbinate at Hebrew Union College in Cincinnati you were trained in modern "scientific" historical and philological criticism, and imbued with a faith in the University as a redemptive, civilizing force. Now, at the end of a century of barbarous slaughter, you write movingly of your "loss of faith in the intellectual and cultural pretensions of modernity," and in the power of the University. You have become, as you aptly phrase it, "skeptical of skepticism."

Like you, my ancestors were also Litvaks. I am a product of highly assimilated suburban Chicago of the 50's and 60's. In one sense, our generational differences are strong. But in another sense, we are both Jews who keenly feel effects of the shoah, the failures of modernity, and are skeptical of the University as an arbiter of value and ideals. We both seek a return to the particular Jewish self defined in a binding relation to G-d, other Jews, and community. We are both engaged in a kind of *teshuvah*.

Halakhah

But unlike you, I have chosen to be a halakhic Jew, and I believe that one of the key unmet tasks of postmodern Jewish thought is to overcome what I would call—forgive me—a secularized Christian antinomianism. That is partially a legacy from the German philosophers who also inspired the Jewish haskala and modernist thought. Especially Kant, that great proproponent of morality defined as duty observed out of inner conviction (reason and autonomy), as opposed to duty observed due to externally commanded law (authority and heteronomy). In his schema, Judaism becomes an inferior religion of heteronomous law, rightly superseded by a higher Christian religion of inner freedom. Kantian autonomous reason as Natan Rotenstreich once put it, is an equivalent or transformed version of Protestant grace or "inner illumination."

When I say that postmodern Jewish thought needs to recover the meaning of law in Judaism, I should insist on using the word halakhah, originating in the Hebrew root for "path" or, "walking." But, Gene, I don't want to rehash worn old arguments between "orthodox" and "reform" Judaism—terms that I am not comfortable with in any case. What I do want to emphasize here is that halakhah cannot be understood in terms of modernist categories of "autonomy" and "heteronomy." As Emile Fackenheim once wrote, Kant did not understand the nature of revealed morality in Judaism because it is outside the realm of both autonomous and heteronomous morality. Its source and life "lies precisely in the togetherness of a Divine commanding Presence that never dissipates itself into irrelevance, and a human response that freely appropriates what it receives."

Postmodernism, I think, can help move us beyond the sterile antinomy of autonomy/heteronomy. For one thing, the autonomy/heteronomy dualism presupposes an independent isolated self, a notion that is heavily critiqued in postmodern thought. For another, it is a mistake to identify the obligation, the "must" of a *mitzvah* with the "must" of rational propositions and deductive logic. Rosenzweig and Levinas well understood the need for this "third term" beyond the heteronomy/autonomy dualism. The paradigm for their construction of the self is the biblical cry of *hineni*, "Here I am." These are the words with which Abraham responds to G-d before the *Akedah*, and with which Moses responds at the burning bush, and which the prophets use when they are called by G-d.

Let me quote Peter Pitzele, who eloquently describes what is so difficult for us moderns to understand about Abraham's "obedience":

> "History has given obedience a bad name; too many docile lambs led to the slaughter, too many obedient functionaries murdering the lambs. Whenever we hear of talk of obedience, we are likely to feel ambivalence and fear. And a personal revulsion curdles the word as well . . . Obedience is a giving over of one's personal power; it is a loss of control."

But there is another kind of obedience, Pitzele notes:

> The word obey in English comes from the Latin word meaning 'to listen, to hear.' Abram listens to the call to leave his native land. And his father's house. He obeys. He experiences the call as something coming from a G-d who is felt to be Other and outside him. But this G-d is also inside him. Deep speaks to deep . . . Abram is not being obedient to some external dictate, to some chain of command. On the contrary, he breaks with customary conventions. . . . What Abram obeys flashes upon him like a beacon, points a way, then disappears. . . . On each step of his journey he must renew his commitment to his task, for his obedience is voluntary, not compelled (*Our Father's Wells*).

So often you reiterate, Gene, that central to your project is the need to protect our integrity in the face of the G-d who commands. But I would say that this is what the interpretive tradition of Oral Torah has always done. And as you know, the Talmud already voices your concern about an external compulsion which invalidates the revelation at Sinai in the famous passage in *Shabbat* 88a. I want to quote at some length from the Talmud here, for as much as I cherish those personal moments in *Renewing the Covenant*, so as much do I sorely miss in it the embodied texture of classical Jewish discourse—the cacophonous yet melodic weave of voices from different eras and times in the commentaries and super-commentaries, the dialogic voices of Talmud and Midrash.

The biblical text (Ex. 19:17) tells us that the Israelites stood *b'tachtit ha har*—translated idiomatically "at the foot of the mountain," but having a more literal sense of "at the underside." Here the Talmud comments:

> Rav Avdimi bar Hama bar Hasa said: this teaches us that the Holy One Blessed be He turned the mountain over on them like a cask and said: "If you accept the Torah, all is well; if not, here will be your grave." Rav Aha bar Jacob said: "Based on this, a major complaint can be lodged against the Torah." Rava said, "Nevertheless they reaccepted it willingly in the days of Ahaseurus, for it is written [Esther 9:27]: "the Jews [*kimu v'kiblu*] confirmed and accepted." They confirmed what they had accepted previously.

Rashi explains the nature of this complaint: "For if they were brought to judgment about why they had not fulfilled what they had accepted upon themselves, they could answer that they were compelled by force to accept it." In other words, it was not of their own free will. Nevertheless, they reaccepted it a thousand years later in their exile in the Persian Kingdom of Ahaseurus—"from," says Rashi, "the love of the miracle that was done for them."

In other words, what the Book of Esther is referring to in verse 9:27 is not just the Jews' confirmation and acceptance of Mordecai's instructions about how to commemorate their miraculous rescue from Haman's plot to slaughter them all . . . but to reaccept the entire Torah. They confirmed and accepted what had previously been "forced" upon them a thousand years earlier at Sinai; only now they did it out of free will.

Levinas, in *The Temptation of Temptation*, his commentary on this passage, understands this midrash on the relations of Sinai and Purim as indicating a "third way" beyond the dualistic alternative freedom/violence or autonomy/heteronomy. It signifies that there is a certain "non-freedom" prior to freedom, one which makes freedom possible, a prior saying of *n'aaseh ve-nishma* (Exodus 24:7), "we will do and we will hear/obey/understand," a prior calling to responsibility which is what in fact constructs the self. The self is defined by saying *hineni*, "Here I am for you." Moreover, Levinas notes, the thousand years of history between Sinai and the Persian exile were filled with the difficult consequences and suffering resulting from that first acceptance of the Torah. In reaccepting it at Purim, we do so in full cognizance of its price; it is a free taking on of the burden of that history.

In this light, I also find Rashi's comment even more poignant—the motivation for reaccepting the Torah was "from love of the miracle." Acceptance out of love, and in a time of threatened mass annihilation. For Purim is, in its own way, a holiday made for a postmodern sensibility . . . a holiday of masks, inversions, comic mockery, concealment of G-d whose name is never even mentioned in the Megillah; for the rabbis to make out of this a second Sinai is an act of hermeneutical genius and profound theology.

And this is the continuing task of any Jewish theology, of course, to continue Sinai. The great climactic scene at Sinai filled with thunder, lightning, and the Voice from heaven, is followed in the biblical narrative by a seeming let down: the minutiae of law regarding goring oxen, Hebrew bondmen, and so forth. Then come the long, seemingly tedious narratives of the building of the mishkan, the Tabernacle, descriptions of its boards and nails, the dress of the high priests; and then we proceed on into the book of *Vayikra* (Leviticus) and its elaborate descriptions of the sacrificial system.

Now these are the parts I usually skip when I teach "The Bible as Literature" to my mostly non-Jewish undergraduates. But perhaps this is a mistake. For these are also the parts that are also so distinctly Jewish. . . . These are the ways in which the elevated abstractions are brought into the concrete world. This is what halakhah is: second Sinai.

Revelation cannot remain an awesome inchoate Presence. It needs to be concretized and brought into the realm of the everyday. . . . A more "orthodox" way of saying all this would be to characterize it as the "will of G-d." And I am not hesitant to say that the Divine Will must manifest itself and be reflected in the minutiae of daily life. Where else should it manifest itself? Where else do we make a *mishkan*, a holy dwelling for G-d, if not in those areas of life most central to human finite existence: food, dwelling, clothes, sex, economics.

Our Jewish postmodern world is a post-shoah world as well. And the hermeneutic theories of postmodernism have helped us gain a new appreciation of the radicality of rabbinic ways of reading and re-reading. These insights fortify me on my path of *teshuvah*. But it is not just in the realm of *aggadah*, that humans are partners with G-d; that partnership has always been part of the traditional halakhic imperative. That is the whole notion of the Oral Torah. It is a caricature to describe the classical notion of "Torah *mi-Sinai*" as something handed down by a dictatorial G-d which takes away autonomy.

The Problem of Authority

But somehow, I do not think I have persuaded you. The problem is not so much with these general ideas. It is really, I have a hunch, the notion of authority that bothers you. "Why," you ask, "should thinking Jews consider giving up their self-determination to follow the rulings of decisors who have Jewish learning but otherwise no greater access to G-d's present will than the rest of us possess?"

. . . One Shabbat, Rabbi Barry Freundel of Kesher Israel, [the Georgetown Synagogue in Washington D.C.] made an intriguing distinction between "power" and "authority". Pharaoh has "power," he claimed, but no "authority"; Moses has "authority" but not "power." What does this mean? Pharaoh, the paradigmatic political authoritarian, speaks the language of "power." Like contemporary anti-Semites, he has an exaggerated fear of "Jewish power," far in excess of the reality of Jewish social position and influence. In coming to Pharaoh, Moses does not speak the language of "power" but asks instead that the Jews be allowed to go the desert to sacrifice to their G-d.

"Today in many circles," said Rabbi Freundel, "everything—politics, religion, literature, the family—is discussed only in terms of the power relationships involved. Hierarchy, patriarchy, racism, sexism, etc, . . . is all about the language of power. . . What has been lost is, first, the Jewish opposition to seeing the world only in terms of the dynamics of power. Second, we have lost the distinction between power and authority." Citing Erich Fromm, he defined authority not as a quality one has, but referring to "an interpersonal relationship in which one person looks upon another as somebody superior to him." Put another way, while power is a quality that flows from the top down and carries with it coercion, oppression, and tyranny, authority comes from the bottom up and begins with the acceptance of something larger and better."

This dynamic is modeled in the relation between Sinai and Purim: When the Jews at Mt. Sinai say "we will do and we will obey," and then re-confirm their acceptance of it in the days of Esther, they then establish G-d's authority. In other words,

"G-d's authority begins from those in a position of less authority, accepting that something special exists in the higher authority."

The contemporary educational theorist Parker Palmer has some eloquent and strikingly similar things to say about the relation between knowing, freedom, hearing, and obeying. And what it means to teach and to learn. Noting that the English word "obedience" does not mean slavish adherence but comes from the Latin root *audire* which means to "listen," Palmer writes:

At its root, the word "obedience" means not only "to listen" but "to listen from below." How fascinating that this is also the common sense meaning for the word "understand," which suggests that we know something by "standing under" it. Both obedience and understanding imply submitting ourselves to something larger than any one of us, something on which we all depend. . . .

I find in these words a wonderful "Quaker" dash on the rabbinic interpretation in *Shabbat* 88a of the Jews standing "at the underside of the mountain."

But I still probably have not convinced you, Gene, because your ultimate authority is the autonomous self, even though you are pained by the narcissistic excesses that has led us to in contemporary society. Your entire book is meant to redress that imbalance. But I do not think that a Covenant, as a binding over to the other, and the kind of "sacrificial ethic" you want to construct can emerge from your model.

Let me restate your question again: "Why" you ask "should thinking Jews consider giving up their self-determination to follow the rulings of decisors who have Jewish learning but otherwise no greater access to G-d's present will than the rest of us possess?"

What, indeed, is "Jewish learning"? True Jewish learning is not something one possesses like an exterior piece of property.

Not a list of publications on a CV. The true teacher is not simply a repository of knowledge, but an embodiment and performer of that knowledge. Perhaps this is why the rabbis talk about the importance of *shimush hakhamim*, attending to or serving one's teacher: Who is ignorant? He who has studied scriptures and mishna, but has not attended or served the scholars (*Berachot* 7b). This is not a slavish, mindless act, but a way of learning by attending to the personhood of the *Rav*. Torah cannot be obtained only from books or by oneself or through one's "inner light." It is not a "knowledge" in that sense, as I have argued elsewhere.

In all our academic discussions of the hermeneutics of Oral Torah, we tend to forget that ultimately it is also the world made personal by being mediated through another—through the living voice, face, and being of the teacher. Not the assertion of absolutist authority but the recognition that knowledge has a face. We are not the People of the Book; we are the People of the mouth. It was the Moslems who dubbed us the "People of the Book." That is a mistake and misnomer. Books are fixed, rigid. Protestants are People of the Book, and therefore they need the inner voice of grace to illumine the text. For us, the Oral Torah illumines, breathes voice and life and personal presence into the Written Torah through the collective voices of the teachers and their students through the generations, whose dialogues and debates it records.

Tzimtzum

I reread what I have written. From the confusion of my beginnings, I see a pattern has emerged, and that I have been more or less following the traditional Jewish exegetical path of the four levels of interpretation: *peshat*, *remez*, *drash*, *sod*—from the literal, to the intertextual, to the homiletic . . . now, to the last level, *sod*, the mystical.

It is interesting to me, Gene, that you use one of the fundamental kabbalistic metaphors, that of the *tzimtzum*, to describe one of your central "postmodern" moves. The *tzimtzum* is the kabbalistic notion of G-d's primordial self-contraction in order to open up a space, a void, *halal panui* in which the finite universe could be created. (I find it interesting that the "Ari," Rav Isaac Luria developed this notion in 16th century Sefad, coincident with the rise of Early Modern Europe. The modernist focus on the self seems to here already have its postmodern counter-echo in the Ari.)

Among those Chasidic masters who knew how to inhabit that void, spoke from it, and tried to cross and recross it was the inimitable Rabbi Nachman of Breslov. As I move here to the level of *sod*, the mystical meaning, I find myself again dealing with those same texts about Exodus and Sinai, which have been presenting themselves to me throughout my meditation. Rabbi Nachman has an extraordinary teaching in his *Likkutei Moharan*, #64 on "*Bo el Paroh.*" G-d tells Moses in Exodus 10:1,2 "Come to Pharaoh, for I have hardened his heart and his servants' hearts, so that I may place these, my signs, in their midst; and that you may tell your son and your son's son how I made sport of Egypt and my signs that I did among them; that you may know that I am G-d." Rabbi Nachman's exposition is quite complex, and I can here give only a small piece of it. He interprets the word "Pharaoh" to refer precisely to the vacated space, the *halal* created by the *tzimtzum*. The word "*paroh*," he says, comes from a root meaning "annihilation" and "removal" as in Exodus 5:4 where the Pharaoh says to Moses "You have removed (*tafriu*) the people from their work. And it is also related to the root meaning "uncovering and revealing."

So, says Rabbi Nachman, in the vacated space, from which G-d has withdrawn, there arise all the philosophical questions which have no answer, which pain and confuse us . . . and in which our hearts become hardened. But Rabbi Nachman then interprets the name "Hebrew"—*ivri*, in a reparative sense as coming from the root *iver.* In this sense, it means "to cross over, or ford some space," thus signifying that the Jews, the Hebrews—*Ivri'im*—have the task and power to cross the void created by the *tzimtzum*, the empty space where G-d is absent. And that is also why G-d is called in Exodus 5:3, "G-d of the Hebrews." The root also yields the word *ever*, meaning the "sides" of a river. In the Lurianic notion of the *tzimtzum*, the empty space is created by the image of G-d contracting his light to the "sides."

The notion of this vacated space, an absence where there is also yet a presence of G-d, is an epistemological and ontological paradox: unsolvable in terms of human intellect. Needless to say, a postmodern world, a post-shoah world is one in which we seem to be in an empty place from which G-d is withdrawn and absent. Postmodernism in its deconstructive modes leads us right into this emptiness—this undoing of the notion of solid being, this vision of flickering presence in absence. The key question is, how do we find G-d there? Yet, Rabbi Nachman reminds us, somehow G-d is still "there"; for without some trace of the Divine, even the Void could not exist. And so, Moses has to come to Pharaoh, the place where G-d cannot be found, to ford the void, cross to the other side.

Rabbi Nachman's ideas on debate, language, song, silence, vacated space, take up all the themes I have been preoccupied with in my "meditation." I look back and see that I have been arguing for the need for postmodern Jewish thought to reconstruct the shattered vessels of authority, halakhah, faith. It often happens that friends and readers of my academic work are surprised when they hear me speak in these terms. They assume that a person who wrote books about deconstruction and who is a contemporary Jewish woman, would be seeking to "deconstruct halakhah" or practicing the "hermeneutics of suspicion" and writing critiques of modern Judaism in terms of gender, class, race, not quoting Rabbi Nachman or arguing that Chasidut is postmodern. The academic forms of postmodernism I encounter in contemporary literary and cultural theory generally value "transgression, subversion, interrogation"; these, too, are moves into the vacated space, ways of clearing space, but they do not take that next step; they do not help me cross the Void.

So how, I ask myself, is the way in which I quote and learn from Rabbi Nachman different from that of a "pre-modern" reader? . . . With what accent or intonation does a postmodern speak? The postmodern accent may be more on rupture, break, fragmentation . . . trying to construct its melody out of fragments and pieces; self-contracted. We are called to come to Pharaoh, slow of speech like Moses. We have entered the vacated space stuttering; yet we do not seek to prematurely fill or try to negate it. And we need to remember that we are *Ivri'im*, that we must cross and recross that void. We do so not only with the complex words of our debates and disputes, but also with our silence, and our *emunah*. For there is something of the "pre-modern" in both of us, Gene. . . . In the way we both understand that there is indeed a wisdom of faith in Israel.

. . . So I deeply respond, Gene, to those moments in your book when you speak of your *emunah* in simple terms. And to the condition in which it was sparked . . . a moment in a Manhattan fast-food restaurant when the halakhic prescription to saying a blessing over a sandwich causes a flickering transfiguration of a mundane reality. . .

Academic systems of thought and theories of discourse come and go . . . and fairly quickly. There will no doubt soon be a "post-postmodernism," which will probably be called the "New . . . X," and the blindnesses of our own work will be incisively analyzed by those who will come later . . . in the same way that we at present critique the blindnesses of "modernist" thought. I think you sense this as much as I, Gene. Your own postmodernism, like mine, is provisional and instrumental. . . .

The following story is told of the Rebbe of Mezritch: A stranger once came and knocked on his front door. The Rebbe asked, "Who is there?" The response was, "I." The Rebbe was shocked that a Jew could utter "I" so easily. He opened the door and invited the stranger inside. He asked if he had eaten yet and, upon receiving an answer in the negative, told the guest, "Go to such-and-such a place, a certain distance from here, and eat there." Since the Rebbe had instructed him thus, the Jew went on his way. The road was long and tiring, and he walked and walked, becoming covered with dust along the way. After a hard journey he arrived at the place, filthy and exhausted. A wedding was just about to begin in the village and, as was the custom, a festive meal was offered at the site for the poor. The man joined the poor guests and ate with them. At the end of the meal it was discovered that a silver spoon was missing. Immediately, all suspicion was focused on this Jew, since he was the only stranger, and everyone turned to him accusingly: "You stole!" The Jew replied, "Not I!" They continued to torment him and accuse him, and he steadfastly repeated, "Not I! Not I!" Eventually he managed to escape from them, and started his journey back towards the Rebbe, wondering all the way what the Rebbe's reason could have been for sending him to that place. He arrived at the Rebbe's house, knocked on the door, and once again, the Rebbe asked, "Who is there?" The Jew was about to answer "I" as he was accustomed to do, but suddenly he caught himself and answered, "Not I." Only through suffering and pain had the message penetrated his consciousness—now he knew that he was "not I." There is only one "I"—and that is "He."

Understanding the Dead Sea Scrolls

Lawrence Schiffman

IT WAS A COLD, RAINY DAY IN JERUSALEM, IN DECEMBER OF 1991, just a few months after the historic release of the Dead Sea Scrolls from the hands of the so-called cartel, the group of Christian scholars that had controlled access to the scrolls and their publication from the early 1950's, under both Jordanian and Israeli rule. The scrolls had only recently been made available to the wider scholarly community, initially as the result of the publication of bootleg editions and photographs, and later by a formal decision of the Israel Antiquities Authority (IAA). Already months before, the IAA had appointed Hebrew University professor Emanuel Tov to head up a new and expanded publication team, and I had been asked to join in this project.

Now, in December, I sat in the "scrollery," the room in the Rockefeller Museum in East Jerusalem, where the scrolls were housed and studied. I arrived to find that the manuscripts I had requested were waiting and that I would finally, after some 25 years of scrolls scholarship, be able to work with the originals and to make use of the full corpus.

People often ask me: if the scrolls were kept hidden and secret, how did you work on them? Even before the release of the scrolls I had written several books on the Dead Sea Scrolls. Some 25% of the titles, comprising about half of the material (if you count words), had already been published before the great "battle of the scrolls" which unfolded in the headlines. That material was enough for a lifetime of scholarship, and it was to these scrolls that my research and that of other "outsider" colleagues was devoted. But we were always haunted by the incompleteness of the picture we were painting. How could scholarship be done when access to the rest of the collection was denied?

So now I sat finally, face to face with these ancient scraps of parchment. I cannot describe the feeling that surged through me as I opened the first of the folders (known as paper "plates" in the jargon of the field) to examine an ancient text called "Mysteries" (*Sefer Ha-Razim* in Hebrew) that I had been assigned to edit. Here I was examining the remnants of an ancient Jewish library, a collection of manuscripts gathered in the second and first centuries B.C.E. I sat in front of texts written with pen and ink by people who lived in the time of Judah the Maccabee and his successors, and in the age of King Herod and the Roman procurators who followed him.

Little did I realize how the unfettered access I now had to the scrolls collection would reshape my own scholarly views on the significance of the scrolls. With the plethora of texts now being published both by the official editorial team and by others as well, we are gaining fabulous new insights into the character of the ferment in Jewish thought and practice which took place between the Maccabean Revolt of 168-164 B.C.E. and the destruction of the nation and its Temple in the Great Revolt against Rome in 66-73 C.E. As I sat that day in the scrollery, beginning to do the difficult work of editing these fragments, I felt a connection with our history. The scrolls served for me as a physical sign of the chain that stretched across the generations of the Jewish tradition.

My own involvement with the Dead Sea Scrolls started some twenty-five years ago with a foray into scrolls research for my senior honors thesis at Brandeis University. With this study I was inescapably captivated, and I went on to write a doctoral dissertation on Jewish law in the scrolls and several books thereafter. What was it that fascinated a young Judaic scholar who had studied Biblical and Talmudic studies so extensively? Why are the scrolls so important for the study of Judaism in late antiquity? In a nutshell, it was the opportunity to uncover the missing links between the Judaism of the Bible and that of the Talmud, to trace the links between prophet and priest, on the one hand, and Talmudic Rabbis on the other.

In the Jewish tradition, the oral law, the unwritten, revealed tradition, bridges this chasm. This oral law, when it was finally committed to writing, in the third century or later, preserved some traditions from a much earlier period. Besides the few explicit references to this period in Rabbinic literature, there was virtually no contemporary documentary evidence for this intermediary period. Suddenly, with the discovery of the Dead Sea Scrolls we had material from this dark age, the 4th century B.C.E. through the first century C.E., the years from Alexander the Great to Hillel the Elder. These ancient fragments speak to us across the millennia, helping us to illuminate a period about which previous generations could know very little.

What are the Dead Sea Scrolls?

The Dead Sea Scrolls are a collection of some 850 scrolls or, for the most part, fragments of scrolls which were gathered into a collection by a Jewish sectarian group which made use of a building complex at Qumran on the western shore of the Dead Sea. Near the building complex, collections of scrolls and fragments were found in eleven caves which stretch along a north-south line. These scrolls—containing primarily biblical texts, apocryphal literature, prayer texts, and sectarian documents—were composed over a very long period. The earliest compositions are ancient biblical materials such as the Torah. Fragments of all biblical books except Esther have been identified among the scrolls. The collection also includes texts composed at various times during the Hellenistic period, from the third century B.C.E. on. It is widely recognized that many of the documents found at Qumran were composed before the sect came into being. They were imported to Qumran after the sect occupied the "pre-Qumranian."

Regarding the dating, we must carefully distinguish between the date of composition of the texts and that of copying. The documents were composed over many centuries, from the earliest days of Israelite history up through the turn of the era. They were gathered into the Qumran collection between approximately 152 B.C.E. and 68 C.E. when the Qumran settlement came to an end. A few of the Qumran texts were copied as early as the third century B.C.E., but most were copied between the second century B.C.E. and the early first century C.E. Indeed, this was the heyday of the sect and its building complex at Qumran. This community, like others in the Judean Desert, was most probably destroyed at the hands of the Romans in 68 C.E. as part of their military campaign to crush the Great Revolt of the Jews against Rome (66-73 C.E.).

The Qumran collection can best be described as a library. A large percentage of the scrolls come from cave four, an artificially hewn cave only a five-minute walk from the buildings which served as the sectarian center. Here were found remnants of some 550 manuscripts. It is primarily the material from this cave which remained unpublished and which sparked the raucous controversy of the last few years. In antiquity, this cave had wooden shelves of some type. When the cave was abandoned, the shelves eventually rotted and collapsed, leaving the scrolls on the floor of the cave, which explains their damaged and fragmentary condition. Other scrolls survived with little damage. These were found in neighboring caves where they were apparently placed, some in protective jars, in order to save them from destruction shortly before the conquest of Qumran before the rise of the Romans. These are primarily the almost complete scrolls which are today exhibited in the Shrine of the Book of the Israel Museum in Jerusalem.

Besides their own compositions, the sect also gathered other texts of related groups and placed them in its library along with approximately 225 biblical texts. Accordingly, numerous other compositions—some previously known, others unknown—are preserved here in the original Hebrew or Aramaic. Numerous prayer texts, either those of the sect or other groups of Jews, are also present. Tefillin and *mezuzot*, quite similar to those in use today, were found as well in the Qumran caves. The Dead Sea Scrolls provide for us a broad spectrum of data regarding the period between the close of the Hebrew Bible and the compilation and editing of the Mishnah. They allow us a much needed perspective on the small amount of information about this formative period provided by Josephus, the first century C.E. Jewish historian, and the Talmudic sources.

In view of all the misinformation which has been bandied about as a result of the scrolls controversy, we should also say a few things here about what the scrolls are not. First, they are not the library of the Jerusalem Temple. Clearly, if there is anything which unifies this collection, it is the opposition of its owners to the practices and procedures of the Temple in the hands of the priestly leadership of the day. This was the period in which the Hasmonean high priests became considerably Hellenized and the sectarians protested the manner in which they and their supporters conducted the Temple worship. These, then, are the documents of opponents of those who were running the Temple, not its leaders.

Second, the scrolls are not the documents of an early Christian sect. Contrary to the claims of some sensationalists, the scrolls never mention the major figures in the history of early Christianity. Further, the scrolls in no way reflect Christian beliefs. Most recent carbon-14 dating has confirmed the pre-Christian dating of the scrolls already established by paleography, the study of the history of the shapes of the Hebrew letters. Virtually all the material was copied before the rise of the early church and so the Dead Sea Scrolls cannot refer to those events.

The scrolls comprise a major source for the history of Judaism (its religious ideas as opposed to the political and social history of the Jews) in a period for which little other contemporary information exists. These texts are the earliest Hebrew and Aramaic Jewish documents composed after the books of the *Tanach* (Bible). From these documents, it is possible to learn a tremendous amount about the history of the Jews and Judaism in the Second Temple period.

The Study of the Scrolls

The field of Dead Sea Scrolls research is in the midst of a major transition. With the release of the entire corpus of manuscripts, and the widening of the publication process, many previous interpretations and theories will have to be reevaluated. The first generation of scrolls scholars, primarily a group of Christians who were interested either in the Hebrew Bible (*Tanach*) or the New Testament, did not understand the scrolls for what they really were—documents of the history of Second Temple Judaism. The few Jews who entered the field or who made contributions, labored in vain to get a hearing for this kind of approach. To some extent they were hindered because they were published in Hebrew, as was the case with Israeli scholars. All Jewish scholars were excluded from access to the materials in Jordan as a result of the Middle East political situation. In any case, the main focus of research in this period was on searching the scrolls for what they said, or could be claimed to say, about the background of Christianity. This resulted in what might be called a Christianized explanation of the scrolls.

When I was entering the field of Dead Sea Scrolls studies, there were very few Jewish scholars involved. This meant that the agenda for the field was a Christian one, in which messianism had been severed from halakhah, and in which the scrolls were seen as looking forward to Christianity. The few Jews involved worked on the sidelines, denied access to the unpublished materials languishing in the Rockefeller Museum, then (before the reunification of Jerusalem in the 1967 war) the Palestine Archaeological Museum in Jordanian Jerusalem. In a certain sense, we were second class citizens in the study of our own religious texts.

This strange situation continued until the discovery of the Temple Scroll, a document of halakhah regarding the Temple, sacrifices, and other matters, which was recovered by the Israeli archaeologist and scroll scholar Yigael Yadin during the Six-Day War. This scroll, which was completely halakhic, gave impetus to the realization that these were indeed Jewish texts and that they had to be studied from the perspective of the history of Judaism if they were to be truly understood. For my own research, this scroll turned out to be one of the main keys to understanding the import of the scrolls for the history of Talmudic Judaism. But just as importantly, the discovery of this scroll thrust those of us who could discuss the halakhic material in the scrolls right into the forefront of scrolls scholarship, turning the tables on those who had sought to keep the study of the scrolls *judenrein.*

This new approach has taken hold, and it has wrought profound changes in the way in which the scrolls are being understood. Scholars have finally turned to the Jewish aspects of the scrolls, and it is to that purpose that my own research is dedicated. My recent book, *Reclaiming the Dead Sea Scrolls* (Philadelphia: Jewish Publication Society, 1994) is in fact the first book to see the entire scrolls corpus from this point of view. Finally, we are beginning to mine these Jewish scrolls specifically for what they contribute to the history of Judaism.

The Dead Sea Sect

In my view, the scrolls were gathered at Qumran by a sect whose members left Jerusalem in the aftermath of the Maccabean

Revolt. Soon after 152 B.C.E., the Hasmonean rulers (Judah the Maccabee's family) adopted the rulings of the Pharisees, the forerunners of the Talmudic Rabbis, regarding the conduct of the Temple, leading to a schism. A group of Sadducees left the Temple rather than follow the rulings of the Pharisees as enforced by the Hasmoneans. Thus what eventually became the Dead Sea sect was founded by pious Sadducees, as we now know from the extremely important text known as the Halakhic Letter (*Miqsat Ma'ase Ha-Torah*), the existence of which became known to scholars only in 1984.

We now know that the halakhic (religious legal) tradition of the Dead Sea sect was Sadducean, and so we can begin from the scrolls to reconstruct the nature of this priestly group's system of biblical interpretation and law of which we knew virtually nothing before. Further, it is now clear that the Dead Sea sect went through a process of development and radicalization until it took on the characteristics we recognize from the sectarian scrolls. That sect is identified as the Essenes by most scholars. This identification cannot be definitely established, and indeed there is very good reason to question it. Nevertheless, it can be maintained perhaps if the term Essene is understood to refer to a wider movement, not to one particular sect.

The Qumran sect itself was a small minority of the Jews of the Land of Israel in Second Temple times. Yet because they gathered this library at Qumran, we possess a disproportionate amount of information about this group. The Qumran sect believed in a highly dualistic Judaism in which people were predestined to belong to "lots" of good and evil. All the evildoers were expected to be destroyed in the end of days. The sect was organized in the present age so as to prepare for the messianic era which they expected to dawn immediately. The sect's preparations for the coming age were predicated on the close study of the Bible and strict adherence to Jewish law as they interpreted it.

The Scrolls and Rabbinic Judaism

As more and more scrolls have been published, and as our understanding of the nature of the collection has been widening, it has become increasingly clear that it is possible to learn much more from the scrolls than used to be assumed. The scrolls are emerging as an important source for the study of Judaism in the Second Temple period in all its varieties. From the contemporary point of view, as followers of the Talmudic tradition, we are Rabbinic Jews. Approaching the scrolls, we are entitled to hope for new and important information about the Pharisees, the forerunners of the Talmudic Rabbis, and about the religious ideas, laws and traditions that make up Jewish life as we know and practice it, and in this respect the scrolls do not disappoint us.

Specifically, it used to be believed that we have no contemporary sources for Pharisaism (the Jewish group which bequeathed its approach to Rabbinic Judaism) in the Hasmonean period (152-63 B.C.E.) and that our only sources were the later accounts in Josephus, the polemics of the New Testament, and the scattered references in Talmudic literature to the precursors of the Mishnaic Rabbis. About the Sadducees much the same thing was said, and no sense existed of the various apocalyptic groups the existence of which could only barely be assumed.

Scholars used to think that the library at Qumran was entirely Essene, and initial scholarship sought, as we already mentioned, to reconstruct the nature of this sect, assuming that the entire collection could teach us only about those who gathered it. Only in the last few years have we succeeded in showing that this evaluation was too limited. Certainly, the scrolls inform us about the sect that inhabited the ruins of Qumran. But so much can be learned about the other groups as well, since this hoard of manuscripts includes material representing a variety of Jewish groups and polemics against others.

Let us begin with the Pharisees. This elusive group of lay teachers and expounders of the Torah, who paved the way followed by the sages of the Mishnah and Talmud, is now coming to life before our eyes. The scrolls include material on the Pharisees only in polemical context. This means that we are reading the criticisms of those who rejected the way of the Pharisees, and using them to reconstruct positive information.

In the better known sectarian texts the Pharisees (called by various code words like the similar sounding "Ephraim") are said to be the "builders of the wall," indicating that they built fences around the Torah by making regulations designed to ensure its observance. This is exactly what the earliest of our post-biblical sages, the Men of the Great Assembly, recommended as a means to keep us from transgressing the law. The scrolls, then, prove the antiquity of this basic Rabbinic approach. The sectarians criticized the *halakhot* ("laws") of the Pharisees whom the sect called derisively and in a play on the word *halakhot*, "*doreshe halaqot*," best translated "those who expound false laws." We can understand these criticisms in light of the many disagreements which the sect had with the Pharisees regarding specific matters of Jewish law. Indeed, we must remember that these disputes were all among observant Jews who had differing views on how to understand G-d's word. Yet for us, this information proves beyond a doubt that the designation "*halakhot*" for extra-biblical laws—the results of the interpretations and enactments of what the Rabbis call the oral law—were already in existence among the early Pharisees. One text refers to the talmud of "Ephraim" which the sectarians claim is false. The reference is certainly to the Pharisaic method of deriving laws by logical deduction similar to that found in some early Rabbinic texts. The sectarians, following the Sadducean trend, could not accept this approach. But for us, we learn that this system of logic was already in use in the second century B.C.E., way before the editing of the Mishnah some four centuries later.

All in all, these passages make clear that our traditional system of learning and law was in effect among the Pharisees and their followers even before the Maccabean revolt, as the Talmudic texts teach us. In this system, the Jewish way of life is based on the written Torah, as well as oral law. The oral law is an infinite and constantly expanding corpus which includes G-d-given interpretations of the Torah, along with the rulings and enactments of the sages, based on the interpretation of the Torah and the use of finely-tuned logic. Clearly, in these Dead Sea texts we see that the accounts of Josephus and of Talmudic literature describing the Pharisees and their traditions, the Rabbinic oral law concept, are in fact confirmed by the Dead Sea Scrolls.

There is much more evidence in *Miqsat Ma'aseh Ha-Torah*. This text includes a series of halakhic polemics in which the authors castigate their opponents. In each of these cases the writers speak of their own view and then specify the violation of the law now going on. In a number of these cases the laws of the authors represent views directly opposed to those of the Pharisees, yet matching those of the Sadducees, according to later Rabbinic texts. As such, we have good reason to believe now that we have here twenty or so laws, *halakhot* as they were already called in the Hasmonean period, which were held by the Pharisees. These laws, and many others that can be shown to have been known to the scroll authors, in turn prove that the basic system of Mishnaic Judaism was already in practice in the Hasmonean period.

These laws contribute also to our evaluation of the reliability of Talmudic reports. The letter proves that in two areas the Rabbinic sources were correct, and prominent modern scholars who doubted the reliability of the Rabbis were incorrect. First, the Pharisaic view was indeed dominant for much of the Hasmonean era, in virtually all areas of Jewish law, including even matters of Temple practice. This is not a later Talmudic anachronistic invention as was claimed by some modern historians. Second, the terminology and even some of the very same laws as are recorded in Rabbinic sources, some in the name of the Pharisees, others in the names of anonymous Tannaitic sources, were those which the Pharisees espoused. Put otherwise, Rabbinic Judaism is not a post-destruction invention, but rather a continuation of ancient and longstanding tradition. Its roots reach back even further than the Hasmonean period as can be proven from the Dead Sea Scrolls, as the Rabbinic tradition asserts.

We can also learn about the Sadducees from other Qumran texts as well. In the *Pesher Nahum*, a sectarian commentary on the biblical prophetic book of Nahum, they are termed "Menasseh," the opponents of Ephraim, as we already noted a code word for the Pharisees. The description of the Sadducees as aristocratic members of the ruling class fits that period in which the Sadducees had come close to the Hasmoneans and the Pharisees had fallen out with them just before the Roman conquest of Palestine in 63 B.C.E. All this accords perfectly well with the descriptions of Josephus and shows that in regard to the Sadducees he is generally accurate.

What is more important is the material now available to us in the *Miqsat Ma'aseh HaTorah*. This text shows us some twenty two examples of Sadducean law, which in a number of cases match views attributed to the Sadducees in Talmudic sources. More important, this text proves that the sectarians originated among pious Sadducees who, when the Hasmoneans took over the priesthood, would not toe the new line.

Does this mean that the sect was Sadducean? Not quite. The sect certainly started among pious Sadducees, and many Sadducean teachings lie at the basis of its legal tradition. Yet it seems to us that the community underwent a process of growing radicalization and sectarianization, which led it further and further toward the separatist mentality we observe in many of the texts. As a result, a group of originally Sadducean priests, under the leadership of the Teacher of Righteousness, developed into the group that left us the sectarian texts.

Yet it may be that even more can be learned about the Sadducees. There are a variety of parallels between the laws of the MMT and the Temple Scroll. In some cases the Temple Scroll provides a Scriptural basis when MMT cites only the law. This suggests that some of the sources of the Temple Scroll must date to the pre-sectarian period, when these were indeed Sadducean teachings. The author/redactor of the complete scroll, whether a member of the Qumran sect or of some related or similar group, or a lone author, used these Sadducean sources when he completed the text in the Hasmonean period. As we continue to recover the sources of the Temple Scroll, the views of the Sadducees are starting to come to light. Indeed, we are finally understanding their brand of strict-constructionist interpretation of the Torah, which allowed for exegesis but which required that all laws emerge from Scripture, and their rejection of laws unrelated to the Bible.

Finally, as we read of the ancient debates of Jews of the Second Temple period, we come to realize that the pluralism of that age was a pluralism of Torah observant Jews. No one argued about the obligation of eating only kosher food, or the validity of the belief that the Torah had been revealed by G-d. The presence of two kinds of *tefillin* at Qumran shows that even if there were disputes (as there still are) about how to make or don the *tefillin*, all Jews understood that this was indeed an obligation. Only a small number of extremely Hellenized Jews rejected the fundamental beliefs and practices of Judaism. This faction was roundly discredited and defeated during the Maccabean Revolt, and the rejection of Jewish practice by Jews remained a very marginal phenomenon until the spiritual scourges of modern secularization and assimilation began to take their toll.

Messianism Among the Dead Sea Sectarians

Another important part of the Qumran material related to the subject of messianism. Various sources make clear that some form of messianic belief was part of the Judaism of almost all ancient Jews in this period. After ali, the basic notions of the restoration of the Davidic kingdom and the destruction of evil in the end of days are part of the Bible itself. Unfortunately, the scrolls do not supply us here with information about the Pharisees per se. Our discussion here will be limited primarily to the messianic beliefs of the Qumran sect.

From the very beginning of the study of the Dead Sea Scrolls, it has been clear that the documents of the Qumran sect place great emphasis on eschatology. A number of documents are almost completely dedicated to issues related to the end of days. From the Scroll of the War of the Sons of Light against the Sons of Darkness it can be seen that the sect expected to participate in the battle which would usher in the final age.

According to the Dead Sea Scrolls, two messiahs were to lead the congregation in the end of days, one priestly and the other lay. At the same time the sect expected a prophet who was a quasi-messianic figure. The notion of a priestly messiah fits well with the prominent place of the priesthood in the origins, leadership and organization of the Qumran sect.

The messiah of Aaron was expected to be superior and to dominate religious matters; the messiah of Israel would rule over temporal and political matters. Both messiahs would preside over the eschatological banquet. This model is based on the Moses/Aaron, Joshua/Zerubabel type of pairing and was represented by Bar Kokhba and the High Priest Eleazar in the Bar Kokhba revolt (132-135 C.E.) as well. An alternative system is also found in some scrolls in which only one messianic figure is expected. In this case, the messiah is a descendant of David, as was normative in the later Rabbinic texts.

Thus far we have been describing restorative tendencies based on the biblical prophetic visions. Yet the Qumran sect went much further. Like the apocalyptic trend in Jewish messianism, it expected that the advent of the messianic age would be heralded by the great war described in the War Scroll. It would mean the victory of the forces of good over those of evil, in Heaven above and on earth below. After forty years the period of wickedness would come to an end; the elect would attain glory.

The messianic banquet presided over by the two messiahs would usher in the new age which would include worship at the eschatological temple. Sacrificial worship would be conducted according to the law as envisaged by the sectarian leaders. In essence, the messianic vision was to include the reaching of a level of purity and perfection in the observance of Jewish law beyond that of the present age. The utopian trend in Jewish messianism manifests itself here not only in the destruction of the wicked at the end of a great cosmic battle, but also in the sphere of Jewish law. Only in the future age will it be possible properly to observe the Torah as interpreted by the sect. To the sectarians, as for virtually all Jews, the end of days was to be realized in halakhic terms. Messianism and Jewish law could not be severed. It was only through observance of the law that the messiah could be brought, and his appearance would herald a day of universal perfection in observance of the commandments.

Equally important is the notion of the immediacy of the end of days. The old order would soon come to an end. The forces of evil and those opposing the sect were soon to be destroyed. The new order had already dawned with the sect's removal to the desert from the main population centers of Judea and the establishment of the sectarian center at Qumran. The sect lived on the verge of the end of days, with one foot, as it were, in the present age and one foot in the future age.

We cannot date precisely the elements of Qumran messianic doctrine or their crystallization except to place them sometime in the Hasmonean period. The combination of the two major trends of Jewish messianic thought, the restorative and the utopian, appearing at Qumran for the first time, later exercised a powerful role in the future of Jewish messianic belief.

Unlocking the Secrets

These are some of the secrets unlocked by the recent release of the remaining Judean Desert manuscripts. For me, and for other scholars of ancient Judaism, these materials are the basis of our efforts to reconstruct the complex history of Judaism in this period. The unconscionable delays in publication had slowed the progress of our research, for each new scrap of information is invaluable in refining our theories and deepening our understanding.

This is the fascinating world in which I have been working for already more than twenty-five years. It is easy to see how rewarding this process of discovery has been for me as a Jew committed to the life of Torah in modern times. It is for good reason that the Torah commands us: "Remember the days of old, investigate the years of ages past" (Deut. 32:7). When we study our history, and even more so when we discover our history, we bind ourselves ever more tightly to the chain of tradition which links Jews throughout the ages one to another. I have been privileged to see first hand how our ancestors grappled with the problems of Jewish life and law, and how after centuries of honest disagreement about how to live according to G-d's word, they eventually came to accept the ancient way of the Pharisees, enshrined in the Mishnah and Talmud, as the proper guide to Jewish life. They realized that this approach, based on the unique combination of the written Torah and oral tradition, was the only one which could sustain Jewish commitment, continuity and identity for the future.

The Legal and The Mystical

Eli Silberstein

JEWISH MYSTICISM IS OFTEN PERCEIVED AS ETHEREAL, abstract and beyond the ken of all but a select few. It is often considered to have little relevance to the day-to-day life of an ordinary Jew. Indeed, the laws and commandments found in the Torah and Talmud which form the framework of Jewish living, can be understood and followed without any knowledge of the mystical literature. Chasidic philosophy teaches, however, that there is an essential, fundamental interrelationship between all levels of Jewish thought, reflecting the unity of their Divine source. In particular, Chasidism teaches, there is an intimate connection between the mystical and the purely legal dimensions of Jewish thinking. The former is not merely a lens through which we gain a unique perspective on the latter; it is rather an inseparable part of it, without which Jewish law would not be what it is. If the law is the physical body, explains the *Zohar*, its mystical interpretation is the soul. Through joining body and soul—the legal and the mystical—many difficult-to-understand issues in Jewish law may be clarified.

Mystical Dimensions in Civil Law

It is perhaps not altogether surprising that understanding issues of ritual concern in Jewish law would be enhanced by a mystical approach. Remarkably, however, we also find this dimension in the area of civil law. Although the Torah approach to issues such as acquisitions, loans, torts, and contracts seems on the surface to be in some ways similar to secular systems, it is in reality far more complex.

Consider, for example, ownership—a key concept in the area of civil law. Ownership is central to any discussion of loans, torts and contracts. In secular thought, ownership is normally perceived as no more than a social convention. Society's welfare depends on the implementation of clearly defined boundaries so as to avoid conflict in a world where people compete for the same turf.[1] (An interesting question from this perspective might be whether Adam, while he was alone in the world, owned anything. He had no need to protect objects that he utilized from other potential users.) Jewish mysticism, however, views ownership in an entirely different light. Judaism understands there to be a real metaphysical connection between the proprietor and the property. The Baal Shem Tov explains that every physical object contains a mystical reality, referred to in Jewish mysticism as a divine spark. These sparks are comprised of a G-dly energy which constitutes the essential existence of that object. The purpose of existence, then, is to elevate these sparks from their state of obscurity, and reveal their inherent divinity within the physical; this is accomplished by using the objects in which they are contained to perform divine commandments. Every person is given a share of the physical world—his physical possessions—which are invested of the divine sparks associated with the divine roots of that person's soul.[2]

Ownership, then, represents the association between the soul and the divine sparks present in the object in question. When ownership is transferred, it indicates that the sparks contained in the transferred object require the intervention of more than one soul to be elevated. Rabbi Yehudah Loew, the Maharal of Prague, sees this preordained relationship between owner and property reflected in the following Talmudic dictum (*Kiddushin* 59a): "If a poor man is trying to take possession of a certain cake, and another comes along and snatches it, he can justifiably be called a wicked man, for he has encroached upon the livelihood of his fellow." A man who is attempting to buy an item or enter a business transaction, and another comes along and seizes the opportunity away from him, the competitor has done an ethical wrong, for the initial buyer can justifiably say, "why must you ruin my opportunity to profit? If you wish to profit you can easily do business elsewhere."[3]

The Maharal explains that everything regarding a person's material possessions, from the accumulation of property to the extent of a person's income or the manner in which he achieves that income, is preordained. Negotiations between buyer and seller may be an indication of this preordained bond between buyer and property in question. Thus, depriving the buyer from completing the transaction with the seller is perceived in Jewish law as theft, because it intrudes on the divine establishment of boundaries between territories of ownership.

We find an allusion to this spiritual bond in the words of our sages: "The righteous value their physical possessions more than their bodies."[4] Chasidic philosophy expands this idea even further. When a physical entity enters our possession, it is changed and uplifted as a result of the interaction between the divine soul of the owner and the spiritual constitution of the object. Indeed, in relating the story of Abraham's purchase of land from Efron, the Hittite, we find that the Torah uses the phrase, "and the land rose to Abraham," from which we may infer that simply by moving from the possession of Efron, the idolater, to the hands of Abraham, the land itself rose in status.

It is interesting to note that the word *kinyan*, which in Hebrew means "possession" or "taking possession," is often used in Biblical Hebrew to describe the inherent relationship between Creator and creation.[5] In the Talmud, it is used to describe a special bond between G-d and particular entities such as Abraham, the Torah, and Israel.[6]

The consequence of this intimate bond between owner and property is often reflected in Jewish law, which regards ownership not merely as a legal concept, but as a reality that remains unchanged even when the idea of ownership as a utilitarian notion becomes meaningless. Most rabbinic authorities, for instance, believe that the power of ownership is independent of any use or lack thereof which the owner may derive from his property. Jewish law, for example, prohibits the use of a condemned animal for any purpose, from the time it is condemned until it is put to death. And yet, the owner of the condemned animal is still regarded by Jewish law as its rightful owner, making him liable for any damages it may cause between condemnation and death. Likewise, one is guilty of theft if he steals the condemned animal.

Moreover, even when one owns something which by law he is forbidden to own, title of ownership is not legally revoked. This is clearly illustrated by the prohibition to own leavened food stuffs during Passover. Even so, if a Jew has neglected to sell his leavened foods prior to Passover, he is still regarded as their legal owner.[7] Indeed, it is only possible to violate this prohibition of *chametz* by owning it. We may infer from all this that not only is the legal concept of ownership not defined by the practical use or benefit derived from the object or property, but it is also not diminished by the legal prohibitions against ownership.

We find a striking illustration of this in the laws of contracts. A contract involving an illegal service, such as one regarding the pay due to a hired hit man, has no legal validity in any secular legal system. This is not surprising: the law is established for the sake of providing a moral framework of conduct; it cannot sanction activities that contradict this principle.[8] In Jewish law, however, this is not the case. The validity of a contract is completely independent of its legality.

Take, for instance, a case where someone engaged in a contract in which he hired two individuals to commit perjury on his behalf. Is he legally obligated to pay the perjurers after they have committed the crime as agreed? When this case was brought to the attention of Rabbi Yakov of Lisa, he ruled that the perjurers are entitled to their fee, in spite of the illegality of the service that the fee is claimed for.[9]

A similar situation was recently brought before a Jerusalem rabbinical court, in which an individual interested in purchasing an apartment agreed to pay the seller an amount set by an impartial assessor. The buyer then went behind the seller's back and made an agreement with the assessor to set the appraised value of the property at a much lower amount than its real worth, in exchange for a five thousand dollar fee. The appraiser fulfilled his side of the agreement and the sale was executed. When the appraiser demanded his fee, the buyer refused, claiming that such a contract was legally meaningless. They brought their arguments before a rabbinical court. The verdict was unequivocally in favor of the assessor. The contract was enforceable in spite of its illegal nature.[10]

In Jewish law, illegal contracts retain their validity not only when the crime has been committed, but even when the illegal act has yet to take place. Jewish law, for example, forbids two Jews to participate in a loan agreement in which interest is charged; this prohibition applies equally to lender and borrower. Nevertheless, once the loan was already made under this agreement, the transaction remains valid. In fact, from the perspective of Jewish law, the contractual obligation of the borrower to make his interest payment remains in force; but he is not permitted to fulfill his agreement because of a biblical law prohibiting the taking and charging of interest. So the individual is at once held responsible for his contractual agreement, yet prohibited from fulfilling it by Torah law.[11] While the contract remains valid, it obviously cannot override a Torah prohibition.

This idea is not merely of abstract interest but it has rather tangible legal ramifications. One example of how the laws of usury may be applied in this way concerns the transaction of marriage. If a man gives a woman an object of minimum required value, with the intent (by both parties) of marriage, the two become husband and wife by Jewish law.

Now according to some opinions in the Talmud, the law does not insist upon the transfer of a strictly tangible object to facilitate a marriage contract; the groom may forgive the bride a loan and thus effect the transaction necessary to validate a legal marriage. This raises a question, however, with regards to interest: Would the law find acceptable for the marriage contract, the groom's forgiveness of the interest on a loan to the bride, but not the loan itself? Charging interest on the loan is, we know, prohibited by Torah law. Yet, the interest was agreed upon by both parties.

Many authorities argue that forgiving interest should be no different than forgiving a loan since in principle, the woman owes the creditor interest as agreed upon, but the Torah prohibits her from paying it.

In *L'eor Hahalakha*, the late Rabbi Zevin takes the issue even further: Imagine two people engaged in an illegal contract, in which the money for the illegal service was paid in advance. The party who paid backs out of the deal before the service has been performed, claiming before the court to have changed his mind because of its illegal nature. The other party claims that since the contract is legally binding, and he is ready to perform the service, he is not obligated to repay the advance.

What is the law in such a case? The court can't tell him to perform the service and keep the money, for the act is against the law. Furthermore, he cannot claim that he is able to perform the service (even though it is technically possible for him to do it), for the force of the law prevents him from doing so! On the other hand, the force of the contract protects the defendant from having to repay the money so long as he is willing to abide by the agreement. In a detailed analysis from talmudic sources, Rabbi Zevin shows conclusively that in such a case the willing party is not obligated to repay his advance. Despite its illegal nature, the contract remains binding on its signatories. The implications of this case point to the strength of a contract; even when it involves forbidden activity, a Torah prohibition is powerless to invalidate it.

It seems problematic that the law should be dictated by two mutually exclusive conditions. For if the law really disapproves of certain agreements, logic dictates that it should invalidate them. Why allow a conflict of legal principles within one system? This is especially bizarre in a religious system whose purpose it is to promote moral behavior. It seems so much more reasonable to invalidate such agreements so as to deter corruption.

This peculiarity, however, is a direct consequence of the unique nature of the Jewish legal system, which acknowledges a mystical reality—such as exists between property and proprietor—and the shift in reality when an agreement is made to transfer property, be it money or even a service. Whereas secular law attempts to construct its own reality by the conditions it imposes on a given situation, Jewish law, by contrast, acknowledges an independent reality, and responds to that reality. Hence, a contract between two people is perceived by Jewish law as a creation of a new metaphysical reality. So although the content of the contract may itself be contrary to Jewish law, this does not in any way invalidate the contract itself.

The ultimate challenge of understanding any given law in the Jewish legal system may be to conceive it in accordance with its mystical counterpart. In an anecdote about Rabbi Chaim of Sanz, a 19th century authority on Jewish law, we are told that he was once observed, deeply absorbed in thought. When asked about his unusual preoccupation, he said that he had just received a letter from Rabbi Menachem Mendel of Lubavitch (author of the *Tzemach Tzedek*), containing a very complex legal question.

To arrive at a resolution that would satisfy Rabbi Menachem Mendel, explained Rabbi Chaim, was a very demanding task, for it required that any legal decision be made in harmony with the mystical teachings concerning the law in question.

Indeed, when seen from the perspective of Jewish mysticism, the commandments are not merely practical tools for enhancing human life, but are themselves the embodiment of a Divine reality.

NOTES:

1. John Locke, Second Treatise, Ch. 5; See also Hume's essay on "The Origins of Justice and Property"; Blackstone, *Commentaries on the Laws of England*, Vol. II, Ch. 1.

2. See *Keter Shem Tov*, #218; *Ohr Torah*, p. 101; *Likkutei Sichot*, Vol. 12 p. 118

3. See *Choshen Mishpat* 237.

4. For a discussion on the value of material possession over the value of the body, see *Likkutei Sichot*, Vol. 15, p.288.

5. See, for example, Genesis, 14:19, or the *Amidah.*

6. See end of *Pirkei Avot.*

7. Rabbi Shneur Zalman of Liadi, *Shulchan Aruch, Hilkhot Pesach*, Ch. 435 *Kuntres Acharon.*

8. See Hendrix vs. McKee, 281 Oregon 123 (1978).

9. *Netivot Hamishpat* No. 9:1.

10. Responsum *Netzach Yisrael* No. 17, by Rabbi Yisrael Grossman.

11. *Mishne L'Melech, Hilkhot Malve V'love* Ch. 8:1; *Avnei Miluim* No. 28; *Likkutei Sichot*, Vol. 12 p. 119.

Tying Shoelaces and Other Details

Susan A. Handelman

"R. LEIB, SON OF SARAH, THE HIDDEN *TZADDIK* WHO wandered over the earth, following the course of rivers, in order to redeem the souls of the living and the dead said this: 'I did not go to the Maggid in order to hear Torah from him, but to see how he unlaces his felt shoes and laces them up again.'" So goes a well-known Chasidic story somewhat quaint and strange to our ears. What, one wonders, could one great *tzaddik* learn from the way another tied his shoes—and why concentrate on such trivia to begin with?

In fact, the modern Jew tends to ask the same question about much of the body of Jewish law passed down to us in the *Shulchan Aruch* and various Codes—that is, about halakhah in general. Or perhaps we better say halakhah in its "specifics"; what can one possibly learn from it, and why concentrate on such trivia anyway? That mass of irritatingly minute prescriptions which cover the pages of the *Shulchan Aruch* is one of the greatest stumbling blocks for the modern Jew in search of himself. Its laws appear impossible, extreme. Here are directives about matters such as which shoe to put on first, when to wash one's hands, what to wear and how much of the body should be covered, when and when not to touch one's spouse, how to sleep, eat, drink—even evacuate. Let alone the intricate directives concerning proper observance of the holidays, prayer, litigation, and so forth.

Nonetheless, says the Talmud: "Since the Temple was destroyed, G-d has no place left except the four cubits of halakhah." What kind of G-d, one wonders, cares about shoelaces? No one will argue about the need to strengthen Jewish "identity," "culture," "values"—but that we need to strengthen ourselves in abiding by Jewish law, in all its sticky specifics, is another matter. What does it matter whether one drives to *shul* as long as he gets there, or which shoe one puts on first, and so forth. Justice, morality, being a good person, supporting Israel—these are the true components of Judaism. *Shabbat*, *kashrut*, perhaps even *mikveh* make for a nice "lifestyle"; but let's not go too far; let's not be irrational, fanatic; and above all, let's not call it "law."

Many Factions Have Rejected Halakhah

The validity of halakhah is indeed one of the major issues of contention for modern Jewry. The disengagement of halakhah from the rest of the Torah did not, of course, begin recently. Nor even with the Jewish thinkers of the Enlightenment, those precursors to the liberal-humanist theologians of the past hundred years who helped create the various factions of modern Judaism. There were also, of course, the Karaites in the ninth century—who from a certain point of view were quite "modern"; in essence, they felt that the Written Torah, i.e. the Bible, was perfectly acceptable; but the Oral Torah, that mass of intricate Rabbinic interpretation, discussion, and prescription had veered off the point and could be dispensed with. And before them—the Jewish Hellenists. For to the Greeks, the Torah was neither beautiful nor rational; its directives for behavior were strange and torturously legalistic.

To the Christians, halakhah was (and still is) anathema. The "letter" of the law was pitted against its "spirit," with Paul arguing that in fact the law was the very source of sin. Instead of following halakhah, one need only "believe," feel, and be reborn of the spirit—to follow not the discipline of a burdensome law, but the illuminations of one's inner heart. And it wasn't long before the reforming group of Jews associated with Jesus had completely severed themselves from Judaism, taking along with them some fundamental Jewish concepts, but adapting them so successfully to the philosophy and culture of the pagan world that the Judaic element became an empty shell, filled with anti-Jewish beliefs.

All of which is to say: when Judaism is separated from halakhah, when the flower is snipped from the branch, it might remain fragrant and lovely—but not for long.

How inevitable is the process? Is it also the fate of the reforming movements, which have so influenced contemporary Judaism for the past two centuries, to be subtly, unconsciously transformed into little more than mirrors of Hellenism and paganism in their modern guise? Have we not, in our rejection of halakhah, also unwittingly Hellenized and Christianized those very "essential roots" we seek, abhorring the letter for the spirit? Yet we seek a Jewish "lifestyle," a Jewish "identity." How can halakhah have anything at all to do with this?

Halakhah Unites Spiritual and Mundane

In fact, the popular term, "lifestyle," if we stretch it a bit, might serve as a roughly accurate translation of the Hebrew word halakhah, which as it is well-known comes from the root halach, meaning "to walk." The word does not specifically denote "law" (Hebrew *din* or *mishpat*), but "path," the "way to walk," the way to pattern one's life.

But there is more. Style is not always synonymous with substance. There is a profound insight in the popular cliche, "lifestyle"; we desperately search for lifestyle because we lack life-substance. Style can become a substitute for contents. And so we try to pick and choose, amalgamate and discard, imitate and absorb bits and pieces of other people's lives, cultures, religions, philosophies, politics, struggling to sew some patchwork of ideas together to clothe our nakedness. Like the era which gave rise to Christianity, ours is one of great religious syncretism.

But halakhah is more than style; though it contains its own inner mechanism for dealing with the effects of temporal, cultural, and geographic change, the essence of halakhah does not change. Precisely because the essence of halakhah is the unity of the concrete actions it prescribes, with the "theoretical or conceptual" basis of the Torah, halakhah is that which unites the most "spiritual" aspects of Judaism with the most physical, mundane details of life. Halakhah is that unique religious expression which—overleaping the bounds of other non-Jewish concepts of "spirituality"—somehow is able to connect G-d to . . . how one ties one's shoelaces. Being good, ethical, spiritual, Zionist etc., is, halakhah insists, somehow bound up with the way we eat, dress, cook, sleep, keep the *Shabbat*, and so on. Why?

Because in essence, the Torah teaches that nothing, literally nothing is trivial for the Jew; that there is utterly no aspect of one's life which is unimportant; no action, word, thought, to which one can afford to be insensitive. There is no aspect or moment of life which the Jew does not seek to elevate and sanctify and permeate with Jewishness. That is why in Judaism, soul and body, idea and action, the most metaphysical and the most mundane realms are not separate—as is the case with Greco-Christian culture. And halakhah is this very unity of style and substance, soul and body, spirit and letter, daily life and the Divine. We have a G-d who "*mishes* in."

Halakhah Should Not Be Modernized

Precisely in the detail does one find the whole, or to use more philosophic terminology, only through the particular does one reach the universal; concrete and abstract cannot be separated. Precisely in the seeming small details, in the minutiae, in the concrete *halakhot* is the essence of Torah expressed.

This concept is actually very contemporary. Twentieth century science teaches us the same lesson: the secret of nature, the ultimate strength and power of the universe lies not somewhere in the vast cosmic expanse, but within the infinitely small world of the atom. The biggest explosive force comes from a highly-controlled reaction using the most minute nuclear components.

Those familiar with kabbalah will recognize that the term *tzimtzum*, meaning "contraction, condensation" is central to Jewish mystical thought. The idea is that G-d, so to speak, contracted himself to make a space for the universe, and that he condensed his thought and will through innumerable contractions into the physical letters and words of the Torah.

Halakhah, for the mystic, is the greatly condensed wisdom of G-d, inseparable from the most abstract metaphysical speculation. Which therefore explains why the very compiler and editor of the *Shulchan Aruch* was none other than the great mystic and Kabbalist of the Safed circle, R. Yoseph Caro.

And Caro was not alone—our greatest speculative mystics were also our greatest halakhists. This combination of law and mysticism is unique to Judaism. The most spiritually sensitive of our tradition were also the most attentive to the minutiae of halakhah, for halakhah is the body, the very concrete expression of the soul of Torah. Those who reached the highest levels sought not to abolish, alter, or "modernize" halakhah, but to reinforce it.

Yet the call for American Jewry has been to "modernize" halakhah, to adjust it to the norms of the prevailing culture, until, gradually, halakhah has all but disappeared and it's a matter of each for himself. Each must decide for himself, according to his own "inner light" what is right, wrong, appropriate, inappropriate behavior. How Protestant we have become. Cut the flower from the branch and it can't last for too long. It shrivels and dies. We are left with some abstract, ineffectual spirituality or vague ethical monotheism, and we have created a Judaism in America that is bodyless, content-less, a style without substance that has been alienating Jews in droves.

We Must Seek Meaning in Halakhah

Can halakhah be attractive today? Yes, because halakhah is the very concrete expression, the very ground and bedrock of Jewish "identity," "culture," "values," and all the other abstract words which don't exist in the Bible—because the word "Torah," meaning "teaching, instruction," includes and indissolubly binds together "religion," "ethics," "politics" with one another and with the way one ties one's shoes. One can't separate them; separate halakhah from Torah, Jewish action from Jewish thought, and you separate the Jew from Judaism.

To be sure, some *halakhot* are not congruent with some contemporary styles of thought and behavior. That, however, is no necessary reason for immediately doing away with them, and for rationalizing a Judaism which we adhere to only when it is comfortable for us to observe. And should not we, of all people, be most skeptical of the styles and conceptual fads of modern culture—have we not suffered in this century most from the hands of those who were most culturally and technologically advanced? Did not "liberal humanism" fail us miserably and does it not appear as if it is beginning to fail us again—for oil? Instead of casting away halakhah, let us search for its deeper meaning, its intricate and indissoluble connection to those aspects of Judaism unquestioningly meaningful to us and the world.

But let us search with Jewish eyes—not with the eyes of the Greek who seeks only the beauty of surface, harmony, and rational proportion. Or with the eyes of the Christian who disparages this mundane world of the flesh and seeks his salvation in a purely abstract, spiritual realm. For we will find in halakhah what to the Christian is trivial and "unspiritual," and what to the Greek is unbeautiful and non-rational. The Torah deals not only with the beautiful and rational and spiritual elements of ourselves, ignoring the rest, but also (and perhaps more importantly) with what is not beautiful and not rational, and what is spiritually intractable—with our physical behavior in the world of our everyday life, down to the last detail. For if one doesn't pay careful attention to those aspects of human behavior which are nonrational, they can easily become wildly, destructively irrational—rather than guides which can lead us above and beyond the limits of reason.

Even one who is concerned with beauty, proportion, and aesthetics will tell us that details are important. The artist, above all, knows that one incorrect line, awkward angle, off color, can destroy the painting; the poet agonizes over the exact word. Jewish beauty, however, is not embodied in plaster and paint and poetry, but in deeds, physical actions—the most minute, the most mundane—over which the Jew agonizes and meditates as deeply as does the artist over his composition. Meditation over the proper way to tie one's shoes merges into meditation on the secrets of creation, the *Shulchan Aruch* into the kabbalah. In going to the *tzaddik* to learn how he ties his shoes, one learns all. For the Jew's life, his way of "walking," the specifics of halakhah, constitute the essence of his art, his ultimate masterwork.

First Person

Anthropological Treasures

Barbara Meyerhoff

From a transcript of In Her Own Time, *a documentary film based on the fieldwork of Barbara Meyerhoff, in her study of the Chasidic neighborhood of Fairfax, Los Angeles. The film was produced and directed by Lynn Littman, and distributed by Direct Cinema Ltd. Dr. Meyerhoff, a cultural anthropologist at the University of Southern California was diagnosed with cancer during this project. She died in 1985, two weeks after her project was completed.*

BARBARA: THIS IS NOT THE FILM THAT I STARTED OUT TO make. Originally I intended to do a broad-based depiction of Jewish life in Fairfax, L. A. I hoped for the kind of professional distance that every social scientist wants to bring the subject. But to do anything except something that touched my own life was time I didn't have. When I came into the community after I became ill, they came up to me with these treasures which I hadn't expected, offering resources, offering rituals, offering this deep caring, offering an interpretation of what illness meant and how it fit into a whole cosmos, a whole world. This is a community that is not ordinary. It is not weird, but it's certainly not what you'd expect to find all around you. It's as if I walked into a New Guinean village in the middle of my own backyard. . . . You step inside these little worlds that they have all over their streets and there's something there you never could have dreamed existed.

They have what everyone is looking for in religion, and that is a community and spirituality. I certainly didn't intend to make a film about the orthodox per se, but they turned out to be somehow the most compelling and drew my life into theirs so deeply that they became the focus.

And in a way that was kind of familiar and satisfying. This is really what anthropologists are taught to do. You study what is happening to others by understanding what is going on in yourself. And you yourself become the data-gathering instrument, so that you come from one culture and you step into a new one. And how you respond to the new one tells you about them and it tells you about the one you came from.

Voiceover: Barbara began her personal journey with the ritual purification [mikveh]*. As both a scientist and a sick woman, she was intrigued by the* mikveh's *promise of renewal.*

Going to the *mikveh* to purify yourself before making love must be very erotic. My experience in being around orthodox families is that there is a special kind of bond between them very often, and I think it comes from the fact that they're not available to each other half the month, sexually.

Voiceover: Barbara interviews a baalat teshuvah, *a woman who has "returned" from a secular to a Torah lifestyle.*

To tell you the truth, I can identify [with the *baalat teshuvah*] in that I can understand what she's talking about. And probably more than with anyone else I know, I feel envy because I think she stepped through that invisible barrier. I can see through the membrane and I can't walk through it. And the membrane is thinner now than it's ever been because there are times when in this illness I realize I can't do it alone. I really need help. Something has to come from outside of me, or it may be inside of me. But it's not the regular stuff. I can't use my head in the same way that I always have in my life.

I came to this work with certain antipathies to the way women are treated, to the exclusions of women, to the secondary status of women in the faith, to the fact that this is a very patriarchal religion. There's no getting away from that. What I had left out was the return value.

Could I be one of these women? Unfortunately, when I look at the women, it's across an affectionate distance. It's so much not possible for it to be me. One reason—this woman we spoke to earlier articulated it perfectly: she said how she loved the restrictions, how they give her order. Now part of me is deeply attracted to that, that's why I've always loved ritual, but a part of me is profoundly rebellious and independent, and I do not love restrictions imposed on me from outside. I don't think I could bear that for a quarter of an hour. Certainly, the men have more of the kinds of things that I myself would want and value. But the men don't get cheated the way they do in my society, of participation in the family; and they don't get cheated of intimacy.

. . . They presented me with an organic life, a life that was all of one piece. It had a totality. Because of the way the people knew each other, because of the deep intertwining of their lives at every moment, at every level that enfolds them all. So that there almost can't be a separate word for religion. It's not a separate category. It's in every relationship, and because of this envelope of belief, it's embedded in everything.

Several months later.

The replies that I gave you to the question of restrictions and the loss of freedom and independence, when I spoke about it several months ago, are not the ones I would say now. Mostly, then I was thinking about restrictions as coming from the outside. Things I would have to do because they were laws. I was thinking about, of course, the priesthood, religious laws, G-d giving me rules. There was no sense in this of the G-d within, let's say, or the restrictions coming from something I carried, not that I bowed to. Suddenly here are restrictions. I can't walk the way I did, eat, breathe—the basic functions—mother my children the way I did. Everyday presents me with new restrictions. And I have some choice still, some days more than others, as to whether I see those as restrictions or doorways to other possibilities.

Voiceover: As Barbara became increasingly fragile, she continued to struggle with the unfinished business of her life. Her friends from the Orthodox community offered their own traditional forms of help.

One of the rituals that they were most eager for me to have from the very beginning was to get a Jewish divorce. Rabbi Z. told me, "Your civil divorce doesn't talk about your soul." He said, "How are you going to get your soul back, because when you're married, your soul is wrapped around your husband." And indeed, I had lived with and loved the same man for 30 years, and I didn't feel I had gotten my soul back. And I knew I needed to. So I put myself in their hands.

After the divorce.

These people have a fundamental human heritage that the rest of us have lost—spirituality and community. That's probably what they show me more than anything else. How will those figure in my life in the future? I have no way of knowing. I know I want them, I know they've made them accessible to me. I don't know what my future will be. I have no way of anticipating my health, my freedom. I'll never be the same after doing this work.

I will never want to lead a life where I have to do without those things again. And I can't think of any other people to whom I could have turned, where I would find these offered to me so abundantly, and in a way, so simply. And here it was, it was in a way mine all along, it was what I belonged to without knowing it and I suppose that's a treasure that they've given to me.

If I can, in my work as an anthropologist, at the same time make it clear to others who they are and what they feel and what they have, if I can take what they've shown me and pass that through me and out into the world, then my work is done.

From Feminism to Chasidism

Chana Shloush

HAD I KNOWN THAT THE DECISION TO KEEP KOSHER AND *Shabbat* in 1971 would eventually lead me, many years later, to walking around Brooklyn in a wig and modest clothing, I might have been too paralyzed to have done the first *mitzvah*. There I was, 19 years old and thrilled about being a college student in Boston, exploring all the "isms" of the day: pacifism, socialism, vegetarianism, meditation, feminism, mysticism and Judaism.

My involvement in Torah Judaism came through an Orthodox relative, a woman in her 50's who welcomed me into her home like an adopted child. She was a European refugee like my father, able to fill in blanks about the vanished world I yearned to understand. Particularly in the context of her lifestyle she described much: "This is the tune your grandfather sang for the Grace After Meals. Now you are mixing up the cake your grandmother baked for *Shabbos*. These teacups were a gift to me from your aunt who died in Auschwitz." She was not an intellectual and also had no formal Jewish schooling, so she could not answer my why's about the performance of *mitzvot*, but she did them all with a compelling *joie de vivre*. She was also able to talk a little, in her down-to-earth way, about her relationship with G-d. She obviously had no hangups about that relationship, and she tried to convince me that there was no reason for concern. But Jewish spirituality and mysticism, which greatly interested me, were not part of her vocabulary—she did not radiate them or discuss them. Thus she could not give me some key information I required, and I had no recourse but to work through those issues in my own way. Thankfully, she also accepted me exactly as I was at every step.

My Torah commitment came about after many basic questions about observance and lifestyle had been answered. There was a moment when, with an English Bible open to Exodus 20 (the *Shema* prayer), I had an overwhelming inner experience. *Kabbalat ol*, acceptance of the yoke of Heaven, is perhaps the most correct description. One might call it a leap of faith, yet afterward I found myself walking, not in midair, but on very solid ground. I committed myself to *Shabbat* and *kashrut* observance and was determined to eventually keep the rest of the *mitzvot* as well. Months and years actually passed before I had the intellectual knowledge and emotional readiness to take on many other *mitzvot*. I had also been forewarned about doing too much too fast, as there were others who had apparently taken that route and then abandoned their observance.

In 1971 feminism was a brand new, hot issue on campus. Those present at my first Women's Liberation meetings included an editor of the original *Our Bodies, Ourselves* and a woman who later wound up on the FBI's Ten Most Wanted list for bank robbery and murder, committed for the sake of "the revolution." I belonged to a women's literary circle which read and discussed feminist literature. I studied poetry and received personal advice from feminist poet Adrienne Rich. I came to find radical feminism frightening and distasteful because it bespoke such hatred of men. I didn't hate men: I was simply resentful whenever they seemed to get a better deal than women. One day a friend said, "You're interested in Judaism and also in feminism—why not explore the two together?"

My desire to establish a women's *minyan* arose from intense spiritual frustration and doubts about the status of the Jewish woman, based largely on my synagogue experience. At the time, praying in Hebrew was difficult, especially for one who had learned little more than *alef-bet* in Reform Sunday School. Trying concomitantly to pray in, and understand the Hebrew was even harder. Attempting to juggle all this and have a spiritual experience in the women's section of a traditional synagogue caused me terrific problems. When everyone sang spiritedly in unison, I managed well. But usually I sensed an uncomfortable silence, especially among women. I yearned for good concentration, warmth and openness during prayer, from myself and others. Instead I was confronted with furtive whispering or mouthing of the words of prayers. Usually by the end of services the atmosphere warmed up a bit, but then all too soon it was time to leave. I wondered why these women, who were saying the same words as the men, seemed, in my perception, to be lacking something in their self-expectations regarding a personal relationship with G-d. I had been told that women were not second class citizens, but how could I not begin to have doubts when so many women behaved as if they thought that perhaps they were? My Orthodox relative did not act like a second class citizen, but then, neither did she intellectualize, so I thought that maybe some wool was being pulled over her eyes without her knowing or caring. If G-d had created a system in which I was a second class citizen, could I trust him enough to have a close personal relationship? On the other hand, what about the times when I did have positive spiritual experiences, which certainly occurred without my having any thoughts of feminism? The issue was paradox-laden, and I was confounded. Precisely at the time when I needed a spiritual boost, I found frustration. So I continued praying in a traditional synagogue, meanwhile seeking alternatives. A visit to a *havurah* group proved disillusioning because of the members' lack of consistency in their Jewish commitment. A more intense practice of meditation served temporarily as a satisfying spiritual outlet, but I did not believe that I could ever transform it into a positive Jewish group ritual experience.

The idea to establish the first women's *minyan* in America (to my knowledge), took root in my mind late in 1971, during a lecture at Harvard Hillel by a Conservative rabbi. About ten days later, our "Women's *Minyan*" was born, with seven women in attendance. Our beginnings were tenuous; everyone seemed nervous and self-conscious. I was frustrated, but we plugged on with the group, meeting bi-weekly and having Torah study sessions together on occasion. I was spurred by one of my professors, the late Dr. Pauli Murray, a lawyer who nominated herself to be the first black female Supreme justice in the early 1970's, and later entered the Christian clergy. She encouraged me to keep a log of the group's progress. I don't believe there ever really was any progress, despite the fact that women in other places caught wind of the idea and set up similar groups. I didn't give up, though, and our "*minyan*" continued for the remaining year and a half until I graduated. I reasoned that other *mitzvot* had felt awkward and uncomfortable at first and had grown to feel like second nature; I kept hoping that I would eventually experience our group that way as well. However, I never found spiritual satisfaction in our "*minyan*" or any of the other women's *davening* groups I attended sporadically over the course of the next six years.

Not everyone in the "*minyan*" viewed it as I did. The student I recruited to be the co-founder of the "Women's *Minyan*" went on to become a Reform rabbi and made headlines a few years ago as the first female member of the Rabbinical Assembly, the Conservative rabbinical organization. In fact, I helped her draft a letter in 1972 to the chancellor of the Jewish Theological Seminary, requesting an application to Conservative rabbinical school. While I toyed with the idea of becoming a rabbi, I had to reject it, because I knew that the truth I was seeking had to lie somewhere within traditional Judaism. Instinct told me that finding it would involve a search—and I was prepared for a lengthy one if necessary—but not the kind of battle my friend was waging.

Concerned over missing out on important spiritual experiences, I did other kinds of Jewish feminist experimentation at the same time. I made my own *talit*, in beautiful pastel colors, learning from a man how to tie the *tzitzit*. I also created a very feminine headband which I wore for about two years. I thought that wearing the *talit* would help me shut out the external distractions, and sometimes this was the case. However, the *talit* induced other, greater inner distractions: the fact that I knew many pairs of eyes were on me, and the fact that deep down I sometimes enjoyed the attention and notoriety my behavior was bringing me. My initial basic motives were quite sincere. But whatever spiritual highs I experienced started to be clouded by the awareness of such falseness at the root of motivation.

I once put on *tefillin*. The woman who owned them asked for them back after ten minutes: at that point I did not want to take them off. I knew I could have some incredible meditations wearing them. But I was also overcome by immense awe and sensed that *tefillin* were too holy to wear if there were even an iota of an ego trip involved, especially if there were no *mitzvah* for—and some prohibitions against—my wearing them.

I also felt a sense of loss at not being able to come close to the physical Torah, to watch over the shoulder of the *baal koreh* as he *lehned* (read aloud)—or to actually be that *baal koreh*. So I learned the *trup* (cantillation) for Torah, *Haftorah* and the Song of Songs. There was some exhilaration in *lehning*, and it greatly aided my following the Torah reading in synagogue as well as personal learning, but I found the study and memorization of each *parsha* difficult and painstaking. With time, I also came to suspect that a great percentage of the exhilaration was an ego trip.

In retrospect, I believe that my stiff feminist principles became burdensome at a certain point, preventing me from trying out new *mitzvot* or delving deeper into already familiar ones.

They also kept me from meeting the kinds of people I needed to encounter in order to gain the knowledge I craved.

A key transitional experience between feminism and Chasidism occurred in 1974. I spent that school year after college graduation in Jerusalem, studying Torah—mainly Talmud—in Hebrew, in an effort to gain the skills for independent text study. A group of Americans would study *Chasidut* one evening a week with a Chasidic rabbi in Meah Shearim. If he had an address, we didn't know it; we knew only which alleys to go down, which courtyards to cross. He spoke no English and taught quietly and patiently in the simplest Hebrew. One warm evening, a friend and I stayed after class to ask questions. His wife appeared with a glass of water which she handed me with a smile. Suddenly I was riveted to the floor. There was something intensely spiritual about the way that woman gave me the glass of water. I didn't want to leave. I wanted to grab her and shake her and beg her to tell me what the secret was, to say that I had been waiting for this moment for years and had to understand. But I couldn't. It seemed to me that the gaps in language and culture were too vast to even attempt it. So I went home that night and, without understanding why, carefully packed away my *talit* in an old footlocker. Today the reason is clear: I could no longer afford the luxury of alienating Torah-observant and Chasidic women who might bear the keys to locked doors I desired to open.

Perhaps the woman was a mystic. Or perhaps she changed my life with very strong *kavanah* (positive intention and concentration) in performing the *mitzvah* of *hachnassat orchim*, serving guests. Had I never put away the *talit*, it is hard to imagine ever having learned of the latter explanation.

Another incident greatly changed my attitude toward Torah study. I was not blessed with the analytical *Gemara Kop* that best absorbs Talmud. However, I was determined—again, partially on the feminist principle of not missing out on anything—to maintain an ongoing study of it. I had picked up an attitude from a number of supposedly learned men, that other parts of Torah were somehow lacking in comparison with "the sea of Talmud," and that one could not attain any respectable level of Torah knowledge without mastering it, much less gain wisdom. After the year in Israel, I moved to New York, where I found a genius of a teacher who taught Talmud to women on weekday evenings. A small group spent as many as six hours a week learning Tractate *Berachot* (Blessings) *b'amkut*, slowly and intensively. Our teacher loved to search within the discussions for deeper generalizations. I recall his spending several weeks on a brief passage in trying to understand the nature of a blessing, and his excitement over his conclusion. A blessing, he found, is like the economic principle of pump priming (my analogy), in which we open up the gates of Heaven so G-d can grant us His blessings.

Several years later, just before moving to Crown Heights, I attended the Bais Chana Women's Institute in Minnesota. Shortly after my arrival we went to wash our hands for bread before lunch. One self-appointed young woman helped everyone wash, as most were newcomers to observance. She was obviously quite new herself. As we waited, I could not help but perk up my ears as she explained to another woman the purpose for the blessing: "*Chasidut* says. . . ." Would the reader like to guess the rest? This was not a case where, as often happens, someone accidentally misquoted a source, since my teacher had worked for weeks to come up with an original explanation. In a manner totally uncharacteristic for me, I viewed that girl as a G-dly messenger. Never again did I force myself on principle to study Talmud. Today I will open a volume of the Talmud if I have a specific reason, but my basic daily Torah study focuses on other works. Perhaps the real inner process of my transition out of feminism becomes clearest with the struggle over the *mechitzah* issue. I had never battled the notion of *mechitzah*, yet neither had issue. I had never battled the notion of *mechitzah*, yet neither had I ever really trusted the explanations which I had received. In particular, the protests that those men who led the services weren't really the focus of attention on a community-condoned ego trip smacked of "The Emperor's New Clothes." I accepted the *mechitzah* because it was part of the package deal of Torah, but for many years my mind was not at peace with it.

The eve of Yom Kippur, around 1980. Men and women alike were packed into Lubavitch international headquarters for *Kol Nidre*, somewhat like passengers on a Jerusalem bus during rush hour. The *baal tefillah* took his place to begin the service. I was anticipating an inspiring voice, a poignant melody to sweep me into the mood of the holiday. Instead, a man with an ordinary voice began the prayers with an atonal melody and then broke down in what appeared to be sincere sobs.

He sounded ridiculous. I was annoyed. An instant later, I was forced in all honesty to redefine my emotion as terror. I had no inspiration, no melody to hide behind. The *baal tefillah* was not about to lift me to any spiritual heights. Here was a man leading the prayers for thousands of Jews, including no less a personage than the Lubavitcher Rebbe, yet he was on anything but an ego trip. This meant that I was missing absolutely nothing on the other side of the *mechitzah*. At that moment, the *mechitzah* figuratively came crashing down once and for all, hitting me with what the issue had been in the first place. There were contradictory feelings involved: on one hand, a concern that somehow G-d was present only on the other side of that divider curtain, and on the other, a fear that if He weren't, I wouldn't be able to cope with the confrontation. In a way it had been easy to hide behind my anger. Now that the reality was clear, it would just have to be me and G-d—me facing up to my real self in front of G-d.

I was not able to cast off the women's *minyan*, *talit*, and the rest—nor was I interested in doing so—until there were other spiritual resources to take their places. A crucial factor in the change process was the study of *Chasidut*. Part of what helped me trust the system was finding that *Chasidut* is replete with feminine imagery. The subject would be interesting and inspiring in itself, but it is beyond the scope of this article.

I did not find Chabad *Chasidut* accessible until I was living in Crown Heights and attended classes, local synagogues where I had role models for proper concentration during prayer, and the Rebbe's *farbrengens* (Chasidic gatherings). With a deepening of study and *mitzvah* observance has come a heightened awareness of what was superficial in the past, and a natural wish to reject it. Hence, the change has mainly come gradually, like casting off clothes which neither fit any longer nor are needed. I suppose I entered into my feminist Jewish experiments with the soul of an innocent child. On one hand there were wide-eyed openness, beauty and wonder, which remain a refreshing source of inspiration when I recall the early days of observance. On the other hand, there was a passivity, as if important spiritual experiences should be conferred upon me from Above simply by virtue of, say, wearing certain accoutrements. I used to assume that G-d was providing all kinds of lovely merry-go-round rides for men as they performed their particular *mitzvot*. Hands-on experience, Torah study and discussions with men led me to the conclusion that the men were unlikely to be getting free goodies any more than I ever had. With time came a gradual shift away from initial unrealistic and hence unfulfilling expectations.

There was an acceptance of my responsibility not only to fulfill my requirements in *mitzvah* observance, but to infuse energy and enthusiasm into each *mitzvah*. Originally I had demanded that my role models—including all those women behind the *mechitzah*—be perfect. When I stopped expecting so much from my fellow Jewish women, and had gained enough self-confidence to realize that perhaps I was meant to try to set an example for them, prayers and other *mitzvot* flowed more easily.

It is impossible to minimize the significance of tremendous female role models. I have met human dynamos, whom I believe rank among the spiritual Green Berets of the Jewish people. They have the shortcomings of all of us mortals, but their maximization of potential is astounding. During my early feminist years, the praises in Torah literature of the Jewish woman had sounded like so many platitudes: "A superior wisdom was granted to women," "A woman of valor, who can find?" etc. In meeting women who exemplified these verses, my views had to change radically. Even more, when I married and started a family I began to appreciate that the spiritual fortitude, the *mesirat nefesh*—the total giving of one's best—with which the Torah challenges a Jewish woman, is no less than the highest form of mystical practice I could ever have imagined, as different in form as it might at times appear to be on the surface. I seem to have come around full circle in trying to live up to models like the Meah Shearim woman, and the relative who first inspired me with her *joie de vivre* in *mitzvot.* I am grateful to be connected to a community where, spiritually speaking, the streets are paved with gold. In fact, who knows? Had my eyes been open all those years ago to see that gold, performing the first *mitzvah* might not have been paralyzing at all.

Handwashing and Other Rituals

Marjorie Ordene

"HOLDING THE CUP IN YOUR LEFT HAND, POUR THE WATER over your right hand. Then take the cup in your right hand and pour the water over your left. Now dry your hands and recite the blessing. After that, return to the table and do not speak until you have said the blessing and eaten the bread. During the meal keep your conversation away from weekday talk or gossip. Stay in the Sabbath mood."

As the rabbi gave instructions to a group of twenty students on Friday night, I couldn't help but recall another group of students receiving similar instructions one weekday morning a decade ago. "Holding the scrub brush in your left hand, scrub your right arm and hand with overlapping strokes until every millimeter of skin is covered. Then place the brush in your left hand and do the same." No mention was made of saying a prayer or observing silence, but ten years later, I found myself thinking, it would have been appropriate if it had. After all, I thought, if we say a prayer and observe a silence before eating bread, how much more important it would be before cutting open a human body. At the time, however, it never occurred to me—I was much too worried about accidentally touching something and contaminating myself or worse still, getting yelled at by the scrub nurse or surgeon. But looking back on it, I think how nice it would have been if the surgeons had meditated while scrubbing, observed a solemn silence while being gowned and gloved, and then, after cutting the skin, spoken only in respectful tones, mindful of the gravity of their work.

A year or two ago, an article appeared in the health page of the *Times*, describing a study by anesthesiologists in which it was found that patients under general anesthesia remembered what was said in the operating room, and that those whose surgeons had said they would make a speedy recovery, did so. I remember looking back on my own experience in OR and thinking, "Oh, no, what did we do?" True, we didn't wish the patients ill, but the term "respectful" wouldn't quite apply either. I recall a lot of horsing around, off-color jokes, and verbal one-upmanship. Is it still the same, I wondered, or did that study revolutionize the operating room?

A few years ago my parents went on a tour called "Jewish Friends of Scandinavia." It was led by a rabbi, and my parents were just about the only non-religious people on the trip. "Everything we did, they said a prayer," my parents told me. "We went on a bus, they said a prayer; we went on a plane, they said a prayer. See? We have the book." They showed me a little book, Prayers for Travel. "We never felt so safe." I was used to these jokes. My father comes from a very religious family. Fanatic, we would say. I imagined they did have a prayer for everything: talking on the phone, doing the laundry, taking a walk . . . We joked about it, but now I'm beginning to have second thoughts. My friend Dorcas is a religious Christian. Whenever I tell her my problems, she says, "I'll pray for you." I thank her politely. Then one day I was telling her about a very nasty person who came into my medical office demanding care. Dorcas, who counsels patients at a local clinic, told me, "Every day before I open my door, I say a prayer that whoever walks through that door will bring their good energy with them and leave their bad energy outside." Now there's an idea, I thought.

It's Friday night again, and my friends Nancy and Bob have invited me for the Sabbath dinner. As I enter their apartment, the two kids are running around making enough noise for ten. Seth, age four, is demanding a glass of apple juice, and Jed, seven, wants to know, "When are we going to eat?" Amid the noise and confusion, we manage to get to the table, light the candles, and later, gather round the table to say the *Kiddush*. Then, Jed jumps up and shouts, "Let's wash our hands!" Finally, the room is still as, one at a time, we pour cold water over first one hand and then the other, recite the blessing, and sit back down in perfect silence, waiting to eat bread.

Fundamental Truths

Tziporah Unger

GROWING UP IN THE SIXTIES AND SEVENTIES AS AN American Jew was a confusing experience, to say the least. We were the "baby-boomers," the post-war generation who had known no Depression, educated to meet the challenges of the space age, the generation which—it was assumed—would continue the spiral upwards in material success. In this we were completely American.

The Jewish part was the source of the confusion. Yes, we should be completely assimilated into our public schools. But go to Hebrew School afterwards. We were taught to get along with everyone—but don't date non-Jews.

At home, everyone ate chicken soup on Friday night, but the chicken wasn't always from a kosher butcher. And everyone ate pizza out. If you "kept kosher" you just told them to hold the pepperoni.

This nebulous Jewish identity had somehow been enough for our parents' generation. They still remembered a parent or grandparent who had had stronger ties to Judaism, memories of anti-Semitism which had left their mark, a feeling of the "old neighborhood" which they had left for the better part of town and then suburbia. Jewish food was a piece of their heritage, so chicken soup made from non-kosher chicken was still comforting to them if there was enough schmaltz floating at the top.

But mine was the generation that scoffed at schmaltz. For the most part, my peers have rejected the ersatz Jewishness of our parents. Many have rejected their own Jewishness as a result. Others are now in Israel, consoling themselves by practicing secularism among other Jews. And the lucky ones have rediscovered the source of their parents' emotions, the *kashrut* that had been rendered into mere schmaltz, and have reversed the process.

I count myself among the lucky ones.

The message I received growing up at home was somewhat schizophrenic. I was expected to act like everyone else but to feel Jewish. My home was relatively observant. We kept kosher. We went to Hebrew School. We went to Temple every Friday night and Saturday morning. We were discouraged from bringing non-Jewish friends home. My mother lit candles every Friday night at six o'clock—summer and winter.

My father believed in G-d and wanted us to believe in Him too. But if his faith was purer because it lacked intellectual understanding, it was all the poorer in its transmissibility to his children.

I knew that I was different because I was Jewish. My parents never quite made it to the suburbs, so by the early sixties we were in a gentile neighborhood by virtue of social immobility. I read a lot and wanted to read about Jewish things. But there were no Jewish books in the local branch of the public library. My first attempt at writing came at the age of nine; I tried to write a Jewish version of the *Bobbsey Twins*. I only wrote two pages and then I had to quit. A book has to have action; and while I knew that the Jewish Bobbseys would feel differently than the originals, I didn't quite know how they would act differently.

When the sixties reached their peak, I was still in high school. The initial message of the sixties wasn't bad: One should find absolute truths and guide one's life by them. That message lasted about ten minutes. Then it became formulated into generalities like peace, love, and brotherhood. The final equation looked like this: peace = burning down the campus; love = indiscriminate distribution of one's bodily favors; brotherhood—rejection of established morality/religion as a divisive factor.

The social law established in the sixties was: thou shalt not follow any rules.

The intellectual result of the sixties milieu was not nearly so direct nor easy to see through. On the one hand, intellectuals pursued the goal of finding the absolute truths of social science. On the other hand, one could prove himself only by proving that someone else's absolute truths were false. Academic success required total arrogance and the ability to convince others that the arrogance was justified. Belief in anything higher than one's own intellectual ability was a badge of shame and dishonor. Finding a reason to disagree with anything and everything was the ultimate sign of brilliance.

As I entered college in 1973 I planned on being intellectually successful. But world events collided with my plans, and the feelings that I had never understood took over.

I had (as had everyone) been influenced by the sixties. I knew my parents did not possess absolute truths and therefore I had to find my own way—with all the arrogance, stubbornness, and obnoxiousness of my generation.

Jewish youth had produced its own particular questions. There had been a few heroes presented to us. Meir Kahane with his shout of "Never Again!" led us to recognize that we were part of a people. Elie Wiesel was my personal choice. While his books never advised Jews to act differently, they were based on the assumption that the Jewish experience had made Jews into a people who felt differently, who asked different types of questions, whose natural state was to be somewhat alienated from the general world.

Acting on those feelings I dropped out of college in my first semester and went to Israel to be a kibbutz volunteer in wartime. Ten thousand American kids went that year, most against the wishes of their parents who thought such Jewish identification to be a bit extreme. And why? Because we knew that our people were in trouble and we chose to be with them. *Ahavat Yisrael* drove us, although we boned up on Zionist philosophy to claim a rational basis to our actions.

Our parents still identified more strongly with America than with other Jews. Their hopes were pinned on their children achieving professionally and financially, and they were all uneasy about the prospect that we might just decide to stay there. Jewish peoplehood was not a big deal to them; they felt chicken soup should be enough.

So I spent six months on a communist kibbutz in the Negev as an act of Jewish identification. I had thought that Israel would be the place where I would feel relaxed as a Jew, but instead found that the ideology of the kibbutz was to rid the Jew of any feelings of being different. If there are no gentiles to make you feel alienated then you can feel comfortable acting like a gentile. I didn't act Jewish on the kibbutz; I acted less Jewish than I had in America.

So it was with a secret sense of relief that I went home to my angry parents, and back to school. I felt Jewish—but wished I could feel better about it.

I decided to major in History. Somehow, I felt that by understanding the past I could understand where I stood in the world.

The Holocaust is the obsession of any self-respecting Jewish history buff and I was no exception. But Jewish history in the University curriculum rejects a priori the reality of Judaism. All topics of study are based upon the assumption that the best thing a Jew can do is escape from Torah.

In the pursuit of the Jewish past, I immersed myself in the study of the Haskalah movement, the Enlightenment as pursued by Jews. The irony of it was that the individuals and movements I studied were those that advocated the rejection of Judaism, while I was trying to find it.

There were Torah-observant Jews around. There was a Chabad House; I knew the rabbis, and some of my friends went there. But my academic training indoctrinated me to believe that anybody who could keep the laws of a Medieval religion in the twentieth century had to be intellectually deficient, or crazy, or both. I would have nothing to do with them.

So I devoted myself to the writings of Jews who dealt with modernity: atheists, reformists, humanists, communists, etc. Each admitted that he was a Jew, but felt that Jews had to be something else in the modern world. And of course I studied anti-Semitism. It is paradoxical that I somehow thought I could come to grips with my own identity by wading through the thoughts of intellectuals (some of them Jewish) who had devised new and different ways to revile my great grandparents.

Most of these courses were offered under the heading: "Judaic Studies." One class in particular shook me to the core. It was a seminar on German-Jewish intellectuals, taught by two very eminent Jewish professors who had themselves escaped Germany in the thirties.

It was toward the end of the semester that we read Freud's *Moses and Monotheism*. For those who have had the privilege of avoiding this polemic, it theorizes that the Jewish people originated as a low-class rabble led by an incestuous Egyptian prince.

Something snapped in me. Yes, I was a rationalist. Yes, I believed in evolution and the A scroll and the J scroll and all that stuff anthropologists said about the Bible. But this was too much. I knew in the pit of my stomach that my ancestors had not suffered for two thousand years because they had been deluded by an egocentric Egyptian con artist.

"Freud went too far," I said through clenched teeth. The student near me, a German-born son of a Nazi, smiled. We had argued all semester and now he had me. "What's the matter?" he sneered. "What are you? A FUNDAMENTALIST!"

There it was. The dreaded word of the intellectual world. Everyone literally gasped in horror. It meant you believed there might actually be something higher than the human mind, even higher than the mind of a professor. If I was a fundamentalist then I was an academic heretic.

I took a deep breath. I said nothing. I didn't owe him an explanation. This son of a Nazi had, quite possibly, in his German accent, inadvertently taught me a truth. If he was the opposite of a fundamentalist, maybe it wasn't such a bad thing to be.

Mine was the generation that hungered for Jewishness but couldn't believe in G-d. I was taught to pray to Him, but was also taught that the entire Torah had been written by imaginative men who invented miracles and an afterworld to make people behave better. So if the rabbis we grew up with didn't believe that G-d had ever really talked to anybody, why should we believe He existed at all?

Something inside of me began to loosen up. I began to realize that people who kept the *mitzvot* of the Torah were not necessarily stupid. And just maybe they weren't crazy.

I had come to what was one of the most humbling realizations of my life.

It was two and a half years before I decided to make a firm commitment to Torah Judaism. Somewhere along the way, I began to suspect that when things didn't go right in my life it was because I was doing something wrong. And the more I began to associate with Torah-observant Jews, the more I liked the lifestyle. It had order. It made sense. It was better than anybody else's lifestyle.

So I made a sociological decision to adopt the lifestyle and beliefs of my ancestors. I then decided to go and study at Bais Chana Women's Institute in Minnesota so that I could really fit in.

The first few days were wonderful. The classes were interesting, the company was good, the food was great. Then it hit me. This was not a sociological exercise. After telling myself for years that I was looking for truth, I came face to face with it.

There really was a Creator of the universe who expected us to behave in a certain way. And I had spent the last 23 years not behaving that way. I couldn't *choose* to change my lifestyle. I *had* to change.

I cried.

I was horrified.

I survived.

Because despite the blow to my ego when I realized that I was not my own clever creator, that the entire value of my intellectual training lay in my rejection of it, it was a relief.

I wasn't schizophrenic—my education was. America has raised three generations of Jews to feel like Jews—but to think and act like gentiles. So when popular novelists and filmmakers portray Jews as neurotics they aren't really distorting the picture; they're telling the embarrassing truth.

The secular Jewish identity promotes schizophrenia.

When one Jew gets another to do something Jewish, to do a *mitzvah*, he's promoting mental health.

And that, Dr. Freud, is a fundamental truth.

My Sojourn in the Garden of Eden

Varda Branfman

HOW WOULD I HAVE KNOWN ABOUT THE GARDEN OF EDEN if I had not seen it with my own eyes? It was a torrential expanse of beauty that hit me like a flood, and my eyes closed by reflex. With my eyes shut, I smelled the sweet mixture of woods and flowers, and I heard the soft chirping sounds and a low buzzing of the wildlife that flourished there.

My eyes opened to see a hummingbird sip nectar from a tree blossom. I had seen that once before, but here it was happening all around me. I appreciated it deeply, but I was also troubled by certain questions. I had found the Garden of Eden and it seemed logical to ask myself who had made it in the first place, and who kept it running? And why did I deserve to be here, after living all my life previous to this time in one of the ugliest suburbs on the East Coast? I had come here from a gray landscape of supermarkets, diners, and bars— iron and asphalt trimmed by ribbons of flashing lights.

In short, I was stunned by the existence of this Garden of Eden in the world and my existence in it. It seemed that I had stumbled on it, and now I could never leave it. How can a person return to Route 46 and the Lincoln Tunnel after a sojourn in the Garden of Eden? Eden Street was the address of the small environmental college where I was teaching English Composition. Apparently, the city fathers back then had made the same connection as I did.

On my way to my class at the college, I passed small stores and houses that made up the bulk of the city life. In easy walking distance from these houses and stores were the glorious fields and forests. In the other direction was the harbor which is a whole other aspect of this Garden of Eden and its magnificence: the sea.

The harbor was the most eastern point of the continent, and so when I looked out of the top floor of my house, I saw an infinitude of sea. A vast depth and length that I tried to comprehend. Up close, the rocky shore was a virtual aquatic Garden of Eden with gorgeous mosses draped over the boulders and vast populations of crusty sea creatures.

I would sit for hours on one of those boulders and watch the seaweed swirling in the shallow waters. The perpetual sound of fog horns punctuated my sleep all night long, and on foggy days, all day long.

At the environmental college, they were busy debating how long the Garden of Eden would last, considering the terrible toll that human negligence was taking. I heard the predictions—no more clean water to drink, astronomical amounts of plastic that had never decomposed, and dying wildlife. According to the experts, our days in the Garden were numbered, and the small heroic efforts we might make to stay would never be able to keep back the tide of destruction.

The doomsday statistics were prefaced with "by the year 2000," and at best, we had until then to get our act together. Considering the state of global consciousness on the subject of saving the world, I would be lucky to reach the ripe old age of fifty.

I tried to do my part. I hoarded my vegetable peels as if they were precious commodities, and I constantly fed the compost heap in back of the house. I never threw out a plastic bag. I ate whole grains and ground my flour with a hand grinder to save on the electricity. I burned wood in the potbelly stove, and when I used the central heat in the house, it was turned down so low that it barely kept me warm. While the college people designed solar heated houses and compost toilets, I taught them how to write grant proposals and reports.

But the whole thing continued to be vast and incomprehensible. When I zeroed in my focus on the trees or the stones or even one tree or stone, I felt the emanation of a spirit or life force, and then when I looked back at the whole thing standing before me—expanses of woods and glacial lakes and vast seascapes—then the whole thing thundered with a life force which was the sum of all its infinite parts.

I felt my connection with it because I was also alive as it was alive. But where did all this life come from? Who was juicing it up? On a cold winter's night, I would walk on the shore path next to the icy waters and feel as if this question without an answer would kill me, as sure as if I lay down on one of the rocks and let the sea carry me out.

In short, I couldn't live without an answer, and no one that I knew had it for me; not one of those massive intellectual minds at the college, and not one of those brawny lobstermen or sunny storekeepers who lived in the town. The lobstermen were busy setting out before dawn, hauling in their catch, and living their lives, while the intellectuals at the college were considering solutions to the practical questions of how to live in the face of these grave predictions for the planet.

Meanwhile, one summer came and went. In late September, the leaves began to turn, and the trees flared up in fiery shades of red and yellow. The background hum of summer was replaced by a thunderous rustling. There was a blast of crisp air as I opened the front door. Then, after the colors had peaked, the first snow gently came down.

And then came winter.

Winter was forbidding, but it had its own exquisite beauty with fields of pristine snow and a profound silence. The cold was intense, and I learned to dress in long underwear followed by several layers of clothing, a down parka and down mittens. I was careful to keep my car well tuned with a full tank of gas because of the real danger of frostbite in case I was stranded.

And then spring came, just when we thought we couldn't take winter a day longer. The cold ebbed away, and the life force surged forth everywhere. It was mighty and exhilarating. I spent the early morning hours standing in the seabed at low tide and hoisting up one pitchfork after another of seaweed. When my wheelbarrow was full, I pushed it over to the garden and carefully made a garland of slippery strands around each tiny seedling that was coming up.

Then summer came again. I went grazing on wild blueberries and picked them to put in jams, muffins, and blueberry ice cream. My pantry shelves were lined with cans of blueberry syrup, stewed tomatoes, and other preserves for the months to come.

I was living with the cycle, and might go on with that indefinitely as others had done. Here I was a creature in the Garden of Eden and could not imagine living in any other spot after being spoiled by its breathtaking beauty. My friends in the City might wait until they retired to settle in the Garden and begin a sylvan existence. But time seemed to be running out, and I didn't want to postpone it in case the statisticians were right with their gory predictions.

I read the books about "just being" and "being at peace with being." I practiced my Zen meditation exercises and struggled with my thoughts. I lay prone for long moments in the corpse pose, as all the cells in my body relaxed, and relaxed yet further. I tried to be at peace, but the question always surfaced again.

If I didn't have the answer to that question, then I would never know what to do with my life besides enjoying the gorgeous beauty and physical highs of sailing, cross country skiing, sitting next to the wood fires, and eating my own fresh tomatoes. Excuse me, but I had to know.

I needed that answer in order to handle all the other tributary questions that haunted me. Where should I direct my efforts and for what causes? Should I get married? Should I have children? And on a more mundane level—what style of clothing should I wear, and what should I eat? Should I even bother to worry about the threat to the whales and sign the petition to save them?

All these secondary questions also became unanswerable without the answer to that first question. I felt myself becoming paralyzed with doubt. How could I make everyday decisions when I didn't know what in the world I was living for and why I had been put on the planet and by Whom?

I had a great job at the college and a perfect view of the sea. But life in the Garden was killing me, and there was no one to understand my misery.

The people at the college were primarily concerned with the material world and its survival, and all those measures towards conservation were really just another form of materialism and the worship of things. They organized conferences on solar heating systems and wouldn't think of serving the potluck suppers on plastic plates, but where were the spiritual dimensions of life? Here were the smartest and the nicest people I had ever met, with many of them ten or even twenty years older than me, and yet these scientists, engineers, and philosophers didn't seem to know any more than I did about the underpinnings of reality.

My best friend and her husband designed a tiny and highly efficient house on the edge of a pond. I admired how it contained everything necessary for human existence at the least expense to the environment. Slowly, I was also working to reach my goal of growing all my food organically and sewing all my clothes from natural fibers. I made plans to build my own little house, but I knew that even once I was planted inside it next to the wood stove on a cold winter's night, I wouldn't be happy.

At best, I was living an animal life of the highest caliber because I was trying not to hurt anything or anyone around me. But the animals, themselves, were doing it better than me, and even better than the animals were the plants, and at the top of my list of enviable entities were the stones whose impassive acceptance and zero toll on the environment were inimitable.

I found myself walking around the Garden and envying the stones at my feet. I would lie on the boulders that lined the shore path and try to feel as they felt— unmoving and mute witnesses to the changing tides and the changing seasons. In perfect agreement with their portion in the universe. I could feel the stony aspect of myself communing with them, and I would lie there trying to experience their timeless state. But then I would always get up, be human again, and move on.

Then something happened that seemed haphazard and even insignificant. One Sunday morning, I was going through a box of books that I had never unpacked when I had moved to the Garden. There was an old Jewish prayer book that I had fished out of the mahogany sideboard and hastily thrown in with the other books as I packed to leave.

I picked it up from the pile and opened it. It had a musty smell, and the English words on the left-hand side were full of "thou" and "thy Lord" in an old-fashioned style. I looked at the Hebrew side. I had a distinct memory of reading the Hebrew words as a child. They had a certain integrity, and I felt that I could succeed in pronouncing them if I put my mind to it.

It was another glorious summer's day, and the sun was still high in the sky. I took the book in hand and drove the few miles to the National Park that bordered on the harbor city. After parking the car at the foot of one of the mountains, I started to climb on a national park trail. Half-way up, I stopped and sat with my back against one of the pine trees. I had a hunch that this old prayer book might have some part of the answer to my questions. I read a few lines out loud—"Let us now praise, extol, exalt the Maker of Heaven and Earth."

I looked around me. I was sitting smack in the middle of this heavenly Earth, and I knew instinctively that there had to be a Maker. It was too perfect and too beautiful. Even the tree that I was resting against had a certain integral grace and wholeness the way the branches were turned towards the sun. And when I looked closer at the minute details, the delicate moss that covered the tree trunk, I had a sense of perfection in every moment of its growth and every aspect of its existence. Just looking at its shade of green was healing to my eyes.

The Maker of Heaven and Earth. This Maker must also be a Maker of me, and unlike the mosses, I felt an insistent desire to know more about this Maker and connect with Him.

There were no thunderous accompaniments to my thoughts and no blinding lights. It was not what they call a breakthrough insight or flash of illumination. I continued to read the prayers out loud, and I clearly sensed that these words were a fitting complement to the stunning beauty around me. I had seen what the Maker of Heaven and Earth was capable of doing. These years in the Garden had been a crash course in appreciating His handiwork.

At this point, I was still not calling this Ultimate Artist and Master Builder by the name I had known in my childhood. In my circles, that Name had fallen out of usage. It was not until a few months later that His name came to my lips in the middle of a sleepless night.

It was at the height of my intense feeling of isolation which was literally driving me out of the Garden. I was suffering from insomnia, and I experienced a very distinct "plunk" as I hit rock-bottom. Then I cried out "G-d!"

I cried out the word from a place deeper than my intellect, because it was certainly not part of my vocabulary, and not mentioned in any of my books on meditation, healing, and Eastern philosophies, at least not in a serious way. From the instant I called to Him, I felt a subtle shift of my being. Now I was pointed in a totally new direction, one that I hadn't even known existed.

At first, I walked forward blindly, and then I began to recognize forms looming in the darkness. There was my new-found and infinitely precious relationship to G-d, and then there was something called *yiddishkeit* which carried with it a way of life centered around the observance of the Torah.

Yiddishkeit would take me into a societal framework and a distinctly Jewish culture. There was nothing wrong with that, just that it took me completely by surprise. I had never imagined that this G-d I had finally found through my apprenticeship with anguish and existential loneliness, where I was literally wandering in the backwoods and on coastal islands, would eventually lead me back to people, and not only individuals, but a veritable society.

But that would come later. Back then, when I was taking my first steps in the darkness, it was still unpopulated with real people. There in the very beginning when darkness lay over the face of the waters, and the light was still hidden away, I became aware of other realities and other times. I immersed myself in reading Jewish history: Poland during the Holocaust, the Chmielnicki massacres in Russia, the expulsion of the Jews from Spain by Ferdinand and Isabella, who were better known for their role in supporting Columbus's voyage to America.

Places and historical figures that I had associated with culture and enlightenment became tainted by their complicity with Jewish suffering. Even in England at the height of its Golden Age of civilization, there were numerous incidents of persecution and slaughter. Throughout history, tens of thousands of Jews had chosen death in the face of conversion to other faiths.

One book written by a non-Jewish sociologist was a study of life in the shtetls of Eastern Europe. I was riveted by the accounts of the spiritual grandeur in the midst of grinding poverty, and the material sacrifice these Jews were capable of making in the pursuit of learning their Torah.

It was not the first time that I had heard that word. I had memories of seeing Torah scrolls in the synagogue as a child and marching with flags around the Torah on Simchat Torah, and my father reaching out to kiss the Torah with his fingertips as it passed by.

It was the same Torah, but this was something else. I was reading about people who chose to die rather than transgress the laws that were written there. And I read about scholars in the shtetl pouring over books with titles like "The Light of the Eyes." They were not academicians or professors, and not even intellectuals. Most likely, they had never set foot in the universities. This was clearly something else. They might live crowded into the ghettoes, but they soared in spiritual landscapes, their Garden even more exquisite than mine.

They studied every letter and every word, every nuance in the Torah, but they had nothing in common with the Bible critics I remembered from my required course in Religion, as an undergraduate in college. For these scholars, the Torah was a gift from G-d who was not an historical Entity who had once created the Universe and then disappeared. Their on-going relationship with Him through study and prayer was the central focus of their lives.

I saw in their thirst for G-d the urgency I had felt in my longing to find answers. I understood their thirst for G-d, because of my own compelling thirst. Here were my fellow travelers.

There was really no one among my friends who could sympathize with my obsession with Jewish History, and there was certainly no one who shared my enthusiasm. One of my students had suddenly been inspired to find his Jewish roots, but he had quickly gone off to Israel.

Meanwhile, the College had invited a well-known Theological Figure who organized a dance event expressing the cycle of life. At its conclusion, everyone put their bag lunches on the altar, and then picked at random one of the bags brought by someone else. It was an attempt to bring people closer and create new rituals for the New Age.

I didn't think of my interest in *yiddishkeit* as a search for New Age rituals and just one other way up the mountain. I knew instinctively that I had stumbled on the Truth, and I believed unequivocally in those forms I saw in the darkness—the people of the shtetl, their holy books, and the long corridors of time called "history" that were peopled by Jews dedicated to their love of G-d and His Torah.

I might be the only authentic Jew for miles, but I had connected to Jewish history in a palpable way so that I felt myself at the tail end of a long stream of people and events, and I was holding onto that continuum for dear life.

The last season that I experienced in the Garden was late Fall and the first snows of the winter. There was one incident especially that precipitated my leaving.

I met an individual whose alienation seemed similar to mine. He was an ex-lawyer who had become disenchanted with just about every scene he had encountered, both in the Establishment and the Anti-establishment. His last frontier was a few acres of land about an hour's drive from the coast where I lived.

He had purchased the land to build a house with his bare hands, digging the foundation and hewing the logs without the benefit of electrical tools. It might take him years before he moved into his house, but he was determined to finish it. In the meantime, he lived in a dirt floor shack with an old wood stove and no plumbing.

This ex-lawyer was quite articulate when he spoke, but the many long hours and days of solitude that he spent in building his house had affected him, as well as the other knocks and disappointments in his life that I knew nothing about.

He seemed to enjoy the company of the people who had grown up in these backwoods, and it was to one of these families that he invited me to come for Thanksgiving. There was a lot of drinking, and a television set blaring in the background. I was feeling like a visitor from another planet where the food, the conversation, and the basic tenets and foundations of life were alien to me.

I tried to be friendly because they seemed to be good, decent people. But the sadness that I was always just keeping back came flooding over me. My ex-lawyer friend had drunk a few beers, and whatever searching we had in common—he had taken the edge off his pain with alcohol.

Now they were clearing the table so they could serve the ice cream and pie. They would see that I hadn't eaten a thing on my plate. Awkwardly, I stood up, thanked the woman of the house, and excused myself. My ex-lawyer friend walked me to the door. It was the last time I ever saw him.

There was a family that lived nearby whom I had heard about from a mutual friend. I drove over and found their spacious log cabin at the end of a dirt road.

They had come from one of the big Eastern cities and homesteaded for a number of years. They drank fresh goat's milk and wore hand knit sweaters handspun from the sheep in their backyard. They also raised cows and chickens, but their main source of income came from raising bees and packaging the honey which they sold throughout New England.

The husband was Jewish and full of dreams of making things happen on a psychic level. Clearly, his non-Jewish wife had shared his vision as far as being totally self-sufficient and developing a home-based industry. But she had stopped following his line of thought years back, if she had ever really understood him, and she stood aligned against him with their two teenage children. When he left the room, she turned to me and confided that lately, he had become very strange and was always talking about his grandfather.

They had worked hard together to realize their dream of living off the land. But now the Jewish half of that couple had begun to feel a longing for his Jewish past, as I had, and the dream had lost its meaning. He had begun to feel his roots reaching deep into the past and reaching even deeper to the Source.

There was no use trying to talk about it with him. He was still firmly entrenched in the Garden, and I was just beginning to feel that powerful thrust of escape velocity. I observed the drama of this estranged family in the light of my own deepening isolation. My last few words had run out, and I was just waiting to drive back to the Coast early the next morning.

Their log cabin had a wing with a guest room, and I lay in bed waiting out the night. I followed the soft outline of the mountains against the dark velvet sky. In my state of mind, I was desperate for even a small measure of peace, and it couldn't be anymore jarring outdoors than it was inside that room. I got dressed under the warm down quilt, quietly made my way downstairs, and opened the front door.

There was a full moon and a foot of pure white snow on the ground. I stopped at the end of the driveway. To the left, I would be passing houses every few hundred yards. I turned to the right and took a footpath through the thick woods.

At this time of night, there was a stillness, more still than I had ever known. I knew that I had gotten as cold as I could get in one lifetime. It wasn't only the deep-freeze of below zero. It was so cold that my heart was turning to ice. I felt as if it had been years since I had felt any real warmth or real nourishment for that matter. Here I had been living in the Garden, and it had turned into a veritable wilderness for my soul.

I must have walked for several hours, just hearing the sound of my boots cracking the snow. I felt that with each step, I was making a pact with the Creator of this existence, that it was only Him and me from then on. The part of me that was more than just animal and alive, the part that was me, what I was beginning to think of as my soul, was pushing forward with the only way it could express itself at that time, the movement of me walking in the stark coldness among the shivering spines of trees.

The next morning, I drove back to the Coast. The whole way my car made strange noises and finally ground to a halt as I pulled into my driveway. When I turned on the ignition, it wouldn't start up again. I took that as a sign.

Without explanations to the college administration or my friends in the Garden, I packed up some of my things and left on the Greyhound bus a few days later.

Finding One's Way

Tamar Frankiel

SOME YEARS AGO, AS I WAS WAITING TO GIVE A LECTURE before a group at my synagogue, the rabbi came up to me and said confidentially, "I hope you aren't going to talk too much about other religions." He was referring to my work in comparative religion. I had spent fifteen years studying and had a master's and a Ph.D. in the subject. But at his remark, I was startled. "What do you mean?" I asked. "Well, you know, Jews don't bother with that stuff." Actually, I wasn't planning to talk about anything except Jewish material. But I rapidly began reviewing and censoring my speech in my mind. I had two reactions: one resentful; Is he trying to tell me how to think? And one fearful—maybe I'm not really "kosher"—not Orthodox enough.

My two opposite feelings were hints of what was almost my double personality. First, I was a creation of the secular world: I had spent years learning the ropes of academia; I knew the challenge of intellectual life, the stimulation from University colleagues. At the same time, I had accepted the way of Torah. I wanted most of all to grow in my relation to G-d, to develop a deep spiritual practice. Up to this point, I had believed that my previous studies had enriched my understanding of Judaism. I found in Jewish practice many echoes of what I had learned. The setting aside of sacred times, the holiness of certain places, rich symbolisms of the natural world and ancient cultures, complex systems of sacrifice—the religions of the world were full of these phenomena, and I was finding them alive in Judaism.

But now I began to wonder. Were there conflicts between my studies in comparative religion and my life as a practicing Jew? If I had been a computer technician or a doctor, perhaps it would not have been so great a problem. But I was studying things that seemed very alien to a Jewish philosophy and way of life. I loved teaching about everything from Buddhism to Judaism, from bizarre rituals to esoteric philosophy. I saw the world through the lenses of my studies of the history of religions, sociology and psychology. But perhaps these were not things I should be thinking about. I even considered giving it up entirely.

I had the good sense, at one point, to ask a rabbi if I could continue to seek professional work in my field. I received his approval, so my concerns about making a living were relieved. But many personal and intellectual issues remained. Some of these issues turned out to be superficial, and my problems quickly disappeared; others were deeper and required considerable inner work and intellectual searching to resolve them.

Many people, for example, assumed that it would have been difficult for me to believe in G-d or to practice one religion exclusively. They thought studying comparative religion discourages a person from believing in one G-d and promotes a relativistic morality wherein all beliefs and practices are equal. Comparative religion supposedly teaches that all religions are really one—they have basically the "same" myths, the same ethics, and the same ultimate purpose. But this is not really true of serious scholarship in comparative religion. True, for purposes of classroom teaching, questions of belief are temporarily set aside. The instructor does not put forward a particular religious viewpoint, because s/he must encourage students to ask significant questions fearlessly, and to develop the intellectual discipline to think through to some answers and to criticize all answers.

The result of this teaching method—it is a method, not a conclusion—is that many university students come away with the idea that there are no respectable religious answers to questions of goodness, truth, or divine reality; that every argument has its counter-argument; and that truth is relative. Simplified even further, some students hold (and vehemently affirm to their teachers) that anyone's opinion is as good as anyone else's in religious matters, so how can the teacher dare give low grades for their opinions! This argument ad absurdum shows its own fallacy: it is not that there are no answers, but that one must be very careful about putting forward one's own culturally limited viewpoint as the answer.

But then, are there answers to ultimate questions in the study of comparative religion? No one so far has been willing to stake a scholarly reputation on a definitive answer, for there is always an element of faith involved. Yet, in my opinion, there has been progress. The inquiry has proceeded to the point where a simple atheism is no longer possible. Over and over again, the attempts to explain away religion as a function of social, psychological, or political forces have been demonstrated as inadequate. Positivists still struggle to come up with a more adequate explanation, but more and more scholars have left that narrow-minded enterprise behind. In that respect, the field is more open to serious discussions of faith than it was twenty years ago. For me, the further I inquired into the matter, the easier it was to accept a belief in G-d. In 1970, I was an agnostic if not an atheist; in 1980, I had no difficulty believing, though I was still searching for how to conceive of a relationship to the G-d I believed in.

G-d was one thing; accepting a Torah way of thought was another. Sometimes I wondered if I was consenting to my own brainwashing. "Everything is in Torah," I was told. You don't need to go anywhere else. For someone who has sampled the richness of other traditions and the works of great authors, this seemed impossible. I considered it a statement coming from very intelligent but very narrow-minded individuals, designed not to encourage discussion and exploration but to cut it off. For after all, I didn't know much Torah—I only knew that strange other stuff, the ways of thinking taught in universities—so what could I say? Go and learn, they told me.

I went and learned. And I found that the deeper I went into Torah, the fewer conflicts I found within myself. For example, I was interested in depth psychology and its relation to religion. I found in Chasidic teachings and in certain commentators on the *Chumash* ideas that preceded Freud and Jung by scores, if not hundreds, of years. I was interested in associations of symbols and the use of language. I found the poetry of the siddur and *Tehillim* not merely beautiful but inspiring and challenging. And to see a mind at work on the intricacies of language, one need go no further than the *Likkutei Moharan* of Rabbi Nachman of Breslov. I liked sociology and anthropology: it surprised me to find that our sages were enormously sophisticated in such areas: they knew about crowd psychology, social pressure to conform, radical differences in cultural viewpoints, and the difficulties of being fair and objective. Was everything really in Torah, then? Certainly the phrase didn't mean that Chinese history or modern art was in Torah. But everything I needed to know to improve the quality of my life was in Torah, from spiritual inspiration and intellectual challenge, to depth of ethical thinking and practical advice.

Still I had problems arising from my scholarly background—for example, the matter of similarities among religions. I had learned to look at the larger patterns which many religions seem to have—for example, similar symbolism, common ways of marking off sacred space or sacred time.[1] Traditional Jewish thought simply didn't recognize such parallels as having significance. It took me some time to understand why.

The history of Judaism is replete with examples of having to fight the incursions of other religions. We need only remember the golden calf: "This is your G-d, O Israel, who took you out of Egypt!" Together with all the great commentators, we wonder how the Jews who had just received the Ten Commandments at Sinai could have fallen for that one. Later on, we have the famous contests organized by Elijah between the Baal of Canaan and G-d as understood in Jewish tradition; these are followed by many examples of the prophets' denouncing Jewish involvement in other religions.

Certainly no Israelite of ancient times intended to offend G-d by having a comforting little amulet of a goddess in her home, or participating in a seasonal ritual of a Canaanite god. But all such practices were consistently weeded out, as much as possible, by those clear-sighted leaders of biblical times whom scholars call the "Yahwists" (and sometimes refer to, less objectively, as the zealous fanatics). These prophets and sages recognized how easily alien practices diluted the reality of the historic Jewish experience of G-d: the G-d who transcended nature. Other religions tended to return the mind to the easier, more comfortable affirmation of "god" in nature, "god" in the forces around us. Judaism affirmed a G-d who was beyond all this, beyond all of reality as we know it.

Today, even the most innocuous-sounding statements about religion can lead in the same direction, toward a kind of "nature-religion" and away from the distinctive impulses of Jewish thought. We can see this, for example, in the work of Joseph Campbell, the well-known popularizer of comparative religion whose interviews with Bill Moyers on PBS attracted thousands of viewers. Campbell promoted the view that the many religions are similar paths to the same goal (except for Judaism!—his anti-Semitic views were well known to his acquaintances). He emphasized the personal spiritual quest over the communal dimension of religion, thus tuning his ideas to American individualism. At the same time he presented his views, ambitiously enough, as a foretaste of the "planetary religion of the future."

But what was the goal of this religion? Not G-d in our sense—or what he disparagingly called the "supernatural"—but rather oneness with all life, the universal will in nature. This is a form of the same essentially pagan approach that Judaism has always challenged—the affirmation that nature is the ultimate. It is really an affirmation that "I" am the ultimate (hence, "Follow your bliss" was Campbell's motto), and a refusal to recognize G-d's transcendence over all the created world.

Our tradition, in short, is right to be suspicious of comparative religion. There are many genuinely spiritual dangers lurking down those attractive paths. It is true that one can find similarities among religions, but there are quite obvious reasons for that. All religions, even those which are based on a divine revelation, have some elements that are humanly constructed (in Judaism, an outstanding example is the prayer book). Since all human minds have certain patterns of imagery and understanding, we will find similar structures. Even in the category of what religious people regard as direct revelations, G-d certainly intended them for human minds, so one might find similarities even there.

For me, the examples of similarity became less and less important, because it became increasingly clear that Judaism's own strengths were so great, intellectually, communally, and in the daily life of observance, that there was virtually nothing to compete with it. The issue was not occasional striking parallels, or structural similarities between religions, but the comprehensive way in which these were interpreted, the coherent view of the world that had evolved, and most of all the effects on one's life.

I recall hearing a rabbi at a lecture, responding to a young man in the audience who had taken the opportunity of the question period to detail his wondrous mystical experiences. He asked if the rabbi would consider them authentic. The rabbi asked simply: Have these brought you to do more *mitzvot*? Have they brought you to lead a better life? For me, the same was true of my ventures into comparative religion. If they helped me to deepen my belief in the wonders of G-d's universe, or to have greater purpose in my performance of *mitzvot*, then they were fruitful. Otherwise, they were of academic interest only.

But, I am often asked, hasn't comparative religion undermined belief in the Divine revelation of Torah? As I mentioned above, all religions have some human elements. But the tendency of scholarship since the Enlightenment is to regard all of religion as humanly invented; in other words, to regard Divine revelation as impossible—or at least impossible to discover by rational means.

For a long time this assumption prevented me from appreciating even the written Torah itself. After all, I had been receiving strong doses of biblical criticism since I took my first course in "Old Testament," as it was called, when I was sixteen years old. For years I had to struggle just to read the text of the Pentateuch "straight," let alone understand what Rashi or the Midrash were trying to communicate. Gradually I began to realize that my difficulties were related to the fact that I had been taught that there was really no such thing as communication from G-d to human beings. "Religious experience" was some sort of emotional fluke, and anything that claimed to come from religious experience was really a fake. The guy's followers made it up later.

The main target of this argument in the college courses I had taken was Christianity; and indeed, it has been proven to be true, beyond the shadow of a reasonable doubt, that most of what was attributed to Christianity's founder (who in any case never claimed to be a prophet like Moses) was reconstructed later by the early church. But the assumption that people "make things up" after the fact and then persuade, delude, or force others to believe them ran through almost all of the scholarship on Western religions.

But, I realized, each case had to be understood on its own terms. I discovered that recent research done on the books of the Bible was finding more historical reliability than scholars had previously thought. As far as revelation was concerned, scholars had been unable to call the Biblical Prophets into question in the same way as they had the New Testament; these men and women we call the *nevi'im* apparently did receive messages while in an unusual state of consciousness. I knew, too, that parallels are found universally of individuals undergoing unusual experiences and then bringing a message—usually a vision, sometimes a verbal message—to their people. Often the ability, or susceptibility, for such experiences is inherited.

Scholars were claiming that religion was a human invention, but now I realized that scholarship had presented me with its own invented story, one with little believability. The story went something like this: A group of priests and scribes who have inherited powerful positions decide to rewrite all the traditional narratives to favor themselves. They invent laws which keep them in power, and attribute them to ancient authorities. They create (or borrow from other tribes) rituals which keep money coming into their temples. Power is kept in the hands of an elite, and the common people believe because they have no way of questioning what they are taught.

This pseudo-Marxist version of religion is, of course, beyond the pale of credibility. No one would believe a sudden, new rewriting of tradition. It would be as if someone came and told me that, contrary to everything I knew, I was really adopted and belonged to an ancient race from Atlantis. Theories about a small elite holding onto power and forcing others to accept their version of history are equally implausible. In the complex society of ancient Israel, prophets, priests, tribal and national dignitaries, traders, and agriculturalists all coexisted, none of them necessarily "common," i.e. ignorant, people. One could say there was a natural system of checks and balances that kept any one group from pulling the wool over the others' eyes (indeed, this was true of many traditional societies).

We have our own confirmation of this in the remarkable tradition that all the people heard the revelation at Sinai. This is unique in the history of religions. Often a group makes a claim that its leader is specialty endowed, that s/he is enlightened or has contact with the Divine. But in no other case (except Christianity's Pentecost, which is clearly a copy of Judaism's Shavuot) do we have the claim that the whole group received a revelation. In addition, we have stories of the elders receiving part of Moses' prophetic spirit, and of people prophesying "in the camp," suggesting that many had additional experiences of revelation. Indeed, in such a situation it was difficult for Moses to hold onto his leadership position—we are told that many people, including even Miriam and Aaron, expressed jealousy of him.

If you were making up a religion, you wouldn't claim that everyone had a revelation. On the contrary, you would try to prove that the privilege was very limited. Otherwise you would be opening yourself to all sorts of challenges, as indeed Moses experienced. The result was that Judaism, while acknowledging the primacy of the revelations to Moses, became a very open religion. Prophets, priests, scribes, and people of various lineages all made their contribution to the biblical dialogue; all had their distinct claims to authority and understanding. Later, with the development of the academies of the sages, Judaism continued to be open to discussion, to different opinions ("three Jews, four opinions").

What this meant for my understanding of our written and oral tradition was even more mind-boggling. It became pointless to ask whether a section of the Torah was written by J, E, P, or

D. I might as well ask whether Moses was writing with his right or his left hand. Instead, I had to be convinced—and I was becoming convinced—that the tradition as a whole was authentic. After all, even the most Divine document could have been distorted if its transmission was controlled by people of evil character. I recognized that those who wrote down, selected, and copied the books of the Bible had to be committed, as fully as humanly possible, to the faithful transmission of the Divine word. So did the teachers who passed down the oral Torah. I had to believe that each link in the chain was faithful, down to the present day, down to my rabbi and my teachers; that none of them would knowingly deviate from the Word that had come down at Mount Sinai and the teachings that had been passed down for generations after.

A tall order? Yes—but not as difficult as it might seem. I had been learning with men and women of incredible dedication, of personal integrity and devotion such as I had never known before, They were also intelligent, inquiring, critical in their thinking. They told me that they were but midgets standing on the shoulders of giants: the generations that came before. They told me inspiring stories of their fathers and mothers, grandmothers and grandfathers, on back to the great scholars and great tzaddikim of earlier times.[2] At the same time, the tradition was not merely a series of eulogies. The stories of even the greatest men and women showed their faults as well as their strengths, and this made them believable. I came to understand that this was an incredibly strong chain of human faithfulness, to one another, to Torah, and to G-d.

I realized that G-d had taught our people, through Torah, how to create human bonds of love and learning, compassion and wisdom, which could in turn sustain faith in G-d and in the Torah. The centrality of those bonds reminded me of the story of Ruth which we read at Shavuot. Ruth was the first convert, symbol of the whole Jewish people at Mount Sinai, the great event when we all accepted G-d, when we all "converted." Yet Ruth's story tells of a human bond that cements her to the Jewish people, namely, her relation to Naomi. Ruth tells Naomi: "Where you go, I will go; where you die, I will be buried; your people are my people, and your G-d, my G-d." Naomi, her mother-in-law, had been an example of faith, honor, and integrity during all the difficulties they had encountered in Moab. Her character impressed Ruth so much that she said, "This is the way I want to live." Ruth is not only the first convert; she also shows us the human chain of faithfulness on which our lives depend. It is people of faith, dedication, and good character who guarantee the Torah itself, and connect us through more than thirty centuries to the word of G-d.

As I came to understand the nature of the Jewish people and Jewish tradition, I understood better the nature of Torah itself. Slowly, then, the conflicts between my intellectual training and my Jewish life had begun to resolve themselves. I had peace of mind. I no longer felt brainwashed. I had discovered that Torah ways of thought were deeply connected to a Torah life. Both were not only rich sources of inspiration and challenge, but also an intricate melody that resonates in the mind, finally creating its own space for itself.

Then I began to understand at another level the statement that "everything is in Torah"; Torah is the space in which everything else comes to be thought. As we all live and breathe "in G-d," so we understand our existence "in Torah." This does not mean that we must be exclusive, or that there is no room for anything non-Jewish. But everything is filtered through our understanding of the purpose of life, how we and others play our part in G-d's plan for all humankind.

Other religions, then, serve a purpose, and not just the negative one of warning us about idol-worship. They remind us of our common humanity, the world we share on this planet, and the search of all human beings for G-d. We can appreciate the spiritual achievements of non-Jews as well as Jews, just as we can appreciate achievements in art, music, or science. We can acknowledge the moral leadership of a Gandhi, the grace of a Japanese tea ceremony, or the inner discipline taught by a master of meditation. These should inspire us to seek higher levels in our own practice. For Torah outlines the structure of our practice; but the human side of our religion, the way we respond to G-d, is not just to do the *mitzvot* in robot-like fashion. We should "beautify the *mitzvah*," as it is said, externally by adding to its aesthetic quality, internally by increasing our level of devotion. In these respects, we can learn from others—as the sages said in *Pirke Avot*, "Who is wise? He who learns from everyone."

We will do this wisely, however, only if we are continually enriching our personal relation to G-d, our Torah learning, and our sense of ourselves as part of a people. The Sages said that "God, Torah, and Israel are one." These three are the mutually interdependent conditions of our existence. To be fully and vitally alive, we must connect ourselves to these—and each will lead us more deeply into the others. Through prayer, through the study of Halakhah and Bible and Talmud, through extending our knowledge of our history and our exemplary leaders, and by becoming more involved in community life, we are inscribing a circle within which we can live consistently, richly, faithfully. Everything significant to life can be encompassed within this circle; nothing we deeply care about, nothing that nourishes us need be left out. We need not fear that we are missing anything out there in the world. As we deepen our practice and our learning, all that we need will come to us, as it is written: "You open your hand and fulfill the desire of every living thing" (Psalm 145).

NOTES.

1. For readers familiar with studies in comparative religion, I am referring to what are known as "archetypes"—a word one finds used, with different nuances, in the work of psychologist Carl Jung, comparativist Joseph Campbell (whose thought largely follows Jung), and historian of religions Mircea Eliade. Whether one regards archetypes as part of the psychological "collective unconscious," as does Jung, or as transcendental in their referent, like Eliade, they remain common structures in all thought. Examples: associations of the moon with the feminine, sun with the masculine; themes of death and rebirth; rituals of immersion in water, rituals of sacrifice; stories of the hero who conquers a monster and wins the princess.

2. I am often asked whether there really are *tzaddikim*, people of such a high degree of righteous behavior that they stand out as perfect or nearly so. There are. What is difficult is to find unambiguous statements about who they are. Interestingly, however, those who stand out as great Jewish sages seem to have received fewer personal criticisms (i.e. on moral, as distinct from intellectual issues) from opponents than is usually the case in other religious traditions. Even the rabid anti-Semites who invented many attacks on Jews as a group seldom found anything to say against the impeccable character of the individuals who were the guardians of tradition—the Rabbi Akivas and Rashis and Rambams. They were essentially beyond suspicion.

Through A Chasidic Lens

Joining Worlds

Naftali Loewenthal

"ALL THAT IS ON DRY LAND IS IN THE SEA," SAYS THE Talmud. One's imagination is caught by the idea of the silent world described by Jacques Cousteau and other deep sea divers. In some sense it is not just another world, but parallel, linked to this one and mirroring it. Chabad Chasidic thought takes up the theme: the "sea" represents the spiritual realm, the "hidden world." The "dry land" signifies the "revealed world," our tangible universe.

These worlds are joined. The spiritual is the source of the physical; Chasidic teachings keep reminding us about that fact of life. Yet, they also tell us, the goal is in the physical world, on the land, daily reality, rather than in the mystical sea. The ultimate aim is a fulfilled, perfected reality, when the spiritual and physical merge, as when Moses split the sea and one could walk through on dry land.

Judaism connects these worlds in many varied forms. At the most basic level, the world of humanity connects with G-d; the finite connects with the Infinite. Torah from Sinai, the fiery Law given to Moses, is the mediator. It reveals G-d's infinite Will and Wisdom applied in the context of a practical, human world. Moses split the sea before the eyes of those who knew him, and revealed the Torah which would continue to do so for the future.

In order to join the many dimensions of world, the Torah itself has revealed ever more inward depths. Beyond the Law and its discussions in the halachic parts of the Talmud are the subtleties of the *Aggadah* and the Midrash. Beyond those are the esoteric teachings, culled from the "white spaces between the letters," found in *Merkavah* literature, the *Zohar* and the thoughts of the sages of 16th century Sefad. Yet another level of mediation is disclosed by the Baal Shem Tov and the early Chasidic masters. If the kabbalists explored the mystery of prayer, showing in detail how every word relates to another level of the Divine emanations, the *sefirot*, the Baal Shem Tov explored the mystery of ordinary life, showing how one can connect with the Divine at every step.

At each stage of this revelation of Torah there is generally a parallel dimension of "Moses": Rabbi Akiva, Rabbi Judah the Prince, Maimonides, Rabbi Yitzhak Luria, the Baal Shem Tov and many others. Looking back at them, we see the chain—or web—of our Sages in their different epochs: Tannaim (Sages of the Mishnah), Amoraim (Sages of the Talmud), Early Codifiers, Kabbalists, Later Codifiers and so on.

This model concerns the sages of the past. But there is another dimension in the disclosure of the Torah. This concerns the sage of your own time, your Rebbe. This is the teacher who joins the worlds for you, in your particular generation, in your special situation. He splits the sea that confronts you, turning its depths into dry land where you and your children can walk comfortably.

In our time, for most of us, our own teacher would have to help us deal not only with life and death, the Infinite and the world, but also with the yawning gaps between sacred tradition and secular modernity, between the spiritual and the material in daily experience, between the particularized Jewish past and the universal present, between the theme of freedom of the individual man and woman and the exigencies of social life, not to mention the delicate structure of Jewish law. Our teacher would help us perceive Torah as truth in a fragmented, documentary, relativistic age, make marriage and children a tangible and realistic goal, and even bring meaning to the theme of the Messiah.

Thus your own teacher, your Rebbe, joins worlds: the point where the sea and dry land touch, perhaps transforming the sea to dry land, as Moses did, or sometimes—more poetically, when faced by an unbending present—giving you a path through the sea. Yet this very concept, your teacher, itself joins worlds. Can you see your teacher? Can you understand him? Can you truly follow him? Chasidism emphasizes this gulf, at the same time that it draws Rebbe and Chasid together. One could suggest that the Rebbe reveals to you who you should be, and who you are (to the extent that you can bear this). By virtue of one's recognition of this chasm, to some small degree, one begins to serve G-d. . . .

We therefore have the following model. The Sage of your time, your Rebbe, in some sense splits the sea for you, or at least shows you that it needs to be split. He seeks to help you join the spiritual sea, G-dliness, with the reality of dry land: your life. His teachings, which are addressed to your generation in the widest sense of the word, continue this process in the unique manner of "Torah." Not just a literary heritage, but a bonding of worlds.

The Chasidic Discourse

One of the ways the Lubavitcher Rebbe (1902-1994) achieved this, is through his Chasidic discourses. A discourse of this kind is known as a *maamar.* In the second generation of the Chasidic movement, one of the disciples of the Maggid of Mezheritch (d.1772) described the way one delivers Chasidic teachings:

> Once I heard the Maggid tell us explicitly: "I will teach you the best way to deliver Torah teachings. One should not be aware of oneself at all, and just be attentive to the way the Divine is speaking through you: the person himself is not speaking. As soon as he begins to hear his own words he should stop." Many times my own eyes saw the Maggid:

> when he opened his mouth to deliver a Torah teaching he seemed to everyone as if he were not in this world at all, but as if the *Shechinah* were speaking from his throat. Sometimes, even in the middle of a theme or the middle of a word, he would stop and wait a while.

A special Chasidic melody, without words, "the *maamar* nigun" would precede the saying of a *maamar* by the Lubavitcher Rebbe.

While the melody was being sung with great fervor and intensity by the Chasidim, the Rebbe would sink deeper into himself. In Chabad sources it says: "when you are preparing to say a *maamar*, it should seem to you that you are walking in the street and people are throwing stones at you." In a *tzaddik*, a true Rebbe, the *aniy* of the self has been transformed to *ayin* (nothingness), a metaphysical level giving access to the realm of the holy. It is this that speaks during a *maamar*. Unlike his usual very expressive speaking voice when giving a *sicha*, "talk," when the Rebbe delivered a *maamar* he would intone a kind of melodic chant: words drawn from another world.

The Chasidim, for their part, tried as much as they could to be receptive to this revelation. Unlike at other times in a Chasidic gathering with the Rebbe (*farbrengen*), they would all stand. There was a mood of focused attention transcending our normal concepts of these terms. Some of the Chasidim, such as Rabbi Yoel Kahn, are famous as *chozerim*, scholars who could repeat by heart hours of the Rebbe's teachings after hearing them once. Yet everyone tried to make the first step in this process: to hear. "If a person listens to the *maamar* without having any thoughts of their own, they remember it." The idea is often repeated. But how do you get to not having any thoughts of your own? Well, the researcher might be told, that is part of the inner step of being a Chasid.

When you heard the *maamar*, you were present at the Splitting of the Sea. When today you study the *maamar* (or other teaching) this joining of worlds takes place in terms of your life, your reality.

On 3 Tammuz 5754 (1994), the day the Rebbe passed away, I was traveling to New York for the funeral. From the London airport I called a colleague, a noted international scholar of Hasidism, who would nonetheless claim to be living a "secular" lifestyle. She had followed with interest the last years of the Rebbe's life, and the messianic enthusiasm in the Lubavitch movement. When I called she had already heard that the Rebbe had passed away: another colleague had informed her from New York. "What now?" she asked me. "The hundred volumes of the Rebbe's teachings will bring the Messiah," I replied. "That," she responded, "I can accept!"

It was not only my answer: it is one that has been heard repeatedly in Jewish history. Moses dies but the Jewish people enter the Land of Israel, carrying the Scroll which Moses had written, and bearing in their minds his oral teachings which explain it. Among these was the instruction to build the Temple. Fourteen centuries later the Second Temple is destroyed but the Torah lives on—its scholars confident that study of its laws will bring the Redemption.

How does the theme of joining worlds relate to the yearning for the Messiah which is expressed daily in the Jewish liturgy? How does it link with the Rebbe's much publicized teaching that the Messiah is an imminent reality?

As expressed in Chasidic thought, joining worlds, in general, is the very function of Redemption: revealing the dry land in the sea, bringing together domains that seem disparate. This helps one understand the way Isaiah depicts the coming of the Messiah in terms of "splitting the river" (11:15). The Redemption means the discovery of the ultimate oneness between world and G-d, finite and Infinite: yet this takes place in the world rather than beyond it.

This was always the task of the Torah: transforming the lives of the Jewish people so that their physical person, their home, their community, their society in its widest terms became an expression of the Divine. Maimonides in his Guide for the Perplexed describes the difficulties in the early stages of this task: weaning them away from idolatry. There are always further stages, and each level of revelation of Torah both broadens the frontier yet further, and also brings an even more intimate dimension of spiritual realization. Rabbi Menachem Mendel of Kotzk (mid 19th century) spoke of reaching a person's "guts"; the previous Lubavitcher Rebbe tells of his discovery, as a child, that there is not only an ordinary Evil Desire but also a *frum* (pious) Evil Desire, and even a Chasidic Evil Desire: ever more subtle areas which need to be transformed.

The Talmud and Codes of Law bring us to one level of this process of inner transformation and redemption, which leads necessarily to the "general redemption," (eventually the Jewish people will repent . . . and they will be redeemed at once." The teachings of the mystical and pietistic traditions aid us to go further. Chasidic thought, and particularly the Rebbe's teachings, help us cross yet more borders both within our own being and in society at large.

However, for the Lubavitch Chasidim, this process continues to link to a personal relationship with the Rebbe. This is consistent with the tradition of Chasidism which always emphasized not only the ideas of the great Sage, but how he tied his shoelaces; not only general statements which would guide the nation for centuries, but a special teaching for you.

Gimmel Tammuz 5756

On 3 Tammuz (June) 1996, Lubavitch Chasidim from round the world came to New York for the second *yahrzeit* of the Rebbe.

Judaism is a strong affirmer of life in all aspects: the main form of impurity mentioned in the Torah is a corpse.

Nonetheless, for many centuries the ongoing relationship with those departed has been a significant feature of Jewish thinking. The *yahrzeit* candle in the glass and the *Kaddish* are expressions of a Jewish reality not confined to the here and now. Grave visiting has long been an aspect of a spiritual relationship with the Land of Israel. For the pre-modern visitor, the essential itinerary apart from the Western Wall of the Temple were the graves of the Patriarchs at Hebron, Rachel's tomb and further north in Meron the grave of Rabbi Shimon bar Yochai.

Many would also visit Maimonides' grave in nearby Tiberias—despite his objections to this practice: "one does not build a monument at the grave of the *tzaddikim*: their teachings are their memorial." But Rashi, the standard commentary on the Torah (especially for the Ashkenazi Jew) tells how Caleb, one of the Twelve Spies, went to pray at the graves of the Patriarchs at Hebron. Apart from Joshua, who had been specially blessed by Moses, he was the one spy who gave a true report.

How does one combine these apparently disparate approaches? The Jew of the Middle Ages seems to have found a way: both study their teachings and visit their graves.

This was also the view of the Kabbalists in 16th century Sefad. In their writings we discover more about the power of this relationship which spans the worlds. Rabbi Chaim Vital, the leading disciple of Rabbi Yitzchak Luria, tells of a Sefad scholar whose son had unfortunately left the path of Judaism. At that epoch this probably meant conversion, but whether to Christianity or Islam he does not say. The scholar went to the grave of one of the *tzaddikim* buried in Sefad and carried out a mystical practice termed *yichudim* (Unifications). Through this the soul of the tzaddik was linked to the soul of his son. The result was, says R. Chaim Vital, that eventually the son returned to Judaism.

One of the central aspects of Chasidism is its attempt to import elements of the teachings of the esoteric mystic circle of Sefad—and thus of the tiny elite of European kabbalists who succeeded them—into Jewish society as a whole. Yet the evidence of Yiddish *tekhines* (18th-19th century collections of prayers, often said by women), is that even without this input, at this epoch visits to graves were an important aspect of personal spiritual life. In fact this became a significant feature in Sarah Schenirer's work in revitalizing pre-war orthodox Jewish womanhood through the Beth Yakov school system. She would lead her closest disciples, the members of the Teachers' Training Seminary in Cracow, on visits to the eminent Sages of the past, buried in the Cracow cemetery.

In the literature of most Chasidic groups, the figure of the living Rebbe tends to obscure the significance of the graves of his predecessors. Yet sometimes it is the living Rebbe himself who emphasizes the spiritual power of the grave.

This was the case with Rabbi Menachem Mendel, the Lubavitcher Rebbe. Central in his life was his relationship with his predecessor and father-in-law, Rabbi Yosef Yitzhak (d.1950). Many of the thousands of letters he received were read at the latter's *Ohel* (the sheltered enclosure at the grave), which he visited frequently. In the course of nearly half a century the specific customs relating to the *Ohel* have become well known to most Lubavitch followers.

There is no surprise that on and around 3 Tammuz, large numbers of Chasidim—men, women, youths, girls and young children—packed into a corner of the Montefiore Cemetery in Queens in order to "visit the Rebbe." Typically Lubavitch in style is the creation of a kind of Chabad House nearby, which provides a relatively relaxed, living framework for the more intense experience of visiting the *Ohel.* A tract attributed to the second Lubavitcher Rebbe, Rabbi Dov Ber (d.1827) speaks of five different levels of this experience, ranging from the awe that anyone would feel on entering a cemetery to the mystical attainment of the Kabbalist. The fourth level relates particularly to the Chasid. The Rebbe, in his lifetime, brings the Chasid to a state of self-abnegation so that he can come closer to G-d. According to the author, this power is also there at the grave of the Rebbe, and to an even greater degree, stripped of the limitations of the physical body.

Psychotherapists have been intrigued by the psychodynamics of the relationship of Chasid and Rebbe which would be concentrated in a few minutes of *yechidus*, private audience. One could suggest that a visit to the *Ohel* has a similar power to change one's life.

For some, the *Ohel* today overshadows "770," the Brooklyn headquarters of world-wide Lubavitch since the 1940's. Yet here too, manifesting the special power of a building, is a strong sense of contact with the Rebbe. The book-lined *yechidus* room, where one would meet the Rebbe late at night after days, weeks or even months of preparation, is now used as a small synagogue. The Rebbe's desk is there as it used to be. The power of a Rebbe is to arouse the Divine spark within one's soul. Does one need physical contact for this? How much?

A letter by Rabbi Shneur Zalman, printed in the *Tanya*, speaks of the enduring relationship between a Rebbe and his followers—both those who knew him, and those who did not. A Rebbe's power to join worlds brings him beyond the bounds of conventional distinctions. Indeed, many people feel precisely this kind of relationship with their departed nearest and dearest. A

Rebbe is a person who can enter such a close relationship—with everyone.

On *Shabbat* in "770" there are many different kinds of *minyanim*. Apart from that in the Rebbe's room, there is the *minyan* in the main hall, and also a "slow" *minyan* at the very back of the hall. Here you can indulge in thoughtful prayer in unison with others, one of the goals of Chabad teachings on contemplative prayer. There are at least two other *minyanim* in the *Batei Medrash* upstairs.

At the time of the *Shabbat* Afternoon Service (what the *Zohar* calls "delight of delights") I stray into one of the latter. Here is Rabbi Yoel Kahn with a group of senior students, singing meditative Chasidic *nigunim* one after the other, followed by the recitation by heart of a Chasidic discourse. If you want Jewish spiritual experience today, here is one example. Yet one must remember that it is part of a totality which includes the Chabad House in Hong Kong, or the Lubavitch Summer Camp near Moscow.

Yes, the Rebbe joins worlds. Historical worlds, social worlds, spiritual worlds. The power of the human soul is that we can experience the opening of these borders, the joining of different realms. It is a power we all possess yet, as the old Chasidic story tells us, to make access to this power we need to visit the Rebbe. The visits are still alive in Lubavitch today, together with the hundred volumes of the Rebbe's teachings.

Fortysomething: Turning Points In Life

Susan A. Handelman

"IT IS FORBIDDEN TO BE OLD."
—Rabbi Nachman of Bretslov

A friend recently greeted her fortieth birthday in a state of shock:

"I can't believe it," she said, "this must be a practical joke!"

Something about turning this particular age makes it different from all previous birthdays, and it's often strongly resisted. The cover of a drugstore birthday card reads, "I'm glad you're 39" and the inside flap adds ". . . again for the fifth time." Popular self-help books abound with titles such as: *Life After Youth: Female, Forty—What Next?*, *We Over Forty: America's Human Scrap Pile*, and *Midolescence: The Dangerous Years*. On the other hand, there's *Prime Time: A Guide to the Pleasures and Opportunities of the New Middle Age*, *The Male Mid-Life Crisis: Fresh Starts After 40*, and the famous *Life Begins at Forty*.

These titles reflect the ambivalence and unease that afflict so many people who turn forty. There is a sense that some phase is being completed, but this often gives rise to anxiety—the well-known "mid-life crisis." Feelings of "emptiness" often accompany the completion of any major project or phase of life.[1] One wonders what to do next, how to fill the gap. For "fortysomethings," youth and its seemingly limitless possibilities are felt to be ending, ambitions remain unfulfilled, physical energy is often diminished, and death becomes more of a reality. There are omnipresent reminders: "If you are over forty, consult your doctor," a common warning goes. Social functions for singles and job descriptions are frequently classified into two groups: for those "Under Forty" and those "Over Forty."

The intuition that some "great divide" has been reached can lead to restlessness and putting into question all aspects of one's life. Forty then often becomes a time of turmoil, a kind of "second adolescence" when jobs and spouses are changed in a restless search for a new life. And this sense of disequilibrium is not just a contemporary American phenomenon. The greatest Italian poet, Dante, beautifully expressed it in the famous opening lines of his magnum opus, The Divine Comedy, written in the year 1302:

> In the middle of the journey of our life
> I found myself within a dark forest
> Where the straight way was lost.

What, then, does the Torah as illumined by Chasidic philosophy have to say to those reaching "fortysomething," and further—to all who ponder the passing phases of their lives?

Emptiness In The Middle

Chasidut has a special understanding of that sense of loss and "emptiness." In order for a person to reach any new stage, to ascend to a higher level of insight and understanding, *Chasidut* explains, there has first to be a kind of "self-nullification" (*bitul*), an emptying out of oneself to "make room" for the new. In other words, between the prior level and the succeeding level, there has to be what *Chasidut* terms a "nothingness in the middle" (*ayin b'emtzah*). This psychological principle reflects a spiritual principle, and that—in turn—reflects a cosmological principle. Jewish mysticism explains that the Creation of the world first occurred not through an act of G-d's expansion and self-assertion, but the reverse—through a *tzimtzum* or "contraction." G-d, so to speak, first had to "withdraw" or "contract" His infinite light and presence, and create an "empty space" in order to make room for a world of finite beings.

That pattern is then followed in every aspect of existence: there has to be an "emptiness in the middle" in order to move from one state of being to the next. A seed has to first dissolve in the soil before it can grow towards the light and bloom. In a human being, emptiness becomes spiritual "openness" when one "lets go," when one nullifies one's ego, when one's own ego does not try to fill and control all the space around one, but makes space for the other. The emptiness is the necessary prelude to an entirely new and higher mode of existence.

We find this principle at work in the flood story of Genesis. The flood is described as lasting forty days and forty nights (Gen 7:12). Now clearly, if G-d had wanted only to punish humankind for its corruption, G-d could have done so in a moment. What purpose did a forty-day flood serve? In the Chasidic interpretation, the flood was a kind of *mikveh*, a ritual bath given to the world in order to purify and renew it. One immerses oneself completely in the waters of a *mikveh*, down to every last hair, "nullifying" one's previous state. And by virtue of this complete immersion and self-nullification, one afterwards emerges from the waters "purified, on a different level, a new being."

Interestingly enough, Jewish law also specifies that the amount of gathered rainwater needed to make a *mikveh* kosher is forty *seah*. And the number forty is extremely significant all throughout the Torah: it is associated with critical junctures in the lives of great persons and of the Jewish nation as a whole. Moses, for instance, spent three periods of forty days each on Mt. Sinai: forty days to receive the Torah and the first set of Tablets; forty days to pray and assuage G-d's anger at the Jews after the sin of the Golden Calf (*tefillah*); and forty days to receive the second set of Tablets and effect G-d's complete forgiveness and joyful reconciliation with Israel (*teshuvah*).[2]

Chasidut emphasizes that Moses' life and that of the Jewish people are inter-connected in a profound way: by virtue of the Torah, *tefillah* (prayer), and *teshuvah* (return to G-d) he accomplished in those three periods of forty days, all the Jewish people were also connected to those three things in relation to the number "forty." For instance, the forty days Moses spent on Mt. Sinai from the beginning of the Hebrew month of Elul until Yom Kippur were established as the "forty days of *teshuvah*" and return to G-d for all Jews throughout all the generations. And the Jews were given the Torah in the course of the forty years they wandered in the desert.

On a deeper level, though, what is the link between the idea of self-nullification, "emptiness in the middle," and the number forty?

Forty As the Completion of An Entire World

It's a matter of simple arithmetic but profound spiritual insight. Chasidic philosophy, drawing on the Jewish mystical tradition, explains that all of reality can be described as divided into four "worlds." These are constituted by various states of revelation and concealment of G-d. [The four worlds are named *atzilut* ("emanation"), *beriah* ("creation"), *yetzirah* ("formation"), and *asiyah* ("action").] These four worlds, in turn, emanate from, and are rooted in, the four letters of the holiest name of G-d: Y-H-V-H.

A key tenet of Chasidic thought is that the microcosm emanates from and reflects the macrocosm. So we also find many other sets of "fours" reflected in nature. For example, *Chasidut* speaks of four categories of being in the natural world: the inanimate (*domem*); the vegetative (*tzomeach*); the animal (*chai*); and the speaking (*medaber*). These four types of natural existence levels also exist "within" each person, so to speak. Or, there are four seasons of the year and four directions of the compass. Indeed, the traditional understanding of the physical world as composed of four elements—fire, air, water, earth—could also be translated into the language of modern science: the matter of our physical world assumes one of four states: solid, liquid, gas, active combustion; or the "four" elements can be said to correspond to the four basic chemical elements of hydrogen, carbon, nitrogen, oxygen; or to the "four elements" of subatomic phenomena; or to the four forces known to modern physics (gravity, electromagnetic, strong, weak). On a spiritual plane, there are numerous fours: the four matriarchs; the four wives of Jacob; the four types of sons mentioned in the Haggadah; the four components of a Torah text (cantillations, vowels, crowns, letters); the four basic levels of Torah interpretation (literal, allusion, allegory, secret), etc.

Jewish mysticism also explains that each of the four higher spiritual worlds possesses the entire spectrum of the so-called "ten *sefirot*." The *sefirot* are G-d's creative attributes or characteristics which emanate to, structure, and are reflected in all existence (including the spiritual powers of the human soul).[3] Now four times ten equals forty; so a complete category of being or "world" has forty aspects. In other words, forty represents the completion of a whole mode or way of being, and when one passes the number forty, 'One leaves that mode of being behind and enters an entirely different level . . . another "world."'[4]

So every time one finds the number forty in Torah, its inner meaning is the ascent from one level to the next higher one. But the attainment of a higher level can come only after first reaching and fulfilling all aspects (forty) of the previous level, and then making an "emptiness in the middle" to allow for the emergence of something entirely new. An intriguing story in the Talmud subtly makes this point: When R. Zeira wanted to learn the Jerusalem version of the Talmud, he first fasted forty times to forget all he had learned of the Babylonian version (*Bava Metzia* 85a). Why would he have to "forget" his knowledge of the Babylonian Talmud in order to progress to the Jerusalem Talmud? In the Chasidic interpretation, the reason is that he wanted to absorb the Jerusalem Talmud in a profound and inner way, and he needed to be open to learning the very different style of the Jerusalem Talmud. He had to attain that "emptiness in the middle," "forgetting" his knowledge in order to be able to ascend to the level of the Jerusalem Talmud.

Teaching and Learning Torah at Forty

What, further, are the deeper connections between Torah knowledge and the number forty? For though the Torah was given in the forty days Moses was on Mt. Sinai, it took forty years of wandering and experience in the desert for the Jews to understand it in an inner and profound way. At the end of those forty years, when they were finally about to be allowed entrance to the Promised Land, Moses gave a valedictory address. Reflecting back on all that occurred since leaving Egypt and receiving the Torah, he said to the gathered people:

> You have seen all that G-d did before your eyes in the land of Egypt, to Pharaoh and to all his servants, and all his land; the great trials, which your eyes saw, the signs and those great miracles; but G-d has not given you a heart to know, and eyes to see and ears to hear unto this day (Deut. 29:1-3).

The Talmud has an intriguing comment on this verse: "One does not come to fully comprehend the knowledge of his teacher before forty years" (*Avodah Zarah* 5b; also Rashi on Deut 29:6). This statement connects the number of forty years to the attainment of knowledge and a new state of being.

Regarding Torah scholars, the Talmud also says that "one does not become fit to instruct [in matters of Jewish law] until forty years" (*Sotah* 22b). Rashi, the classic medieval commentator, interprets the number "forty years" here to mean "forty years from birth." *Tosefot*, Rashi's disciples and descendants, dispute this interpretation and argue that the phrase "forty years" means forty years from the time the person begins to actually study Torah, not simply forty years from birth. And their position is supported by the Talmudic statement that "One does not come to thoroughly understand the knowledge of his teacher until forty years." How, then, do we understand and resolve this dispute about the meaning of "forty years"? Does it mean forty years from birth, or forty years from the time one actually began one's studies?

There is further support for Rashi's interpretation in the Mishnah's statement that "Forty is the age of understanding [*binah*]" (*Pirke Avot* 5:22).[5] Now this implies that just as the body follows a natural, programmed course of growth, so too is there a natural and inevitable development of the intellect. At the age of forty, a person's innate faculty of binah "understanding one thing from another" (inference and deduction), becomes fully developed. That is to say, the power of inferential understanding continuously matures until it reaches its full potential at the age of forty.

Other cultures and philosophies sense this development as well. The Roman philosopher Marcus Aurelius wrote that, "Any man of forty who is endowed with moderate intelligence has seen . . . the entire past and future." On the negative side, George Bernard Shaw wrote, "Every man over forty is a scoundrel." But Jewish tradition is far more positive about this development. Forty is the time when a Torah scholar becomes fit to judge and decide halakhic questions. Even though the scholar may have previously studied much Torah, not until this power of *binah* reaches full maturity at age forty, can he best analyze, infer, study precedents, and render legal decisions.

Now the other Talmudic saying, that "one does not come to thoroughly understand the knowledge of one's teacher until forty years," refers to something quite different. It signifies understanding the actual words and ideas of one's teacher—not just the power and potential to understand them. Through actually studying the words of one's teacher for forty years, a student finally comes to understand and fathom his or her teacher's knowledge in depth.[6] In short, we resolve the dispute about the meaning of "forty years" by making the following distinction: at forty years from birth, one develops one's own faculty of understanding; after forty years of learning with one's teacher, one comprehends one's teacher's understanding.

It's also true, though, that profound changes and development of one's powers of understanding can take place in less than forty years.[7] In daily life, we often find that when a matter affects a person's very essence, her or his intellectual powers undergo rapid development—as if she or he suddenly achieved the level of "the knowledge of one's teacher." People who are intellectually underdeveloped or unlearned can create brilliant arguments in a courtroom when a dispute touches their very being; the pressure brings forth an intellectual power that meets the urgent need.[8]

Creating a New Being

But we might then also ask why the Torah appears to imply that forty is the inevitable age of understanding for everyone. For aren't these things—as well as *tefillah* and *teshuvah*—dependent on the varying intellectual and emotional qualities of different people, and their different experiences in life? Some mature more quickly than others; some have special talents, and so on.

Torah, *tefillah*, and *teshuvah*, however, all share a core point, an essence which is independent of any individual's particular measure—and that essential core is elicited through "forty." That essence is a transformative power, a power through which one enters into an entirely new kind of existence. Torah "gives birth" to a person, so to speak; prayer takes one entirely out of one's own existence and brings one to face G-d; *teshuvah* changes one's status from that of a wicked person to that of a completely righteous person.[9]

The essential change from one form of existence to a new one is a kind of quantum leap, to be sure. But this new existence itself then needs to be developed and perfected, and requires the extension of "forty" to become firmly established. In other words, "forty" also represents taking the seminal idea and establishing its general form or structure. After this period of forty, much more time is required for the development of the myriad specific details.

We see this process concretely at work in the conception, formation, birth, and development of a child. The seed is fertilized in an instant, but there are many further phases in the development of the fetus until all the particular limbs and organs are fully completed. According to the Talmud, it takes forty days for the general form of the embryo to develop, and to be able to discern whether it is male or female (*Berachot* 60a). In Jewish law, until forty days after conception, the fertilized egg is considered as "mere fluid." On the whole, an unborn fetus is considered to be a part of its mother's body and not a separate person until it begins to egress from the womb during parturition. But the unborn fetus still has a special status; if aborted after forty days of conception, the mother is required to undergo the same ritual purification process as if she had given birth to a live child.

And after a child is born, of course, it takes many more years for its innate faculties to develop. Learning and development do not stop after forty years; neither do Torah, nor tefillah, nor *teshuvah* cease after the level of forty has been attained. They indeed are limitless, because they contain an ever-renewing, transformative power, and one strives for an ever deeper engagement in them all of one's days.

Growing Older; Becoming Newer

Forty, then, represents both the completion of the previous level, and leaving it behind, "nullifying" it (R. Zeira "forgetting the Babylonian Talmud; the flood lasting forty days), and forty also represents the inauguration and structuring of a new existence (the Torah given in forty days, the development of the fetus, and so forth). The moment of emptiness contains the seeds of the ascent to a higher level. Like the moon, to which the Jewish people are compared, the cycle of waning is followed by a waxing. Jewish history has had many moments of "emptiness," "darkness" and loss, but just as the moon is renewed monthly after its seeming disappearance, the Jewish people are ever renewed, ever reborn.

Rav Avraham Isaac Kook, the great twentieth century Jewish leader and mystic, wrote of this constant renewal as key to the life of Jews and Judaism:

> The perception that dawns on a person to see the world not as finished, but as in the process of continued becoming, ascending, developing—this changes him from being "under the sun" to being "above the sun," from the place where there is nothing old, where everything takes on new form. The joy of heaven and earth abides in him as on the day they were created. . . The time that is an uninterrupted Sabbath [the messianic age] on which eternal peace shines, is the day when, by the nature of its creation, there pulsates a continued thrust for newness. It needs no end, no termination. It is the choicest of days, an ornament of beauty, the course of all blessings.[10]

In the Jewish view, then, getting older is also getting newer. And turning forty is indeed growing up—an ascent to a higher level. The popular saying that "life begins at forty" is right. Forty signifies not a period of decline, nor should it be cause for regret. It is, instead, both a completion and a new beginning, a retrospective understanding and a prospective passage to a higher level, an "emptiness in the middle" and the foundation of an entirely new existence.

NOTES

The ideas in this article are based on talks of the Lubavitcher Rebbe, published in *Likkutei Sichot*, vol. 34 pp. 160-166; *Likkutei Biurim L'Iggeret Ha-Teshuvah* (Korf), *perek* 2, pp. 107-111; and *Likkutei Sichot,* vol. 5 pp. 422-427.

1. The psychologist Carl Jung was quite interested in the psychological transitions and crises that often accompany mid-life. In his view, in a successful "second half of life," those parts of one's personality that were neglected or underdeveloped tend to be strengthened. If, for example, one spent one's first forty years emphasizing intellect and neglecting feelings, this imbalance will often begin to be corrected in earnest around forty. In contemporary society, those who have had to be outer-directed, intensively pursuing careers but neglecting their personal lives, intimate relationships, and spiritual condition tend to turn "inward" at forty. For Jung, these changes represent the process of individuation and the gradual achieving of wholeness of personality as part of the progress of one's life journey.

2. See *Menahot* 99b; Deut. 9:20,26 and Rashi on verses 25 and 18; see also Rashi on Exodus 33:11.

3. Materially, each thing in the world also reflects this "ten-ness"; it can be said to have 9 "sides" or "dimensions": width, length, height; beginning, middle, end; and the tenth aspect is the thing itself taken as a whole.

4. The letter *mem* in Hebrew has the numerical value of 40. And *mem* is the first letter of the Hebrew word for water, *mayim*, which symbolizes the fountains of the Divine Wisdom of Torah. There are also two ways to write a *mem*: open at the lower left corner when it comes at the beginning or middle of a word; and closed (a complete square) when it comes at the end of a word. These are called the "open *mem*" and the "closed *mem*" (*mem petukha* and *mem setumah*). The talmudic sages interpret the two *mems* to refer to "two sayings," the "open saying" and the "closed saying" (*Shabbat* 104a).

Chasidut explains that the "open saying" refers to the revealed dimension of Torah, whereas the "closed saying" corresponds to the hidden dimension, the secrets of Torah; the two also correspond to *galut* (exile) and *geulah* (redemption).

The word Mashiach ("Messiah") itself begins with a *mem*. In the time of the coming of Mashiach, "the earth will be filled with the knowledge of G-d as the waters cover the sea" (Isaiah 11:9); then, even the "closed *mem*" will be revealed. Only once in the entire Torah, in reference to Mashiach, do we find a closed *mem* in the middle of a word: "To increase reign and peace without end" (Isaiah 9:6).

The form of the mem also resembles a womb, and in Hebrew, the word for mother, *em*, also means "womb." Its essential consonant is the letter *mem*. In most languages, *mem* is the basic sound of "mother" (mom). It is also interesting that the Cold War lasted about 40 years (1945—1985), and that the working life of a person until the standard age of retirement is about 40 years.

5. The full context of the quotation is "At five years of age, the study of Scripture [should be commenced]; at ten—the study of Mishnah; at thirteen—[the obligation to observe] the *mitzvot*; at twenty—pursuit [of a livelihood]; at thirty—full strength [is reached]; at forty—understanding; at fifty—[the qualification to give] counsel; at sixty—old age; at seventy—ripe old age; at eighty—[a sign of special] strength; at ninety—the body is stooped; at one hundred—it is as if he were dead, passed away and ceased from the world" (*Pirkei Avot* 5:22).

6. The Lubavitcher Rebbe here clarifies that the debate between Rashi and *Tosefot* about the meaning of forty years is, at bottom, about what is required to render a person fit to become a halakhic teacher and rabbi in his own right. Today, as in the past, one receives *smikhah* ("ordination") from one's teacher, signifying that one has received knowledge of the traditions of the laws from the teacher. The debate between Rashi and *Tosefot* is over the question of what constitutes the completion of this process. For Rashi, the essential factor is the full, natural development of the intellectual power of inference, of *binah*, which comes about the age

of forty. For *Tosefot*, the critical factor is the actual forty years of learning with the teacher, because the ordained student also has to attain a level of "standing in the place of his teacher," in an unbroken chain from Moses. To reach this level, it does not suffice for the student to have only a fully developed power of inference. He needs something additional: the identical understanding and knowledge as his teacher; only then can he be said to stand in his place.

7. The forty years holds for cases when the student and teacher are on entirely different and distant levels; when they are closer intellectually to begin with, it takes less time.

8. And that, too, is reflected in the verses from Deuteronomy 29:1-3 in Moses's address to the people. For there is a tone of rebuke in his words as well: "You have seen all that G-d did before your eyes in the land of Egypt, to Pharaoh and to all his servants, and all his land; the great trials, which your eyes saw, the signs and those great miracles; but G-d has not given you a heart to know, and eyes to see and ears to hear unto this day." That is to say, "Why did it take so long for you to truly attend to and comprehend the meaning of what happened to you at Sinai? You should have been able to really grasp and be thoroughly affected by it earlier." Moses could rebuke the people because the Torah is connected to their very essence and they could and should have attained a deeper love, fear, and knowledge of their "teacher," G-d, before forty years.

9. Interestingly enough, the words Torah, *tefillah* and *teshuvah* all begin with the Hebrew letter *Tav*, and *Tav* has a numerical value of 400, which is 10 x 40. This indicates the power of Torah, prayer and the process of return to G-d to completely affect the ten powers of the soul.

10. Abraham Isaac Kook: *The Lights of Penitence, the Moral Principles, Lights of Holiness*, ed. Ben Zion Bokser (New York: Paulist Press, 1978), p229.

The Waiting People

Naftali Loewenthal

THERE IS A POPULAR JOKE ABOUT TWO PEOPLE WAITING AT A bus-stop, and the bus is taking a long time to come. One person turns to the other and says "We have been waiting so long for this bus! It is like waiting for the Messiah!" The other responds, "Not at all! The Messiah will definitely come eventually; as for the bus. . . ."

Jokes generally provide a good indication of the ethos of a culture. Clearly the Jewish Messianic ideal is one that has inspired centuries of religious thought. Rabbinic Judaism, Kabbalah and Chasidism have each dealt with the theme of Moshiach, the Messiah, in their own way. As contemporary interest in the idea of Messiah heats up, we should perhaps step back and examine the tensions, conflicts and paradoxes inherent in the Messianic theme in Jewish tradition and history.

The opening chapters of Genesis tell us of an idyllic state: Adam and Eve in the Garden of Eden. As a result of sin they are driven out of the Garden. But will they never return? The Midrash on Song of Songs[1] presents an interpretation which gives an insight into what for many generations the story of the Torah as a whole has meant to the Jewish people.

According to this, the essential feature of the Garden of Eden was the manifestation of the Divine Presence. In their pristine state Adam and Eve were intended to live with the Divine Presence in their midst. Through the sin of the Tree of Knowledge, they lost this possibility and were driven out of the Garden. But as the story of the Torah unfolds, a fresh possibility is disclosed in which the Divine Presence will again dwell in the world. This is, initially, in the portable Sanctuary built by Moses. At the foot of Mount Sinai, the Jewish people camp around the

Sanctuary, in which the Presence of G-d is revealed. This becomes a constant feature of their long journey through the wilderness, culminating in the transition to the Promised Land.

Following through the implications of this interpretation, the Torah can be seen as presenting the laws for the individual and community, which are conducive to the manifestation of the Divine Presence in the Sanctuary and later in the Temple. It is made clear that the goal is for this situation to be achieved in the context of life in the Holy Land, although there are also warnings about difficulties which might stand in the way. Further, there is also the idea that this indwelling of the Divine should have a universal effect, reaching beyond the immediate well-being of the Jewish nation (although this is spelled out in the Prophetic and Rabbinic writings, rather than in the Torah, the Five Books of Moses).

This has political and also moral implications. Lengthy passages in Leviticus and Deuteronomy stress that rejection of the Divine will result in political destruction, exile from the Land and concealment of G-d. This will not, however, be permanent. Eventually there will be redemption. Failure leads to exile; but this is not final. Eventually G-d will bring the Jewish people back to their Land, and also "circumcise" their hearts. The great medieval French Bible commentator, Rashi, comments that this means the heart will be unblocked, opened,[2] so that it will be able to express the full intensity of inspired love for the Divine. Then the Divine Presence will again dwell among the Jewish people, this time in a total and fulfilled way, reminiscent of the atmosphere of Divine revelation at the beginning of Creation.

This process described in the Five Books of Moses, especially as understood by the Midrash on the Song of Songs, gives meaning to successive stages of exile and redemption in the context of a wider drama, leading to fulfillment of the Divine purpose for mankind.

Biblical Perspectives

The Torah also contains specific passages that are understood to be references to the Messiah and the Messianic age, such as the prophecy of Balaam in the Book of Numbers:

> I see it, but not now; I perceive it, but not in the near future. A star shall go forth from Jacob, and a staff shall arise in Israel, crushing all of Moab's princes and dominating all the descendants of Seth. (Numbers 24:17)

Seth was the ancestor of Noah, and his "descendants" are all mankind, which will be ruled by the Messiah, here described as the "star" of Jacob. On account of this prophecy the great Jewish leader of the second century, Bar Koziva, was called Bar Kochba, for Kochba or *kochav* means "star." This name expressed the Messianic hopes that were pinned on him by the Sages of the time.

In the teachings of the later Prophets, active in the chaotic and unhappy period leading to the destruction of the Temple, there are repeated prophecies about the future Messianic redemption which eventually would follow the destruction, transforming tears into joy.

A number of further features of this redemption now come into focus. One is the figure of the Messiah as a specific leader, a descendant of the Davidic line of Kings. A second feature is the idea that the Messianic redemption will have crucial significance for all mankind, a concept which leads to the third important theme; the dawn of an era of universal peace.

The following lines are from Isaiah, Chapter Eleven:

> And there will come forth a shoot out of the stock of Yishai, [meaning of the Davidic line, for Yishai was the father of David] and a twig will grow from his roots. The spirit of G-d will rest upon him, the spirit of wisdom and understanding, the spirit of

> counsel and might, the spirit of knowledge and of fear of G-d.
>
> He will be able to scent out the fear of G-d [a phrase the Talmud explains to mean that he will intuitively be able to judge fairly] and he shall not judge after the sight of his eyes, nor decide [merely] after the hearing of his ears. But with righteousness he will judge the poor, and decide with equity for the meek of the land.
>
> He will smite the land with the rod of his mouth, and with the breath of his lips he will slay the wicked. Righteousness will be the girdle of his loins. . . .

This depiction of the Messiah as a leader is followed by a much debated passage describing the atmosphere of the Messianic era:

> Then the wolf will lie down with the lamb, and the leopard will lie down with the kid; the calf and the young lion and the fattling together, and a little child shall lead them. The cow and the bear will feed [in company], and their young ones shall lie down together; the lion shall eat straw like the ox. The small child will play on the hole of the viper. . . . (Isaiah 11: 1-9).

Some commentators interpret these lines literally, as expressing miraculous changes in nature which will take place: there will no longer be any harm nor hurt. But others take them as a parable, expressing political peace. Former foes, the 'wolf' and the 'lamb', will now be at peace together. In another chapter Isaiah overtly stresses this political aspect of the Messianic epoch. Universal respect for G-d, worship at His Temple in Jerusalem, and the charisma of the Messiah will inaugurate an epoch of world peace:

> In the end of days it will come to pass that the Temple mount will be established at the top of the mountains, exalted above the hills, and all nations shall flow to it. And many peoples shall go and say, "Come, let us go to the mountain of the L-rd, to the Temple of the G-d of Jacob. He will teach us His ways, and we will walk in His Paths"—for from Zion will go forth the Law, and the word of G-d from Jerusalem.
>
> Then he [meaning the Messiah, according to the commentators] will judge between many peoples, and shall decide concerning mighty nations. And they shall beat their swords into ploughshares, and their spears into pruning forks; nation shall not lift up sword against nation, neither shall they learn war any more. (Isaiah 2: 2-4)

These and similar ideas are echoed by other Prophets, building up a composite picture of the Messiah and the Messianic epoch. The Book of Ezekiel provides a detailed description of the future Temple, as well as an account of the wars of Gog and Magog which will precede the redemption. The Book of Daniel likewise tells of terrible battles and suffering, as well as giving a number of mysterious dates for the coming of the "End"; these figures were the basis of much of the Messianic speculation in the Middle Ages.

All of these Biblical perspectives on the theme of the Messiah were explored and studied in the Talmud and Midrash, and were thus ratified as a central feature of Rabbinic Judaism. An important aspect of this theme, even in the period of the Prophets, is that the identity of the Messiah was left fluid. At certain times, there was a specific individual on whom Messianic hopes were pinned. If these were disappointed (as in fact they were, repeatedly) the hope shifted to a point further ahead.

The Identity of Moshiach

Thus, in the time of Isaiah the Messianic hope focused on the young Hezekiah, son of Ahaz, King of Judah. Hezekiah is mentioned as the "the child who is born to us" in Isaiah 9:5. When he came to the throne he was under the close influence of this Prophet, following his advice in both political and religious matters. The Talmud comments that "G-d wanted to make Hezekiah the Messiah . . . but the Attribute of Severity complained."[3]

This was around the year 700 before the Common Era. Two centuries later, after the destruction of the First Temple, and when the first steps were taken towards the building of the Second, Messianic hopes were pinned on Zerubabel, scion of the Davidic line and leader of the Jews who were returning to the Holy Land. Although the Temple was eventually rebuilt, it was clear that the Messianic era had not begun. The Talmud states that five things were missing from the Second Temple, one of them being the Divine Presence.

This left the question open as to when the Messiah would come. Rabbinic teachings emphasize the ideal of constant hope and expectancy, despite the worst setbacks. Thus the Talmud describes an incident which took place some time after the destruction of the Second Temple. Rabbi Akiva and three of his colleagues, leading Rabbis of the time, were walking near the site of the ruins of the Temple. Suddenly they saw a fox coming out of the former Holy of Holies. The other rabbis began weeping at this demonstration of the fall of Israel's glory, but Rabbi Akiva laughed. They asked him why he was laughing. He answered that seeing the fulfillments of the prophecies about the desolation of the Temple made him even more certain that the prophecies about the coming of the Messiah would also be fulfilled, "Akiva, you have comforted us!" they responded.[4]

This story helps us appreciate the paradoxical nature of Jewish Messianic belief. One feature of this, clearly separating Judaism from Christianity, is that while belief in the Messianic hopes might be pinned on an individual or a specific historical situation, if disappointed, they are expected to dissolve; the time was not yet right. Of course, there have been instances when this "dissolving" process did not take place. Some of these will be discussed below. The paradox is that even after the most cruel disappointment, from the point of view of the Sages, the hope in a future Messiah should not be weakened. Whatever the setback, Judaism does not surrender its belief and confidence in ultimate fulfillment.

Rabbi Akiva provides us with a further example of this. In the year 132 of the Common Era, the Bar Kochba revolt against the Romans began. The revolt was strongly supported by Rabbi Akiva, who was then the leading scholar of the generation. Rabbi Akiva firmly believed that Bar Kochba was, or rather could be, the Messiah. It is likely that all the other Sages of the time followed suit. With astonishing power, Bar Kochba drove the Roman troops out of the southern part of the country and captured Jerusalem. For two and a half years he ruled. There may have been an attempt to restore the Temple, and special coinage with old Hebrew lettering was struck. Tragically, however, the revolt was put down with ferocious cruelty. In 135, after a long siege, the last Jewish stronghold of Betar fell. Both Bar Kochba and Rabbi Akiba were killed.

Bar Kochba was not the Messiah, but as a hero his memory lives on. Rabbi Akiva was tortured to death, but still today his teachings define the basic patterns of Jewish life in communities throughout the world. His martyrdom affirmed rather than vitiated his effect on the future.

Despite the disappointment and grief at the failure of Bar Kochba, the Sages continued to maintain their belief in the reality of the Messiah. Two generations later the leading scholar of the time was Rabbi Judah the Prince, a descendant of King David and author of the Mishnah. He was the seventh generation descendant and successor of Hillel the Elder, in the long dynasty of the Patriarchate which for fifteen years was to rule the Jews in the Holy Land. One of his greatest disciples, known as "Rav" the Master, who later founded the Sura academy in Babylon, expressed the view that if the Messiah were among the living, he was none other than Rabbi Judah the Prince.[5]

In the year 217 Rabbi Judah died, and he is generally remembered not as a possible Messiah, but as the author of the Mishnah, which has formed the basis of all subsequent Torah study till our own time. It is quite likely that the belief among his leading disciples that he could be the Messiah helped to establish his authority, and that of the Mishnah which he compiled.

After his death his disciples set up a number of different academies, both in Israel and Babylon. An interesting passage in the Talmud[6] states that each of the groups of disciples at various of these academies tried to prove from Biblical verses that the name of the Messiah was similar to, or identical with, the name of the head of their academy. In the next generation too, Messianic hopes may have been pinned on Rav Nachman, a prominent Babylonian Sage who combined great scholarship with political influence. The Talmud reports that he himself explained Jeremiah 30, verse 21, "And their Prince shall be of themselves, and their ruler shall proceed from the midst of them," as implying that a temporal leader such as he could be the Messiah.[7] This Messianic aura might contribute to the fact that throughout the Talmud, Rav Nachman's view is accepted as the Halakhah in matters of civil law.

How can Judaism maintain a stance of continuous expectation of the Messiah in defiance of repeated disappointments of history? The writings of Maimonides, the Rambam, shed some light on the matter.

In the view of Maimonides, Judaism is incomplete without the Temple, the Temple service and other aspects of Messianic Age. This is demonstrated by the fact that his Code of Jewish Law, entitled *Mishneh Torah*, the "Repetition of the Torah," includes all the laws of Judaism including those topics which pertain specifically to the Temple and the time of the Messiah. Even his presentation of other laws often has a Messianic flavor. Thus when he describes the procedure for celebrating the *seder* night on Passover, he starts with a description as if it were Temple times, with the Paschal lamb as the centerpiece of the meal. Then he adds, almost as an afterthought, the explanation of how the seder is conducted "in the present epoch," in the absence of the Temple, and therefore without the Paschal lamb.[8]

Towards the end of his Mishneh Torah, Maimonides gives an account of an aspect of Jewish teaching called the Noachide Laws. These are the laws from G-d which are addressed not just to the Jewish people, but to the children of Noah, in other words, to the whole of mankind. These laws are expounded in the Talmud, based on Biblical texts. As discussed by Maimonides, they include prohibitions against idolatry, blasphemy, murder (including abortion and euthanasia), theft, sexual immorality (including incest and homosexuality), and wanton cruelty to animals, and the positive injunction to society to set up law courts to implement these laws. Other Jewish scholars include in this universal code of ethical monotheism, honor of parents, charity and prayer.

Maimonides states that the Jewish people have the responsibility to communicate these teachings to the world. A gentile who wishes to convert to Judaism may do so, but there is no requirement for him to take this step. Instead, he or she can observe the Noachide laws. The gentile who does this, accepting them as a Divine communication from Sinai, is described as "one of the pious of the nation."[9]

It is clear that the fulfillment of this religious ideal for mankind as a whole will be in the time of Messiah, and indeed this section of the Mishneh Torah helps us understand the nature of the Messianic Age as conceived by Maimonides. The Temple will stand in Jerusalem, with the Jewish people supervising its service and observing all other laws as laid down in the Torah. The rest of the world will be a realm of peace in which the other nations will be dedicated to the goal of fulfilling the Divine Will. How will this transformation of the world take place? As Maimonides tells us in the concluding chapters of his book, by means of the Messiah.

Maimonides writes:

> The King Messiah will arise and return the Kingship of the House of David to its former power. He will build the Temple, and gather the Jews scattered in Exile. In his time all (Jewish) laws will come back into force.
>
> In that time, there will be neither famine nor war, nor jealousy or competition, for there will be great abundance and all good things will be freely available. The interest of the entire world will only be in knowing G-d. For this reason, the Jewish people will then be great Sages, knowing hidden things, and comprehending of the Divine as far as is possible for a human being, as it says 'for the world will be filled with knowledge of G-d as the waters cover the sea' (Isaiah 11:9).

Maimonides emphasizes that anyone who does not believe in the Messiah or await his coming is not only denying the writings of the Prophets, but also the Torah of Moses. He proves this point by quoting at length the prophecy of Balaam we mentioned above. He also emphasizes that the Messiah will not have to perform miracles. To illustrate this he cites the case of Bar Kochba, who was believed to be the Messiah by Rabbi Akiva "and all the Sages of his generation." Nonetheless, no miracle was asked of him to prove his position.[10] Further, states Maimonides, the Messiah will not change any of the laws of the Torah. They are eternally valid. This statement may well be a veiled reference to Christianity. However, his emphasis on the concept of the permanence of Torah law has a more general significance in limiting the likelihood of spurious antinomian and "other-worldly" varieties of Messianism, of which a number of examples are seen in the later Middle Ages.

Perhaps the key contribution of Maimonides is the definition of two stages of Messianic leadership: possible and definite. This distinction enables us to understand the role of the unsuccessful Messianic figure, and also explains why despite repeated disappointments the Jewish hope for the Messiah does not wane.

In the case of Bar Kochba, Maimonides writes that Rabbi Akiva and the other Sages thought he would be the Messiah until he was killed. Then, states Maimonides:

> Once he was killed they knew he was not [the Messiah].

But what is the position of the Messianic leader who does not succeed? Maimonides continues:

> But if he does not succeed in all this, or if he is killed, then it is clear that he is not the one who was promised by the Torah, but he is like all the wholesome and good Kings of the House of David who died. G-d only set him up in order to test the multitude . . . for the time had not yet come.

This rather positive evaluation of the unsuccessful "possible" Messiah depends, of course, on the Messianic claim being dropped as soon as it becomes clear that he is not going to succeed in his mission. This was so in the case of Hezekiah, Zerubabel, Bar Kochba, Rabbi Judah the Prince, and a considerable number of other figures. Since in pragmatic terms they did not succeed in their mission as the Messiah, this aspect of their role receded into the background. The historical problem for Jewish society begins when the Messianic claim continues despite the failure.

The outstanding example of this is, of course, Jesus. However, later figures such as Shabbetai Zvi in the 17th century are also comparable.

False Messiahs

From the perspective of Maimonides it is quite understandable why the Jews should reject the Messianic claims surrounding Jesus. He did not succeed in the primary Messianic objectives. Indeed, this was the Jewish critique of the claims of the early Christians, and why eventually the Christian sect turned to the gentiles with their new message. The Pauline abrogation of the law and eventual Christian persecution of the Jews further reinforced the Jewish rejection of Jesus. Thus Maimonides comments, in a passage censored from most printed editions of his book, that while the Prophets are unanimous that the Messiah will redeem the Jewish people, save them, gather their exiles and strengthen Jewish law, the effect of Jesus was to destroy Jews by the sword, scatter them yet further and degrade them, and to abrogate the Torah.

A similar critique applies to Mohammed, who initially saw himself as a Prophet in the Jewish tradition, in fact none other than the final Prophet, and earnestly wished to be accepted as such by the Jewish clans living in and around Medina. At first he therefore instructed his followers to pray towards Jerusalem. However, the Jews did not take his prophecies seriously. To them, Mohammed's teaching seemed to be a confused version of Biblical texts with which they were familiar. When it became clear that the Jews would not accept him, Mohammed ordered that the direction of prayer be towards Mecca instead of Jerusalem, and around the year 624 he began attacking the Jews, driving some of them away and massacring others.

Although Maimonides commends Islam for its intense monotheism and terms it a "pure religion," quite suitable for the gentile, he completely rejects any prophetic or Messianic claim by its founder.

While the Jews of the Middle Ages were hard pressed in warding off the Messianic overtures of Christianity, it is interesting that they did not do this at the expense of the Messianic ideal. This continued with remarkable intensity. In almost every generation there were "Calculators of the End" who had their hopes fixed on a particular date on which, they believed, the Messiah would be revealed. These calculations stem for the most part from the figures given at the end of the Book of Daniel. There were also many pseudo-Messiahs who arose among the masses, gathering comparatively large followings. Their claims often provoked confrontations with the gentile authorities and they therefore usually came to a bitter end. As might be imagined, this kind of event often brought increased persecution on the Jewish community at large. The Jewish leadership did its best to prevent this kind of disaster. There was a considerable degree of condemnation of the attempt to "Calculate the End," a view expressed also in the Talmud. Obviously, if the "End" is specified in too definite a way, and then passes uneventfully, this could lead to despair in the Messianic ideal and in Judaism as a whole. Even worse, in a number of instances the promised "End" became a date of terrible persecution, as in the case of 1096, the time of the Crusaders' massacres of the Jews in the Rhineland.

Despite this condemnation, among those who engaged in forecasting the date of the Messiah were such famous figures as Judah Halevi, Rashi, and Nachmanides. Even Maimonides, who was at the forefront of quashing the movement which arose around a popular Messianic figure in Yemen, presented a tradition he had received from his father that in the year 1216 the power of prophecy would return to the Jewish people. This statement by Maimonides might be partly responsible for the fact that three hundred leading Jewish scholars of France and England left for Jerusalem in the year 1211, possibly in expectation of the imminent advent of the Messiah.

The most famous, or rather infamous, pseudo-Messiah of the pre-modern period is Shabbetai Zvi. This is partly because for a short time, in the 1660's not only the masses but also many rabbis believed in him. The Messianic mood even affected Spinoza. In a letter to a non-Jew, the President of the Royal Society in London, who had written to him inquiring about the tales about the Messiah, Spinoza described the Jewish Messianic ideal as a realistic possibility. Many Jews laid by stocks of food for the journey to the Holy Land. There was a general air of excitement throughout the Jewish world.

All these hopes were dashed when Shabbetai Zvi accepted Islam to avoid execution by the Sultan. This was a new departure. Previous pseudo-Messiahs, even if utter failures, had at least died as martyrs.

Shabbetai's capitulation provoked horror and despair among the mass of the Jews. But it also had a far more dangerous effect. A small circle of his close followers, led by Nathan of Gaza, claimed that this apostasy was part of a deliberate process intended to bring about the final Redemption. Through manipulation of kabbalistic concepts they explained that since the Messiah will be brought by the power of repentance, it is necessary to sin in order to repent. What greater sin than apostasy? They thus presented Shabbetai Zvi as a hero who had "descended" as a martyr into the worst impurity in order eventually to rise and bring the true Redemption. This approach led to the growth of a small but highly disturbing antinomian movement in which learned scholars would deliberately transgress Torah law, fervently believing they were paving the way for the Messiah. Some followed Shabbetai and converted to Islam. A later similar movement in 18th century Poland developed around Jacob Frank, an highly sinister figure who converted to Christianity.

This phenomenon had some broader ramifications as well. One was a fear of the effect of kabbalistic study, since it was misuse of the logic of the kabbalah which had led to the new antinomian movements. Study of the kabbalah was forbidden to all except a small elite of reliable scholars. Despite this, Jewish society was rent by suspicions and accusations of secret Shabbatean belief.

Fear of Shabbateanism was a major aspect of the hostility to the Chasidic movement. Scholars are divided about the extent to which active Messianism was an integral aspect of early Chasidism. In a famous letter by Rabbi Israel Baal Shem Tov, the founder of the movement, he states that he had a visionary "ascent of the soul" in which he learned that the Messiah would come when the spiritual teachings at the heart of Judaism were spread throughout the community, instead of being reserved for an elite. At the same time, Chasidic thought presents the concept of the "private Messiah" meaning that a great person can achieve now the spiritual state which will generally pertain in the Messianic period. This concept has been understood as neutralizing the danger of Messianic tension. However, complementary teachings present the aim of this great person, the Chasidic Tzaddik, as that of elevating the rest of society so that the "General Messiah" will appear.

Secularization of the Jewish community during the 19th and 20th centuries led to the rise of movements such as the Reform movement and Zionism in which the Messianic ideal was completely reinterpreted: in the one it lost its national character, in the other it lost its religious dimension.

In the Orthodox community, which went through many upheavals over the past century, Messianic yearning remains an important aspect of life in some sectors, while in others it has been spiritualized away into a vague abstraction. A large proportion of traditional sermons end with expression of the hope for the Messiah. Nonetheless there are also accusations that life in contemporary Exile is seen as quite comfortable. A Jewish joke tells of a middle-aged couple discussing a rumor that the Messiah is coming. One turns to the other and says: "Look, we went through the Depression, and we went through the war. So don't worry, we'll survive the coming of the Messiah as well."

Perhaps in response to this dilution of Messianism there have been a number of attempts to revive it as a creative force in Jewish consciousness. Rabbi Yisrael Meir Kagan of Radin, known as the Chofetz Chaim, was a leading halachist and scholar. He saw the events following the First World War as a fulfillment of a description in the Talmud of the period immediately preceding the Messiah. At that time money will lose its value, hunger will prevail, there will be no peace and social hostility will be widespread (*Sanhedrin* 97). He spoke incessantly about the Messiah, exhorting people to hope for his coming. He believed this hope in itself was necessary for G-d to respond and send the Redemption. In his view it was tragic that most people did not fervently await the Messiah. As part of his campaign, in a letter of 1923 he wrote to a colleague, advising him that Talmudists must encourage the study of those parts of Jewish law which explain how the Temple service is carried out, so that when the Messiah comes, the Priests and Levites will at once be ready to perform their tasks in the Temple.

The Lubavitcher Rebbe, Rabbi Menachem Mendel Schneerson speaks of the need for the Jewish people to "want

Moshiach now." He explains the English word "want" as meaning "need." People have to feel the need for Moshiach. Part of his message is not only that through this the Messiah will come, but that without feeling this need, Jewish life becomes complacent and unspiritual.

Throughout history Jewish leaders have seen international events and especially wars as expressing Messianic portents. The Book of Daniel prophecies wars as preceding the Messiah. The Midrash states "If you see nations battling together, you can expect the feet of the Messiah" (Gen. Rab. 42:7). Maimonides saw the spread of Christianity and Islam as a step forward in the Messianic process. In our own time many Jews saw the Second World War as the war of the "birthpangs of the Messiah." Recently the Gulf War excited similar speculation, especially in light of a widely publicized Midrash in *Yalkut Shimoni*, Isaiah, section 499, which states that "in the year that the Messiah will come" there will be a war between many political powers in the region of Iraq and Arabia. This will "alarm the whole world", and particularly the Jews. But G-d will tell them "My children, do not be afraid, I am doing all this only for you, the time of your Redemption has come."

Meanwhile, constant affirmation of hope for the Messiah is repeated daily by millions of Jews in their prayers, and Maimonides includes this constant hope as one of the Thirteen Principles of Jewish Faith. Historians are divided about the effects of this faith: some, like Lionel Kochan, see it as a dangerous source of instability; others, such as Haim Hillel Ben-Sasson, emphasize the benefits of inspiration, activity, revitalization and dedication.

Whatever assessment historians may make, the Jewish people waits on, encouraged by the teachings of the Sages. The Messiah will provide the answer to all the suffering and persecutions through the generations; his coming will make clear why it all happened. Perhaps for this reason there is such certainty.

Thus, for the two Jews waiting at the bus stop, with whom we began, unlike the bus, the Messiah must surely come.

NOTES

1. *Shir Hashirim Rabbah* 5:1.
2. Rashi, Deut. 10:16.
3. *Sanhedrin* 94a. See also comment by Ravi Hillel, *Sanhedrin* 98b, 99a.
4. End of Tractate *Makkot.*
5. *Sanhedrin* 98b.
6. Ibid.
7. Ibid.
8. *Yad. Hil. Hametz Umatza*, 8:1.
9. *Hil. Melakhim* 8:11.
10. This statement by Maimonides follows the Jerusalem Talmud (*Taanit* 4:5) rather than the Babylonian Talmud. According to the Babylonian Talmud, Bar Kochba's claim to be the Messiah was eventually rejected because he did not have the power to judge intuitively, through the Divine Spirit (*Sanhedrin* 93b).

G-d and Patriarchy

Tamar Frankiel

OVER THE PAST FEW DECADES, A NEW AND DISTINCTIVE movement has emerged among Jewish women who are attempting to reclaim some kind of spiritual meaning for their lives. This movement overlaps with the political movement known as feminism, but is by no means identical with it. Politically, Jewish feminism has produced demands for ordination of women rabbis and for changes in synagogue services. But Jewish women seeking their own deeper, inward growth have not necessarily become politically involved—or, for that matter, involved in traditional religious organizations at all. Their focus has been on developing a profoundly personal spirituality, a deep level of self-fulfillment.

Traditionalists have sometimes ridiculed this movement as a female "ego-trip." While this may occasionally be true, we must insist that the paths of inward discovery—psychotherapy, for example, and modern women's literature—have been especially potent for women. The discovery of the self has been the foundation for many women to take the plunge beyond; to search again for G-d—for the G-d we lost as children when we saw too much hypocrisy among our elders, or when we became too intellectually sophisticated to accept a child's view of G-d. The question has been, if we are recovering our connection to the Divine, can we find that connection in Judaism?

The move toward a deeper spirituality has been difficult for some because of the picture of G-d we inherited. The G-d we learned about as youngsters—that distant, kingly figure who watched over us—seemed no longer appropriate, and, for women discovering their feminine consciousness, too blatantly male. Some turned to other religions in search of a G-d beyond gender or a philosophy that did not require a belief in G-d at all. At the same time, in popular feminism, the G-d of the Hebrew Bible, of Jewish, Christian, and Muslim tradition, began to get a bad reputation as "the patriarchal G-d of Western culture."

Is it true that G-d in Jewish teachings is "patriarchal"—that is, thoroughly imbued with male characteristics and values? On first glance, it would seem so. After all, G-d appears to be male. The prayer book and the Bible refer to G-d only as "He." Traditional Jewish teachings point out that G-d is really beyond all attributes, including those of gender. But, feminist writers have argued, while that is a nice theory, we as human beings need to use symbols and words to express our experience of the Divine. Can we not call G-d "She"? Further, the words we have inherited for G-d—Father, Judge, Creator, Lord—seem to spring from male experience, not female. Can a woman have an authentic relation to a G-d named only by male titles? Feminists have suggested that the titles reflect deeper levels of experience and perception that are also thoroughly male. The feminine experience of the Divine, whatever that might be, is simply not available in the tradition.

This longing for something authentically feminine is deep and significant. From it has come the desire to create new women's rituals and new feminine interpretations of the Bible. But how can these be also authentically Jewish? As serious feminists have recognized, we cannot create a new Judaism out of whole cloth. It might be possible in some other religion to create something new and still call it by the name of that religion, but not in Judaism: we are connected, intimately and deeply, to Torah itself, the Torah that was given at Sinai and has been passed down faithfully among our people through the ages. New creations lack depth unless they are connected to the tradition we have received, to our history, even if that history seems thoroughly male.

Two responses to this issue have emerged. One is a radical rereading of the Torah from a modernist historical perspective, suggesting that Jewish women in ancient times had religious resources which were not acknowledged by the men who handed down the Torah. Some feminists argue that we can resurrect the goddess-symbols of the ancient Near East. They suggest that the matriarchs themselves may have worshipped goddesses, and that Israelite women are known certainly to have done so. (We know of these practices from the criticisms heaped on goddess-worship by the prophets, but feminists dismiss those criticisms as mere propaganda of the zealous male followers of the patriarchal G-d.) Therefore, they say, we can borrow from goddess worship its rich feminine imagery; we can speak of the Queen of Heaven rather than just the King; we can use images of birth and fertility as well as of creation and conquest.

A second, more moderate view suggests that we do not need to return to goddesses. But, since G-d is neither male nor female, we can use feminine language and symbols to express uniquely feminine aspects of G-d. We can creatively retranslate Hebrew words, giving them a different nuance that is either beyond gender or has a feminine flavor. We can say "Ruler" of the universe rather than "King," for example, to give a more neutral description. We can speak of G-d as our Father and Mother; we can mention the matriarchs as well as the patriarchs in our prayers and stories. Thus, the remembering and retelling of the tradition can come to have a less masculine cast, while remaining true to the words of the tradition as we have received it, and without passing over into idolatry.

Imaginative as these might seem, there are certain problems with such proposals. First, on ancient goddesses: these figures are not as beneficent as they might seem. We might like to fantasize a goddess as an all-beneficent mother in contrast to a harsh, legalistic father figure. But this is not true to what we know of ancient religions. Goddesses were not always sweet and beneficent. Some of the ritual practices connected to the goddesses were violent and, by modern standards, inhumane. In some cases the rituals involved sexual practices unacceptable to Jewish sensibilities.

Moreover, goddesses were not forbidden merely because they were feminine. Male gods were forbidden also, the Baals as well as the Asherahs. The prophets, from Moses onward, were struggling to unify the worship of G-d in order to ensure that the Jewish people remained connected to their unique historical experience of G-d—the G-d who brought them out of Egypt. We cannot forget that, no sooner had the newly freed slaves received the Torah than they began worshipping the golden calf—a favorite image of a Canaanite male god—even though they said, "This is the god that brought us out of Egypt." It would have been easy to extend the confusion, to become involved in the worship practiced by the Canaanite inhabitants of the land of Israel, and ultimately to forget our own history. In fact, that is exactly what we did; that is why the prophets repeatedly had to call the people to stop worshipping idols. They were reminding us that the Jewish perception of the Divine was connected with history, with purpose and direction that transcended any given place. The G-d who brought us out of Egypt had something bigger in mind, something more than sustaining our life, bringing us success and prosperity, or even life after death.

That sense of larger vision, of greater purpose, has sustained the Jewish people through the ages; and that larger vision assures us also that our G-d is ultimately beyond gender. To borrow from other religious experiences just because they are female can—and in our history almost always did—dilute the reality of our unique Jewish experience.

Women are attracted to goddess figures because it is possible to see in them characteristics women can imitate—strength, creativity, compassion. But this has been for centuries a major emphasis of Jewish thought about G-d: Recognizing that we cannot know G-d's essence, we focus on the Divine attributes or characteristics in order to learn the *derech Hashem*, the way of G-d, the things we can imitate and bring into our own lives. When we ask whether G-d is "patriarchal" or "matriarchal," male or female, we are asking about these characteristics. How indeed has G-d revealed Himself/Herself, that aspect of the Divine that we can understand, to our people?

One would think, from feminist criticisms, that the Jewish view of G-d's attributes would list predominantly negative male characteristics: strength, warlikeness, imperialistic control, jealousy. But what in fact are the attributes which our sages have found in G-d? We can take them from the Kabbalah of Isaac Luria: wisdom, knowledge, lovingkindness, strength, harmony, perseverance, beauty, generativity, presence in earthly life. We can take them from the "thirteen attributes": merciful, compassionate, slow to anger, abundant in kindness and truth, preserving kindness for thousands of generations, ever-forgiving.[1] Indeed, our tradition finds a multitude of ways—more than we can easily translate into English—to describe the love and compassion of G-d for human beings. In any case, there is clearly no justification for criticizing the Jewish view of G-d as full of undesirable male characteristics.[2]

Yet the gender-specific language remains. If G-d's characteristics really transcend gender, why do we speak of G-d only as "He"? Actually, there is nothing wrong with an individual's using feminine words for G-d—to address "her" as "mother" or imagine oneself talking to an intimate female friend. For some individuals (men or women), this helps to develop a richer and more intimate relationship to G-d. We can also write and share our own interpretations of G-d's compassion, G-d's judgment,

G-d's creative work in the world, in feminine terms. This may help us to come to experience the fullness of G-d in our lives.

But this is not a full answer, for there is still the arena of public prayer, where many feminists are eager for changes in language and substance. Some Jewish organizations have rushed ahead to revise translations of the *siddur*, eliminating gender references, sometimes eliminating portions of the prayers themselves. We must say, first of all, that this does injustice to the Hebrew language itself, not to mention the centuries of prayer of the Jewish people, who cherished these words as the channels by which we might address G-d. The issue is not merely introducing some feminine language for our personal enrichment but our relation to the whole of Jewish tradition and the whole Jewish people.

Nor is it only a matter of dutifully respecting the communal tradition. We are easily led astray here because of our cultural disposition to value individual self-expression. We tend to honor the tradition only so long as it feels "authentic" to us. But what this really means is that we do not well understand communal expression, so we tend to brush it aside. We must ask: are there not some powerful reasons why our sages have, through the centuries, kept a certain kind of language for our address to G-d, and have been very careful about what comes to be included in our siddur? Indeed there are.

The mystics tell us—following images used by the prophets—that our relation to G-d, as a people, can be conceived in sexual terms. G-d is male, the Jewish people is female. The *Shir HaShirim*, "Song of Songs," which accompanies the celebration of Pesach and which, in some communities, is sung every Friday night, represents G-d and Israel as two lovers. The holidays can be mystically conceived as representing seasons in the relationship between Israel and G-d: Pesach is the first commitment of the two lovers—the engagement, so to speak—Shavuot is G-d's giving us his *ketubah* or wedding contract, and Sukkot is the consummation of the marriage. In a related set of images, all Israel together is the crown of the *Shabbat* Queen, who is also the *Shechina*, who unites with her husband, G-d, on *Shabbat*.

These images are a way to convey to us that the relation between G-d and human beings is a dynamic model, of which our best understanding is the relation between male and female. If our imagination fails at this point, it is partly a failure of our society, particularly of the widespread weakening of marriage and family in our times. Our grasp of the true meaning of the marriage relationship is dim and vague. We tend either to idealize it as romance (the teenagers Romeo and Juliet), or we criticize it as an instrument of patriarchal oppression, where the husband owns and dominates the wife.

Thus, some feminist writers have severely criticized the Jewish image of the Divine/human "marriage." For example, Rosemary Reuther attacks the images found in some of the prophetic writings which accuse Israel of being the harlot while G-d acts like a petty, jealous husband.[3]

This criticism totally fails to understand the depth and richness of the husband/wife experience in Judaism and, in particular, the notion of fidelity as part of marriage. Most of us today can barely grasp this, so we miss how the symbol of G-d as the "husband" and the Jewish people as the "wife" is the deepest imaginable relationship. Yet this image, this metaphor for G-d and the Jewish people, holds the secret of the apparently "patriarchal" language of Bible and siddur, the masculine terms we use for G-d. In our days of new feminine consciousness, when we are asking what it means to be female or male, this language turns us back to our fundamental relationship to G-d. A woman discovering herself as woman, first questions G-d: Why do you appear as male? Or she questions the rabbis: Why did you write about Him as like "you" and not like "us"? But we must push the question to a deeper level: what do masculine and feminine, male and female, really mean? How are they unique and how do they come together?

We must certainly reject the interpretation that the male (G-d) has all the power and the female (Israel) is his instrument. That would be thoroughly un-Jewish. We need only recall the famous story of Rabbi Eliezer who was intent on having G-d put his personal seal on a certain halachic decision. The sages, however, decided the matter another way. G-d's response was, "Thus my children have decided." G-d might well have said, in the above anecdote, "Thus my wife has decided." For, in another context, G-d tells Abraham, "In all that Sarah tells you, listen to her voice." The feminine has power, influence, and impact on the world just as does the masculine. They are in continuous interaction, an ongoing dance, in which each elevates and enriches the other.

This metaphor of G-d and Israel as husband and wife helps us understand that when we address G-d as a community, we address Him as male. This does not mean that, in our individual prayers, we cannot use feminine words and symbols. It does mean that when we pray in the traditional ways, we are not merely doing our duty by honoring what has been passed down. We are entering into a relationship with G-d—by our speech, helping to create a relationship—that has its own dynamic, the dynamic of the people Israel speaking, in love and intimacy, to her Divine partner. And, as with a marriage, it is only with years of practice that the full richness of this communication becomes a reality for us.

The so-called patriarchal G-d thus turns out to be only one face of G-d. The question once was asked why, in the Amidah, we should address G-d as "G-d of Abraham, G-d of Isaac, and G-d of Jacob" rather than more simply as "G-d of Abraham, Isaac, and Jacob." The sages answered: Because G-d showed a different face to each one. So also with us. We live in a time when many are speaking of the feminine faces of G-d; this brings to our awareness dimensions of G-d that we might have forgotten. We may also see Him in more traditional terms as Creator, Ruler, Redeemer, Giver of the Torah. We need not reject any of these, male or female, but only use them to deepen our understanding of ourselves as individuals, of our people, and of G-d. Learning to live with and think deeply into our words for G-d is part of our spiritual growth, part of the deepening of consciousness we see in our times.

NOTES

1. The list here does not add up to thirteen because one cannot give, in just a phrase, a description of the multiple dimensions of God's mercy, kindness, and forgiveness. See *Tashlich and the Thirteen Attributes*, trans. and commentary by Rabbi Avrohom Chaim Feuer, Artscroll Mesorah Series (Brooklyn, N.Y., Mesorah Publications, 1979).

2. These criticisms usually come from a superficial reading of the Bible without the Jewish commentaries—a common fallacy in our Christian-dominated culture, where non-Jews read what they call the "Old Testament" without a deeper understanding of what it has meant to Jews through the ages.

3. Rosemary Radford Reuther, "Sexism and God-Language," in *Weaving the Visions,* ed. Judith Plaskow and Carol Christ (New York: Harper & Row, 1989), p. 152.

Epilogue

Mutual Destiny, Mutual Responsibility: A Mystical Covenant

Dr. Jonathan Sacks

From a transcript of the inaugural lecture of the Lubavitcher Rebbe Memorial Lectures delivered last September by the Chief Rabbi of England, Dr. Jonathan Sacks, and subsequently published in Wellsprings.

ON THIS MOMENTOUS OCCASION, I COULD NOT DO OTHER than begin with one of the most moving scenes in the whole of scriptures, the scene in the second book of Kings which describes the last days of that great, passionate, visionary leader of Israel, the prophet Elijah. Elijah, we remember, had once stood on Mt. Horeb, and learned that G-d is not in the whirlwind or in the earthquake or in the fire, but in the still, small voice that speaks within the human soul. And it was after that vision that Elijah spread his cloak over the person who was to become his disciple—the prophet Elisha, and finally, the moment comes when Elijah is about to be taken from the world. He is going to die. He knows it. Elisha knows it. The company of prophets who were with them—they all know it. And Elijah says to Elisha, stay here, I have to cross the Jordan. G-d has called on me to make that final journey at the end of my life. I am about to take the one journey that each of us must make alone. And Elisha refuses to be separated from his *Rav*, from his Rebbe. He says "By the life of G-d and by your life, I will not leave you." And the two of them walked together. And it came to pass as they crossed the Jordan and Elijah said to Elisha, "Ask, tell me what I can do for you before I am taken from you and from this life." And he asks one thing: "Please grant me a double portion of your spirit." Just as Moses, commanded by G-d to lay one hand on Joshua, his successor, instead—out of love for his disciple—laid both hands, giving Joshua a double portion of his spirit, so Elisha makes his request. Elijah says, "you have asked a very difficult thing. But this I promise you: if you still see me, if a vision of me still remains with you after I am taken from you, you will have a double portion of my spirit. And if not, not." And then Elisha sees a chariot of fire and horses of fire taking Elijah to heaven. And he cries, "My father, my father, chariot and horsemen of Israel." And he takes hold of his clothes and he tears them in two.

Nothing more precisely captures our sense—my sense—of inconsolable loss at the passing of the Lubavitcher Rebbe. The man who was for hundreds of thousands of his disciples and admirers nothing less than "My father, my father." And yet nothing more eloquently defines our consolation.

Says the Midrash, "Elijah did not really die." He continued to appear to the sages as a kind of living bond between earth and heaven. And why? Because his disciples kept his teachings alive. "If my vision stays with you even after I am gone, I will still be alive in your heart. If what I was, if what I did continues to inspire you then you will still have a double portion of my spirit." And that, in Jewish terms, is immortality.

The Lubavitcher Rebbe was one of the immortals. One of the real immortals. My task tonight is not to paint a portrait of his life. That surely will be done on other occasions by others, but at least let me say this: Among the very greatest Jewish leaders of the past there were some which transformed communities. There were others who raised up many disciples, there were yet others who left us codes and commentaries which will be studied for all time. But there can have been few in the entire history of one of the oldest peoples in the world who in one lifetime made his influence felt throughout the entire Jewish world. Wherever Jews are, there you will find a Chabad rabbi—a direct personal emissary of the Lubavitcher Rebbe. And there you will see him or her reaching out to Jews and rekindling the flame of Jewish life.

Lubavitch went and still goes everywhere. Above all, Lubavitch went before anyone else and at a time when it was fraught with immense danger, to the former Soviet Union to reach out to the Jews of silence and keep the spirit of Judaism alive. It was risky—it was almost impossible. And because it was almost impossible, Lubavitch did it. Under the Rebbe, Chabad recognized no boundaries.

Lubavitch recognized no closed doors, no fences, no boundaries. The Torah says if you are scattered to the very ends of the heaven "from there will the Lord your G-d gather you and from there will He bring you back." And was there ever a religious leader in Israel who took that verse so to heart, and so astonishingly became a partner with the Almighty Himself, in bringing back Jews from every corner of the Jewish world? And I have often asked myself, why? What drove the Lubavitcher Rebbe? Was it, I once thought, that extraordinary statement of the Baal Shem Tov, the founder of the Chasidic movement, who himself spent a lifetime going out to Jews wherever they were—in little villages, little *shtetlach*, and who when asked why he does this, why he doesn't do what a rabbi is supposed to do—sit in his study and learn, the Baal Shem Tov said, "Every single Jew is a letter in the Torah scroll. And just as a Torah scroll is invalid if one letter is obliterated or missing, so the Jewish people, which is a living Torah scroll, is invalid if one Jew is missing. I go around restoring Jews to their place in the Torah." Was it that image that drove him?

Was the life work of the Lubavitcher Rebbe nothing less than a recreation in a secular world of the early days of the Chasidic movement itself, when, as the Lubavitcher Rebbe himself put it, the task of Chasidism was to wake the Jewish people from its spiritual sleep. Was that it? Was he recreating what had once happened two centuries before? Or was it something else? Was it perhaps that the Lubavitcher Rebbe lived through the black hole of Jewish history—the *Shoah.* He had seen his whole world, that world of Eastern European Jewry, go up in flames. And I have often asked myself, what did he feel—he who cared so much? What did he feel about the destruction of one third of our Jewish people, including one and a half million children, Jewish children who never tasted sin?

Chasidut uses a very powerful, highly charged word from kabbalah, *tikkun*—which means to mend this fractured world. How could you mend a fracture so deep, such a hole in the heart of humanity? And I once speculated in a newspaper article that maybe, just maybe, the Lubavitcher Rebbe had undertaken the most daring spiritual initiative ever undertaken in the history of humanity. Would it be possible to search out every Jew in love as Jews had once been searched out and hunted down in hate, and was this the only possible *tikkun*—the only possible mending of a post-Holocaust world. Who can say?

Perhaps the Rebbe had seen, as the Talmud tells us that Rabbi Chanina ben Teradyon had seen many centuries earlier—the *Sefer Torah*—the great scroll of the Jewish people burning, and was he single-handedly trying to rewrite it? I don't know. But all we know for sure is that there are few phenomena like it in the whole of Jewish history, and it owed its inspiration to one man. And one day we will tell our children's children that we were privileged to live in the same age as him.

When I was privileged for the first occasion to meet the Rebbe, to walk into his presence, to share a conversation with him, I discovered something quite stunning. I had met dozens, dozens of other leaders, and from every other leader I had asked questions and I had received answers. The Rebbe was the only one who asked me questions. And what questions they were! "What are you doing for Jewish life in Cambridge?" I remember beginning my answer. "Well," I said, "in the situation in which I find myself"—what a wonderful English beginning—and the

Rebbe interrupted me in the middle of the sentence and he said to me, "No one ever finds himself in a situation. You put yourself in a situation. And if you put yourself in one situation, you can put yourself in a different situation." And at that moment I understood that the Rebbe was not interested in creating followers. He was interested in creating leaders. He was quite the most selfless and self-effacing leader I have ever met. He embodied, to the ultimate degree, that wonderful moment in the Torah when Joshua rushes to Moses and says: "Moses, there are other people prophesying in the camp. Shut them up. They're challenging your leadership." And Moses replies, "Are you jealous for me?"

The Rebbe was an extraordinary man who practiced Torah leadership on an unimaginably vast scale, geographically and, above all, spiritually. And it is about that spirituality that I wish to dedicate the remainder of my words because tonight I want to repay a personal debt that I owe the Lubavitcher Rebbe.

It came about in a most extraordinary way. I had just obtained my rabbinic ordination and I went to the Rebbe to ask his advice as to what to do next. Should I go back to my first career as a teacher of secular philosophy or should I pursue my real ambition which was to be a barrister? And I had been led to believe that what one did was one presented choices to the Rebbe and he said either this or that. Well, he said neither. He said, "You have to become a rabbi. You have to become a rabbi in Anglo-Jewry." He directed every single part of that conversation to the Rabbinate. He spoke to me about how to revive Jews' College, which was then near to closure. He even told me to change the subject of my doctoral thesis, which at that time I was writing in secular philosophy. He said, "Make it something about the Rabbinate." Eventually I chose the topic of the principle that all Jews are bound together—are collectively responsible. And then he said, "When you finish your doctorate, please send me a copy. I would like to read it."

Some years later, I finished it. And I wondered, should I send it? I knew that every single week the Rebbe receives thousands of letters from across the world. All he needs is a 400 page doctoral thesis. But my friends in Lubavitch House said, "If the Rebbe said send it, you send it." So I sent it. Some weeks later, a letter came back. Not typed, but carefully written out in the Rebbe's own handwriting. I didn't realize at the time the value of such a letter so I promptly lost it, but I can still remember exactly what it said. It criticized two things, of which tonight I am only going to speak about one. It criticized one of the words that I had translated in the thesis and then the Rebbe said, "You have written a doctorate on Jewish collective responsibility. I am surprised that you didn't mention Chapter 32 of *Tanya*"—that great work of Chabad Chasidism of Rabbi Schneur Zalman of Liadi. Why didn't I write, he was implying, about the mystical dimension of the love of Jew for Jew which defines us as a people?

I must say I was surprised. I had written a doctorate about Jewish law, about halakhah, and the Rebbe was telling me I should have mentioned in this doctorate something that was not about halakhah—not about Jewish law—but about Jewish mysticism. Certainly, I had included in my analysis the halakhic work of Rabbi Schneur Zalman. But he wanted me to include not only the legal work but also the mystical work. And I couldn't see how it fit in. The Rebbe was saying something quite fundamental, quite daring. He was saying, in effect, that we couldn't even understand Jewish law—the Jewish law of loving our fellow Jews, without understanding the mystical basis for that love. In this case, the *mitzvah*—the command, and the mystical root of the command were inseparable. And I never understood it until now. But tonight I offer, according to my limited understanding, my guess at what the Rebbe meant, what he wanted me to say and what I have not yet said.

I set it out in the form of an extraordinary proposition. We take it for granted as Jews that we are bound by a covenant of shared fate. Nothing could more tragically have reminded us of that fact than the Holocaust itself, where Jews were sentenced to death not just because they were Jews, not even because their parents were Jews, but because their grandparents were Jews. The most fervent and the most assimilated. Even those who spent a lifetime pretending that they weren't Jews were sentenced to the same decree. In that fateful moment, we heard a terrible echo of the words of Mordechai to Esther in the Book of Esther: "Don't believe that you, Esther, in the king's palace will be able to escape the fate of your people." We knew and we know that we are bound by a covenant of mutual destiny and responsibility and mutual love, and the sages defined that in terms of the phrase that "all Jews are responsible for one another." But what I want to ask now is where does that phrase first occur—and on what is it based? The sages never made statements like this without finding some basis in a Biblical text, and in this case what was their text?

The phrase, "All Jews are mutually responsible," occurs in the Talmud in two tractates, in *Shavuot* and in *Sanhedrin*. However, it occurs for the first time in the *Sifra*, which is a Rabbinic commentary to the book of Leviticus from the time of the Mishna, dated somewhere around the second century of the Common Era. And it occurs in the context of a Rabbinic commentary to that terrible passage in the sedra of *Behukotai*, in the 26th chapter of the book of Leviticus known as the *Tokhacha*, the passage that describes the curses that will, G-d forbid, befall Israel as a people if they disobey G-d. It is such a traumatic, terrifying passage that when we read it in the synagogue, we read it in an undertone. And the text says that Israel will suffer terrible catastrophes, it will be exiled from its land, and G-d will make fearful the hearts of those who remain after all the tragedies in the land of their enemies, and they will be terrified by the sound of a leaf blown by the wind. And they will run away as if people were chasing them with a sword, when nobody is chasing them at all. And they will stumble over one another as if they were running away, when nobody is actually pursuing them. And on that phrase—"They will fall over one another," the *Sifra* says: Don't read this phrase "They shall fall over one another." Read it, "They shall fall because of one another. Because of one another's sins." And from this we learn that all Jews share a fate and a responsibility.

It is this Rabbinic teaching which is subsequently quoted in the Talmud in the tractates of *Shavuot* and *Sanhedrin* and constitutes our only source for the principle that Jews are bound to one another in a covenant of shared duty. What I want us to understand tonight and what I never fully understood before is that in this Rabbinic passage, there is a mystery. And if we take time to meditate on this mystery, we will uncover one of the greatest spiritual crises in the history of Judaism. And we will come, I believe, to the inescapable conclusion that 1800 years ago, mysticism saved the Jewish people.

The mystery is this: Why was it, during the second century of the Common Era, 1800 years ago, that the Rabbis chose this text and no other to prove that Jews are united? On the face of it, no more peculiar text is imaginable. Because if you and I were searching for a text to prove that our destinies as Jews are interlinked, the question wouldn't be which text would we choose. The question would be which text wouldn't we choose. Practically every single line of the Torah speaks about our collective fate. Whenever the Torah speaks about reward and punishment, it talks about our collective reward, our collective punishment. Everything about Judaism is collective. We prosper together, we suffer together. We share the same fate. We are bound together.

Could the Rabbis find no other proof than this text of Jews stumbling over one another—a text taken from the curses that might befall the Jewish people—a text which speaks of Israel in exile in the land of their enemies? What were the rabbis doing ignoring every other text and choosing just this one? On the face of it, it is inexplicable, and only if you and I can feel that inexplicability will we understand the depth of crisis into which the Jewish people was plunged by the destruction of the Second Temple.

Let me explain: We tend to think of collective responsibility as a very Jewish idea, but the truth is, it is not a particularly Jewish idea—it is a simple, everyday idea. To be an inhabitant of a neighborhood or to be a citizen of any country, of any state, is to be involved in some form of collective responsibility. The idea is comprehensive but only under one or two conditions: I am affected by those with whom I live in physical proximity—by my neighbors, by the people I live physically close to, or I am affected by those to whom I am bound in a single political entity—by my fellow citizens. What happens to a country affects all the citizens. And that is why during virtually the whole of the period of Scriptures, the idea of Jews being collectively responsible is self-evident and it is there in every line of the Torah. The Torah is full of it because for practically the whole period of Scriptures those two conditions were satisfied. Jews lived in physical proximity to one another and they were a political entity. They were that political entity called a kingdom of priests and a holy nation.

Now we understand the immense crisis—unprecedented in all of Jewish history—of the destruction of the Second Temple and its aftermath: an exile that was to last almost 1800 years, and a dispersion that was to scatter Jewish people across the world. Almost for the first time in history, the Jewish people was no longer a body politic because they had lost sovereignty and autonomy. They no longer ruled themselves. And they no longer lived together because they were dispersed across the world. This had only happened once before in Jewish history, when the Assyrians conquered the Northern kingdom of Israel. And the result of that is that 80 per cent of the Jewish people assimilated and disappeared.

(The Babylonian exile of the Southern kingdom, during the destruction of the First Temple, was something different. It was a brief exile, less than 70 years. That was not a critical test of Jewish survival. They came back soon enough for them not to disintegrate.)

Now we understand the full pathos and depth of the *Sifra*. The question was not, where do we find a proof that the Jewish people is a single entity bound by a collective fate? The question was, where do we find that the Jewish people is still a single entity, even in exile, even in dispersion across the face of the earth. Could it be that the Jewish people were still a people in the land of their enemies, when they had neither of the necessary conditions of being a united people? And clearly, for that you couldn't search the whole of the Torah. The whole of the Torah was predicated on the fact that Jews were together. There are only two places in the whole Torah where you could find a source that might say that even then Jews stayed a people. The only two places were the two passages of the *tokhacha* itself—the very passage in the Torah that talks about this catastrophe befalling the Jewish people, of Israel being exiled and dispersed. That is why the Rabbis had to look just here, and this is where they found it. Even a people broken apart, shattered geographically and politically, remains a united people. That is why they searched for this one verse.

I have explained why they searched for the text where they did. But I have not explained why they knew that they were going to find it there. They say about Michelangelo and his great sculpture of David that he didn't carve it from the stone. He merely uncovered it from the stone. He already knew it was there in potential. Now, you and I and a million others could pass a block of stone for a hundred years and we would see a block of stone. It takes a Michelangelo to look at a block of stone and see in it a David. It needed a Michelangelo of the Jewish spirit to see what nobody else could—namely that even though to all appearances and by all human logic Israel was no longer a people or a nation—nonetheless it was still both of these things. And who was this Michelangelo? He was perhaps the greatest of all Jewish mystics. A man who lived through those times. A man known as Rabbi Shimon Bar Yochai.

What is a mystic? I don't know. My Oxford English Dictionary tells me that a mystic is one who seeks by contemplation and self surrender to obtain union with or absorption into the deity, or one who believes in the spiritual apprehension of truths inaccessible to the understanding—and I'm sure that's right. But I prefer the very simple definition given to me by a fellow student when, 25 years ago, I went to study in Kfar Chabad. He said: "The difference between me and you is that you are a philosopher from Cambridge. Therefore, you believe in the World and you ask whether G-d exists. I am just a Chasid. I believe in G-d and I ask whether the World exists." That is a mystic. A mystic is one for whom the spiritual is more real than the physical. And such a person was Rabbi Shimon Bar Yochai.

In physical, empirical, visible terms, Israel was no longer a nation. It had none of the properties of a nation: not shared territory—the physical definition; not shared sovereignty—the political definition. Visibly it was not a nation. Along came Rabbi Shimon Bar Yochai in the text known to us as the *Mechilta* d'Rabi Shimon Bar Yochai, and he took the Biblical phrase "a kingdom of priests and a holy nation," and he said, "*goy*"—the word "nation"—teaches us that the Jewish people is like one body and one soul. And so it says in Isaiah: "Who is like Israel, a nation one on earth. If one Jew sins we are all punished. And if one Jew suffers, we all feel pain."

That is a mystical statement, and it is not too much to say that this statement, made after the destruction of the Second Temple and the subsequent Roman persecutions, actually saved the Jewish people. Because even when politically and physically we were no longer a nation, mystically, said Rabbi Shimon Bar Yochai, we are still a nation. When there is nothing else visible to hold the Jewish people together, that invisible mystical bond will hold the Jewish people together. And it was that mystical vision which reached its highest expression 16 centuries later in Chapter 32 of *Tanya*—the chapter that the Rebbe had wanted me to quote in my doctorate. Because in that chapter, Reb Schneur Zalman explains that Jews are called literally brothers and sisters to one another, because each Jew's soul is in the one G-d and, therefore, we are one soul. It is only in terms of bodily presence that we are separated from one another. And just as there can be no divisions within G-d, so there can be no divisions within the collective soul of the Jewish people. Therefore, when we live at the level of the soul, there is unity amongst Jews, but when we live at the level of the body there is disunity amongst Jews. When we live at the level of the soul, we fulfill the command that you shall love your neighbor—not as yourself, but because he is yourself. And it is that mystical idea that lies at the heart of Jewish law.

And I finally understood why the Lubavitcher Rebbe had written to me that my thesis was incomplete without this chapter of *Tanya*. Because the whole of Jewish law rests on it. The very existence of the Jewish people for the last 2,000 years depended on a belief that even outside Israel, even without power, even dispersed across the world, the Jewish people remains one nation linked to one another, responsible for one another—a single nation bound by a covenant of mutual responsibility. That is a mystical belief, but it was that belief that kept us as a people since the destruction of the Second Temple to today.

It was, of course, that self-same belief that lay behind every single act the Lubavitcher Rebbe took. If one Jew suffers, we all feel pain. Many of us can understand that sentence as a metaphor, but only a true mystic can experience that sentence as a reality—can actually feel the pain. And that is why the Rebbe sent messages and messengers to every corner of the Jewish world. Because if one Jew is suffering, if one Jew is not yet written into the Torah scroll—the book which is our book of life—he felt pain.

I have read many works of post-holocaust Jewish theology. And they all ask the same question. They ask what unites us—the Jewish people—today, with all our divisiveness and arguments. And in them I read the same answer: What unites us as Jewish people today is memories of the Holocaust, fears of anti-Semitism. What unites us as a people is that other people hate us. The Rebbe taught the opposite message. What unites us, he taught, is not that other people don't like us, but that G-d loves us; that every one of us is a fragment of the Divine presence and together we are the physical presence of G-d on earth. Surely that message—spiritual, mystical as it is—is so much more powerful, so much more noble, so much more benign than the alternative.

I have tried to pay tribute this evening, not only to one of the great leaders of Jewish history but also to one of the great ideas of the Jewish spirit—the idea that even when the physical and political bonds of Jewish unity are broken, as they have been for the last 1800 years, a mystical bond remains, binding Jew to Jew in a covenant of love. I have suggested that that idea, in the days of Rabbi Shimon Bar Yochai, saved the Jewish people from fragmenting and disappearing. And it is that same idea which, in our day, led one extraordinary individual to transform the Jewish world.

I can think of no more visible proof of the power of an invisible force—the force of the mystical *ahavat Yisrael*, the love for every Jew—which the Lubavitcher Rebbe so loved and lived and taught, and how badly we need that message today. May a double portion of the Lubavitcher Rebbe's spirit stay with us, as we seek together to mend the Jewish world.

Biographical Notes

VARDA BRANFMAN, formerly the director of Maine's Poetry-In-The-Schools Program, lives with her husband and children in Jerusalem.

TZIVIA EMMER worked as an editor of *The Spice and Spirit of Kosher Jewish Cooking*. She is a writer and mother, and lives with her husband and children in Brooklyn.

TAMAR FRANKIEL Ph.D. teaches history of religions at UCLA. She is the author of several books, including *The Voice of Sarah*, published by Harper San Francisco.

SUSAN A. HANDELMAN is professor of English at the University of Maryland at College Park. She is the author of *The Slayers of Moses: The Emergence of Rabbinic Interpretation in Modern Literary Theory*, and *Fragments of Redemption: Jewish Thought and Literary Theory in Scholem, Benjamin and Levinas*, and co-translator of a discourse by the Lubavitcher Rebbe, *On the Essence of Chassidus*.

DR. NAFTALI LOEWENTHAL is Honorary Research Fellow, Department of Hebrew and Jewish Studies, University College, London, England. He is also director of the Chabad Research Unit in London, and the author of *Communicating the Infinite*, (Chicago University Press) and other books on Jewish history.

BARBARA MEYERHOFF was a cultural anthropologist at the University of Southern California. Her filmed study of the Jewish community of Fairfax, Los Angeles, *In Her Own Time*, was her final project before her passing in 1985.

MARJORIE ORDENE is a holistic family physician in private practice in Brooklyn, New York. She has written numerous articles on nutrition, and is the author of several short stories and poems.

JONATHAN SACKS, Ph.D, is Chief Rabbi of Great Britain.

LAWRENCE H. SCHIFFMAN is professor of Hebrew and Judaic Studies at New York University. He is a specialist in the Dead Sea Scrolls, Judaism in Late Antiquity, and is the author of numerous works on the Dead Sea Scrolls and Rabbinic Judaism.

CHANA SHLOUSH (nee Forse) is a graduate of Brandeis University. She studied at the Pardes Institute in Jerusalem, and worked for various Jewish organizations. She lives with her husband Nati and their six children in Crown Heights, Brooklyn.

ELI SILBERSTEIN is Rabbi of Chabad in Ithaca, New York. He lectures on Jewish law at Cornell University and is currently at work on a book about Jewish law.

JOSEPH UDELSON is a professor of history at Tennessee State University and the author of several books on topics related to Jewish history. He resides in Nashville, Tennessee with his wife and children.

TZIPORA UNGER is a freelance writer. She lives with her husband and children in the Midwest.